The A–Z of Learning

What is…? How

Designed to provide teachers with answers to the many q... , face every day whether it's:

- How should I tackle bullying?
- What new teaching styles could I try in the classroom?
- How should I deal with office politics in the staffroom?

The A–Z of Learning is packed with facts, expert techniques, practical tips and traps to avoid. Extensively researched and covering all the major educational issues it is a quick, jargon-free solution to the information overload that confronts teachers.

The A–Z of Learning will help when you:

- Need up-to-date information (from ADD to ZPD).
- Want practical advice (from Behaviour Management to Writing Frames).

It also covers useful theories, technical information and recent legislation that will help teachers by:

- Getting more satisfaction out of teaching.
- Managing students (and parents and colleagues!) in what can be an increasingly stressful environment.

This no-nonsense guide is an essential resource for anyone involved in education, from newly qualified and trainee teachers to seasoned professionals. It provides simple answers to all your questions and unravels much of the confusing and contradictory information available.

Mike Leibling (Chair of the Campaign for Learning) and **Robin Prior** have been involved with thousands of students, teachers and educationalists – always focusing on making learning easy.

The A–Z of Learning
Tips and techniques for teachers

Mike Leibling and Robin Prior

First published 2005
by RoutledgeFalmer
2 Park Square, Milton Park, Abingdon, Oxon OX14 4RN

Simultaneously published in the USA and Canada
by RoutledgeFalmer
270 Madison Ave, New York, NY 10016

RoutledgeFalmer is an imprint of the Taylor & Francis Group

© 2005 Mike Leibling and Robin Prior

The views expressed in this book are those of the authors and are not
necessarily the same as those of the *Times Educational Supplement*.

Typeset in Times New Roman and Helvetica by
Newgen Imaging Systems (P) Ltd, Chennai, India
Printed and bound in Great Britain by TJ International Ltd, Padstow, Cornwall

British Library Cataloguing in Publication Data
A catalogue record for this book is available
from the British Library

Library of Congress Cataloging in Publication Data
A catalogue record for this book has been requested

ISBN 0–415–33506–X

Introduction

This book is a concise fact-file of theories, terminology and techniques for teachers.

Plus there are lots of tips ✓, traps ✗ and articles preceded by a star icon ★ that we hope will make learning and teaching even more effective.

We welcome corrections and updates and take full responsibility for errors and omissions, even though we have triple-checked each and every entry. (The third check has come from our Advisory Panel, who also helped select the contents, and we gratefully take our hats off to them, and thank them.)

- **Gill Brackenbury** Associate Lecturer, Institute of Education, University of London.
- **Anna Craft** Director, The Open Creativity Centre, The Open University.
- **Jenny Foster** Educational Consultant and Director of Inner Sense Learning.
- **Dr Bill Lucas** Author, and Patron of the Campaign for Learning.
- **Debbie Prior** Newly Qualified Teacher.
- **Paul Pyzer** Class Teacher, Little Stanmore First, Middle and Nursery School.
- **Dr Michael Waters** Trainer, Consultant and Author (formerly adviser for Personal Development, and Behaviour, Kent LEA).

They have also shared some of their Top Tips on pages 10, 31, 57, 66, 110, 150.

Many thanks also to Richard Griffiths, Kathrin Hardie, Peter Honey and Kenneth Posner for their generous ideas and advice, and to Philip Mudd our editor (again!) for stimulating the idea for this book, and helping to shape it.

We hope you find the book very useful.

Mike Leibling and Robin Prior

PS Please let us have your tips and traps at www.routledgefalmer.com/atozoflearning if you'd like to share your own best and worst practice!

Articles we'd really like you to read!
(Please look for the ⋆)

A Levels Advanced Level General Certificate of Education are GCE (General Certificate of Education) qualifications now made up of A/S units, which are typically taken in year twelve, and A2 units in year thirteen, or at college. This structure was introduced as a result of an Audit Commission report in 1993 concerning the high dropout level in A level courses (where all the exams were typically taken in year thirteen). However, this is again under review since A/S levels are typically taken after only two terms of teaching, and the students are often exhausted from their GCSEs two terms before. And then, in the next year, come the A levels 'proper'. Three years of exams, exams, exams. Anyway, here's the landscape:

- A level is often used to mean an A2 level i.e. the final school or college qualification at age 18.
- A/S level now stands for Advanced Subsidiary, replacing Advanced Supplementary papers (yes, really). The intention is for students to study more subjects (typically four) in the first year of advanced level study, for greater subject breadth and motivation. (Some subjects are stand-alone, and don't lead to A2 courses.)
- A2 level courses follow from some A/S courses in greater depth, but in fewer subjects (typically three).

AA Adult Apprenticeships were introduced from September 2004 for students aged over twenty-five to learn vocational skills to equip them for an occupation.

AB *see* AWARDING BODIES.

ABCs Acceptable Behaviour Contracts are normally devised in consultation with all affected parties (and the process of constructing them often provides valuable insights into the other parties' positions).

Ability Groups or Sets are groupings of students with similar levels of knowledge and/or experience and/or learning ability, put together for specific lessons or activities. The rationale is that not all students in a class will have the same level of ability or will progress at the same rate. You don't want students falling behind and becoming demoralized, or getting bored because they are not being stretched. The 1997 White Paper 'Excellence in Schools' said that 'setting' should be the norm in secondary schools and is worth considering in primary schools. A 1999 report from Ofsted says that setting as early as 5 years old could raise standards. In this way, each student can work as best suits them, and not feel left behind or excessively pushed. However, the evidence is that students recognize when they are being put in a group of low performers. This can demotivate, affect SELF-ESTEEM, make some students feel like no-hopers and create a SELF-FULFILLING PROPHECY of low performance.

✓ *Tips*

☐ When devising the groupings and the tasks for the groups, ensure that you do not label them in any way that can suggest high ability ('clever') or low ability ('stupid'). Putting any age of student into a 'lower ability' group can affect their self-esteem, aspirations and enthusiasm – 'If the teacher thinks I'm not very good then I can't be very good, so there's no point trying'. This also avoids a common trap of teachers focusing on 'higher ability' students. So label them according to the skills that the students have for the task e.g. the VISUAL group, the KINAESTHETIC group: or the group that has no questions, and the group that has questions.

- ☐ Avoid giving letters or numbers to groups, because they'll soon work out that 1 is 'better' than 2, or A is 'better' than B etc. Maybe try colours or fruits or let the groups choose their own names, as this helps with their social skills when choosing, and their involvement with the whole task.
- ☐ Constantly review the students in the sets, as abilities do change.
- ☐ Remind students that success is measured by their own progress, not by comparison with other students.
- ☐ *See also* the traffic light *Tip* under AfL ASSESSMENT FOR LEARNING.

Academic Monitoring is usually an appointed meeting held once a year between teachers, an individual student and their parents to review academic progress. (Behavioural matters are, arguably, better addressed separately and when they arise.) *See* ASSESSMENT, SUMMATIVE.

ACCAC Qualifications, Curriculum and Assessment Authority for Wales.

Accelerated Learning is a fascinating collection of techniques that enable information to be rapidly and deeply fixed in the memory and then recalled. It was devised by Colin Rose, and enables everyone to learn faster and more effectively in ways that work best for them as an individual. The techniques are based on understanding how the brain works, and range from A(ristotle) to Z(eppelin, Led). For example, involving students with all LEARNING STYLES, and using MUSIC and MIND MAPPING® appropriately can make most activities and lessons easier for all concerned.

ACT American College Testing Program Assessment is a US college admission test. (*see also* SAT). Some colleges will accept either test, whereas others will specify only one.

Action Learning happens through working in groups or sets – as in 'action learning sets' – to develop and improve processes, or to prevent or solve problems. The groups may be with colleagues, students, parents – whoever is appropriate – and specific learning outcomes are defined for each session or series of sessions. Typically, once the outcomes are achieved, the group will also spend some time on

- ▪ What processes worked for the group.
- ▪ How they could work even better next time.
- ▪ What other situations might be worth addressing by the group.

Active Concert *see* SUGGESTOPEDIA.

ADD Attention-Deficit Disorder is similar to ADHD but without the hyperactivity. It is more common in females than males. ADD is often overlooked because the teacher does not have to deal with the disruptive behaviour associated with ADHD. An ADD student is often quiet and may appear as a loner or just as a child who keeps themselves to themselves. ADD may be the cause of poor attention, concentration and performance. Exact figures of students with ADD are not possible because many of them simply fail quietly. If you suspect a student as having ADD you should talk with your SENCO (Special Educational Needs Co-ordinator) as a correct diagnosis is essential. RITALIN is sometimes prescribed as a medication.

Additional Literacy Support (ALS) is an INTERVENTION PROGRAMME designed to help year 3 and 4 students who are behind in their literacy skills. Each module includes a practical teaching programme to be delivered during the groupwork session of the LITERACY HOUR, by teachers and/or teaching assistants. The modules cover PHONICS, reading (guided and supported) and writing (shared and supported).

ADHD Attention Deficit Hyperactivity Disorder is both a medical condition and a behavioural disorder affecting around 2 per cent of the population (more males than females). Research suggests it is genetic because it often occurs in more than one member of a family. A key feature is an imbalance of dopamine and nora-drenalin which are involved in transmitting messages between cells in the brain during tasks. (RITALIN is often prescribed to redress this balance.) Symptoms include

- Lack of attention – short attention spans which create difficulties in learning even where they have academic ability.
- Hyperactivity – not sleeping well, suddenly disrupting others.
- Impulsiveness – acting spontaneously, not thinking about the consequences.

Combining the effects of these behaviours, a student with ADHD may be rejected in their efforts to make friends (leading often to low SELF-ESTEEM, depression, anxiety, substance abuse). They may acquire friends of 'the wrong sort', and lack social skills. They constantly need very specific instructions about what to do in different situations.

At home their behaviour can often be seen as destructive as, for example, they need less sleep than most people and so they may keep others awake. There may also be overlap with other disorders e.g. AUTISTIC SPECTRUM DISORDER or ATTACHMENT DIS-ORDER. The disorder does not diminish with age, but people can learn very effective coping strategies.

US research suggests that most ADHD students are under-achievers, with reading and writing as well as social difficulties.

With milder forms, a great deal can be achieved by noticing what triggers the outbursts, in order to avoid 'trigger situations' in the future. Changes in seat-ing, class size and teaching practices can have an impact on the frequency and strength of outbursts. If you suspect a student as having ADHD you should talk with your SENCO (Special Educational Needs Co-ordinator) as a correct diagnosis is essential.

✓ *Tip*

☐ You can make a difference by being very precise about the type of behaviour that is expected. Help the student achieve the desired behaviour by recognizing danger signals and planning ahead. Having recognized negative patterns, work with the student to avoid the negative triggers in the first place. Explain the benefits and consequences of this desired behaviour, and reward them when appropriate, to reinforce success and/or effort. It may also be useful to have frequent contact with the student during lessons and seat them near you.

Administrators (in education) are here to help.

✓ *Tips*

☐ Remember, they are doing their job, and trying to do their best.
☐ They have chosen a job with systems and organization, not people and learning.
☐ They are likely to have good attention to detail and to follow the rules, and may be frustrated by those who do not.
☐ You may not have noticed the things that smooth your path for you, only the things that get in your way.
☐ It is best to find ways of working with them rather than against them.
☐ Understand how their minds work and what they are looking to achieve, and try to speak their language, and help them achieve their goals.

☐ If you ever become frustrated by bureaucracy then your frustration will affect only you and not the administrators.

☐ And finally, please remember, when you think you're dealing with an idiot, so do they!

ADSL Asymmetric Digital Subscriber Line is a regular phone line which is much faster than regular lines and can receive (download) up to 1.544 mb of data per second, and send (upload) data at 128 kb per second. It is an alternative to BROADBAND for computer networks, Internet etc.

Adult Education refers to 16+ lifelong learning and personal development within colleges, communities, and correspondence courses, for people no longer in full-time education.

Adult Literacy and Basic Skills Unit *see* BASIC SKILLS UNIT.

Advanced Skills Teacher *see* AST.

AEA Advanced Extension Awards are more challenging A level papers that replaced Special (S) A level examinations in England, Wales and Northern Ireland in summer 2002.

Affective Learning can be thought of as largely below-the-neck emotional learning (i.e. feelings, emotions and values), rather than cognitive above-the-neck thoughts and beliefs. Examples include 'gut-feel', 'heart-felt' and other forms of distributed cognition. (*See also* EMOTIONAL INTELLIGENCE.) Affective *skills* are those of feelings and emotions. There are five commonly quoted, based on Benjamin Bloom *et al.*'s Taxonomy (=classification) of Affective Skills:

1 *Being aware* – e.g. listening respectfully, noticing non-verbal communication.
2 *Being responsive* – e.g. participating in a discussion, asking pertinent questions.
3 *Being tolerant* – e.g. respecting other people's values and cultures.
4 *Able to prioritize* – e.g. negotiating between different points of view or needs.
5 *Able to internalize* – e.g. aware of their own and others' values, accepting change, working comfortably with different groups of people, and working alone – as they are relatively self-aware.

AfL Assessment for Learning – *see* ASSESSMENT.

Age There are three main measurements in education:

■ Chronological – how old they are (the main meaning, unless otherwise specified).
■ Mental – their IQ (as measured in INTELLIGENCE TESTS) compared to their chronological age.
■ Reading – their ability compared to the average (e.g. 'how old chronologically would an average person be who could read at this standard?').

A student might, therefore, be 10 chronological years old, have the mental age of a 15-year-old and the reading age of a 6-year-old.

 FACT

Some tabloid newspapers have a reading age of 9. Some government forms demand a reading age of 25 (i.e. having had a post-post-graduate education!).

Agreement, Home-School (HSA) is intended to enhance partnerships between students, parents and the school, as they define the roles and responsibilities of each party. Students who can understand the agreement should also be encouraged to sign as an indication that they understand and accept the school's expectations of them. From September 1999 governors of maintained schools must have a statement explaining:

- The school's aims and values.
- Its responsibilities towards its students.
- The responsibilities of the student's parents.
- What the school expects of its students.

Parents should be consulted in drawing up the agreement, and the parents of students of compulsory school age should be invited to sign their acceptance.

Example

Here's one we like for its simplicity and clarity:

Our School will

- Respect all students, staff and parents (verbal and physical abuse are not acceptable).
- Provide a safe and caring environment.
- Have mutually acceptable and clear goals and outcomes for students and staff.
- Listen to and seriously consider, improvements from students, staff and parents, in order to....
- Facilitate learning to the best of our ability according to each student's needs.

Our Students will

- Do their job (i.e. learn) to the best of their ability.
- Arrive on time, regularly, and be physically and mentally prepared to learn.
- Respect other students, staff and parents (verbal and physical abuse are not acceptable).
- Take responsibility for their own learning needs.
- Help others when needed.
- Ensure that the school's reputation is enhanced by their actions.

Our Parents will

- Ensure that students arrive punctually, regularly, and be physically and mentally prepared to learn.
- Contribute to discussions about the student's needs and goals and outcomes.
- Work with the school and the student to achieve the agreed goals and outcomes.
- Support the student in achieving their goals and outcomes.
- Respect all students, staff and other parents (verbal and physical abuse are not acceptable).

ALS *see* ADDITIONAL LITERACY SUPPORT.

ALSA Accredited Learning Support Assistants are TEACHING ASSISTANTS who are certified to help students with specific learning difficulties.

AMA Advanced Level Modern APPRENTICESHIP (1995–2004).

Analysis is seeing the parts, and patterns of parts, that make up a totality. Practical examples could be

- Troubleshooting a situation.
- Finding a bottleneck in a process.

✓ *Tip*

☐ To find out students' analytical skills, ask questions beginning with analyse, find, identify, sort out, deconstruct, etc. (*See* BLOOM'S TAXONOMY OF THE COGNITIVE DOMAIN.)

Analytical Thinking *see* CRITICAL THINKING.

Andragogy is the study of adults' education (sometimes referred to as the education of equals, with the teacher as FACILITATOR of learning). It contrasts with PEDAGOGY (the study of child education) which is sometimes known as education from above, as the teacher directs the processes, rather than facilitates them. Andragogy was defined by Alexander KAPP in 1833 and it incorporates parts of PLATO's education theory. It was developed by Malcolm KNOWLES in 1980 and andragogy vs. pedagogy has been much debated ever since.

Knowles' key assumptions, in a nutshell, are

1   Adult learners have their own internal motivation to learn, as they can see the purpose of their learning and are self-directed; children need to accept from others, externally, the need to learn, and be willing to be led.
2   Adults draw upon their life experience when learning, whereas children have less to draw upon.
3   Adults learn what they need to learn, for more immediate use, whereas children tend to learn 'subjects' as building blocks for longer term use.

Much of the debate is about these and other assumptions. Much is also about the belief that education should be 'facilitated' rather than 'led' by teachers.

★ **Anger Management** helps students to handle this potentially damaging emotion in a way that minimizes negative consequences to themselves, others, their school and/or family. If possible, it is taking anger (which is a perfectly natural emotion) and turning it into a positive force to drive achievement. But if anger becomes persistent or violent then specialist help should be sought.

When dealing with anger it is essential to know your own limitations as a teacher. Although learning by doing, and by making mistakes, is part of a teacher's development, anger management is not an area in which to make mistakes. The stakes could be too high. Bottled-up or suppressed anger tends to increase until it explodes. However, in most cases there will be actions you can take as a teacher that will manage a student with anger (or indeed a colleague or friend).

There are a number of reasons why a student may be angry. As a teacher you need to understand these reasons before you look to handle the anger. If you do not understand the reasons behind the anger then you are trying to change behaviour without knowing or dealing with the force behind the behaviour. However, there are boundaries to how intrusive you can be. Again, this may be an area for specialist help, although very often the causes are well known and obvious. It is *essential* to take each student as an individual, and find out their needs, rather than to categorize them. Here are some common situations you might come across:

■   Domestic problems, the break up of relationships, divorce, siblings in trouble.
■   Abuse of some sort.
■   Lack of self-esteem, with anger being a projection of self-hatred.
■   Frustration because they are slow to learn or have a special learning need that has not been identified or dealt with.
■   Frustration because their learning style does not suit the teacher's teaching style.
■   Being bullied.
■   Feeling deprived or victimized in some way.
■   Copying parental or peer behaviour.
■   Physiological and/or hormonal factors are affecting their moods and/or they are not being helped to understand the changes taking place.

✓ *Tips*

☐   Let the student know that it is normal to experience the emotion of anger.

☐   Be a good listener for the student.

☐   Model the behaviour you want them to adopt, rather than retaliate.

☐   Recognize their anger in words and show empathy, e.g. 'You look angry', or 'I'm not surprised you're so angry'.

☐   Avoid saying anything like 'I know just how you feel'.

☐   Make time to help them, e.g. to find goals and positive objectives in life.

☐   Help build their self-esteem by getting them to list all the things they are good at, pleased about, or not angry about. Express confidence in them. Add to their list of positives anything that you think the student is good at.

☐   Describe the behaviours that come with the anger as being atypical of the student, not commonplace.

☐   Make them aware (possibly by bringing in other students) of the impact of the anger on others.

☐   Make it clear that hurting or damaging other people, themselves or property is not acceptable. Let them know the behaviour that is not acceptable and the impact of that behaviour on others. For example, 'shouting is not acceptable, it upsets others'.

☐   Help them identify what causes them to be angry, what the triggers and the stepping stones are towards being angry, and how to take action during this build-up stage, to express the anger in a positive and non-destructive way.

☐   Identify what the anger gives the student, and what the pay-off is. And then find another way of getting the end result without using anger. For example, if the pay-off is that the student releases the tension in their body, find some other physical activity that will give them this release.

☐   Find out what the root cause of the anger is.

☐   Find a way of redefining anger so that it becomes a positive force. Show how anger and frustration can be the driving force behind success.

☐   Don't force apologies if it is not the right time for the student to apologise. The apology may come days later.

✗ *Trap*

☐   Remember, you're a teacher not a psychiatrist. If in doubt, and instead of getting out of your depth, consult.

Annual Report to Parents *see* ASSESSMENT, SUMMATIVE.

⭐ **Answering Skills** as with so much in teaching, these work best with a calm composure and a relaxed, yet alert, frame of mind. Otherwise, students' questions can be the most testing events in a teacher's day. In order to answer you need to

■   Stop your flow.

■   Evaluate the reason behind the question.

■   Consider the effectiveness of your communication.

■   Check what the rest of the class is doing.

■   Attempt to maintain your control and composure.

■   All at the same time as providing a response that will clarify understanding.

(If it wasn't for having to answer questions interactively we could employ actors to present lessons.)

When a student asks a question you need to work out their reason for doing so. It could be one of the following:

■   They want more information.

■   They want the information explained in a different way.

- They want it repeated because they have not been listening.
- They are trying to trip you up or set you up.
- They are trying to look clever.

Normally if a student asks a question for a negative reason they will tend to look (maybe only slightly) to their friends for recognition and validation. If their request is genuine they will tend to maintain eye contact with you and therefore their question should be handled with respect. Your ability to read BODY LANGUAGE is important here. With genuine questions, never make it wrong to ask.

✓ Tips

☐ When you are asked a question by one student it is essential to involve the whole class with the answer. Even if the question could be answered quickly and then put aside, you might be losing a learning opportunity if you answer and move on. Therefore, when appropriate, offer the question to the class by saying, 'The question is (and repeat the question)' so that even if they hadn't bothered to listen to their classmate, your repeating the question will gain their attention. Then expand and clarify the question by asking the student who asked it to rephrase or expand on the question or to define specifically which aspect of the subject they are not clear about. When the question is full and clear ask the class if they have an answer. (This might also provide valuable time for you to think if you need to.) If the class can answer, then all well and good. If you have to answer then do so and then check with everyone that the point in question is now clear.

☐ 'Can you say that again, I (still) don't understand?' is a frequent request that can be communicated both verbally and non-verbally. Sometimes people get offended when asked this, as if they are being made to feel inadequate, provoked or tested. They often feel the pressure of time because they'll need to 'repeat themselves'. And, if it happens too often, it can create self-doubt. They can read all sorts of meaning into students asking them to clarify or repeat what they said. It should, therefore, make us examine whether the way we have presented information is not the best way for one or more of the students to receive information. It's not that we are a failure. It's that, with the best will in the world, we failed to put it in a way that could be received successfully. So, what is our best response? The priority is to maintain a positive frame of mind. If we demonstrate being flustered or annoyed then students are less likely to seek clarification in the future (unless they want to wind us up). See the question as an opportunity to impart more learning. Be pleased that a student is showing so much interest that they want clarification.

☐ Because the way we have said something makes complete sense to us, when asked to repeat ourselves we tend to use the words that we ourselves understand i.e. we say the same thing again in the same way. So, if you are going to repeat yourself, find new phrases or words. Simple repetition of what they didn't understand the first time, is unlikely to help.

☐ It is not often that all that you have said does not make sense, so if a student asks for repetition, ask what parts of what you have said have not been understood. This will not only give you a tighter focus for your clarification, it will help the student use their own thinking to understand you. And it will give you a few seconds to maintain your composure, and breathe.

☐ Remember that the real meaning of your communication is the message that they receive. Never put blame on the student for lack of understanding. It is your job to bring about understanding in whatever way is necessary.

☐ If the communication was just verbal, use some VISUAL and/or KINAESTHETIC demonstration to support the words.

☐ If you don't have an answer, then admit you don't know. Unless your acting skills are excellent, students will read your BODY LANGUAGE and know you are not certain. We have to model the values and behaviour we expect from them, so maybe say, 'I don't have the answer to that now, but I know where to get the answer and I'll come back to you.' or, 'I don't know – who can help us with this?'. Being comfortable with not knowing is essential. No-one is born with all the answers to all the questions that all the people might ask us. Unfortunately many people feel pressured to answer quickly rather than correctly or usefully.

✗ Traps

- ☐ Saying something louder or quicker does not bring greater understanding.
- ☐ When we feel we are being tested, it is tempting to confront someone with a challenging response such as 'and what do you think I mean, then?'. On an individual level this may work but it gives a negative message to the other students.

APEL Assessment of Prior Experiential Learning is where a student's previous non-formal learning (e.g. work experience) is credited towards a new course. *See* CAT(S).

APL Assessment of Prior Learning is where a student's previous formal learning is credited towards a new course.

★ **Appearance Bullying** is a common term for name-calling. There is an old saying that 'sticks and stones may break my bones but names will never hurt me'. But anybody who has been called an unpleasant name will know that this isn't true. Name-calling hurts because it singles out a physical or personality characteristic that the caller knows is a hot button for the recipient. What makes it extremely hurtful is that it's hard, if not impossible, to change appearance, which makes the victim feel trapped. It can affect a person of any age with tragic consequences.

Bullies choose the softest target. They find a quick route to real pain and often disguise or add extra mockery to their name-calling by saying the opposite of what they see as the truth. The slow person is called Speedy and the overweight person Skinny. Appearance bullying is hard to detect because it leaves no physical scars. The names can also be whispered or even mouthed silently. Students being bullied by name-calling are often reluctant to confide in teachers because many teachers do not recognize the severity of appearance bullying, and the students may be ashamed to repeat the words that have been used.

✓ Tip

- ☐ Emily Lovegrove is a psychologist who advocates that physical differences should be acknowledged openly, so that they are defused (e.g. 'Yes, I am fat.') She also teaches a process called fogging which is a response that leaves the bully puzzled. It works by responding to a bully with, 'And your point is?' when the name is called. If the name is used again, the 'fogging' response is, 'I still don't get your point'. This process is generally effective when taught and practised.

Application Activities are where, having explained a theory or concept, you then set an activity through which the students confirm for themselves that the theory or concept works in practice. Contrast this with DISCOVERY LEARNING and DISCOVERY ACTIVITIES.

Application is applying a concept in a new situation, e.g. applying existing knowledge to solve new problems.

✓ Tip

- ☐ To find out students' application abilities, ask questions beginning with apply, solve, experiment, discover, etc. (*See* BLOOM'S TAXONOMY OF THE COGNITIVE DOMAIN.)

Apprenticeships are, from September 2004, available to students age 14 plus with no upper age limit. They are based on Modern Apprenticeships which were introduced in 1995 – with an upper age limit of 25 in England – to enable young people to learn on the job, gaining qualifications, knowledge and skills, while earning money. There are two levels, Foundation and Advanced, and both lead to nationally recognized VOCA-TIONAL qualifications e.g. NVQs. Subjects range from health and beauty, through administration, to agriculture and transportation. *See* AA (ADULT APPRENTICESHIPS) and YA (YOUNG APPRENTICESHIPS).

AQA the Assessment and Qualifications Alliance is one of the three English unitary awarding bodies and was formed in April 2000 from the merger of the Associated Examining Board and the Northern Examinations and Assessment Board.

ARCS Model is a four-step sequence to motivate learners, developed by John Keller.

1 Gain the learners' *Attention*.
2 Ensure that the learners are motivated by the *Relevance* of the learning to them.
3 Instil *Confidence* in the learners that the learning can be successfully completed.
4 Leave the learners *Satisfied* that they have achieved their learning goal.

Top Tips from Bill Lucas

■ If a group or class finds it hard to get started, take it in turns to talk about what went 'wrong' last time, and having identified the issues you all care about, decide how best to move on.

■ Never say something is 'easy' to a student who is having difficult, especially if they have special educational needs. It may be easy to you, but probably not to them.

■ Don't forget the school grounds outside. Much of the important stuff happens here. Get your student to tell you how they would like to develop your school's grounds.

ASBO Anti-Social Behaviour Order.

ASD Autistic Spectrum Disorders (e.g. AUTISM and ASPERGER'S SYNDROME) are brain-based dis-abilities affecting language and/or information. They mainly affect males. People with ASD have difficulty understanding how others behave and how they themselves are expected to behave. Social skills and communication skills are particularly challenging. Their use of language may be pedantic, and they may take things very literally. Some, but not all, also have a learning disability.

They can find it hard to

1 *Talk Sociably*

■ To understand what people mean rather than what they say.
■ To know what to say.
■ To have a conversation.
■ To form social relationships.
■ To understand others' feelings.
■ To be concerned about other people.

2 *Act Sociably*

■ To know how to behave appropriately.
■ To join in social activities.
■ To hide their feelings of pleasure or displeasure.

3 *Imagine*

■ To pretend.
■ To accept novelty, change and disruption, preferring routine and repetition.

✓ *Tip*

☐   Don't jump to any conclusions or cause alarm by labelling someone 'autistic' without sensitive exploration of other possibilities (e.g. shyness) and a professional diagnosis.

✗ *Trap*

☐   A medical diagnosis of 'autistic' requires the local authority to support that person. Since this support can be hugely expensive (e.g. a residential school can cost £100,000 per year) there is a financial reluctance to diagnose autism. Patience, persistence and support will be needed for the person's carers.

ASM Auditory Sequential Memory is the ability to remember information given verbally (e.g. lists or instructions) in the 'correct' sequence. A dis-ability may first be noticeable when a child is limited in their ability to learn and recite nursery rhymes or songs. When students with poor ASM carry out these tasks they may appear to 'lose track'. Or, if they are asked to pick up several items they may come back without some or all of them and be in a confused or agitated state. (Be aware also that most people can only remember a maximum of seven items at a time, and so ASM may be an incorrect diagnosis of the above behaviours.)

✓ *Tip*

☐   ASM disabilities often occur in DYSLEXIA but when observing students with possible learning disorders it is important to consider all possible causes without leaping to conclusions. Symptoms need to be persistent before you take action to get a formal diagnosis.

Asperger's Syndrome was identified in the 1940s by Austrian paediatrician Hans Asperger (1906–1980). It is a 'mild' ASD (AUTISTIC SPECTRUM DISORDER). People with Asperger's may not have any learning disability, and may function well throughout their life without being diagnosed.

Assembly is a gathering of the whole school, or specific classes, year groups or tutor groups, as appropriate. The purpose can be to build the ethos of the school or groups within the schools. Or it can be purely administrative.

✓ *Tip*

☐   It is essential that all present have a stake in the information to be imparted or discussed. If not, this should be done only with the relevant groups, to avoid boredom.

✗ *Trap*

☐   Collective worship can sometimes be confused with assembly, and a school should be clear about the separate outcomes for each gathering. This is not to say that the two cannot on occasions be combined, so long as the intentions of each section are clear.

Assertive Discipline is a controversial means of behaviour management, based on the belief that the teacher has the right to determine what behavioural rules are best for students, and to expect students to comply with them. It was developed in the 1970s by Lee and Marlene Canter in the belief that students should not prevent teachers from teaching, nor prevent other students from learning.

The approach states that

■   Teachers should establish rules that define acceptable and unacceptable behaviour.
■   Teachers should teach students to follow these rules.

- Teachers should expect participation and support from parents and colleagues.
- Students should expect to have a teacher who will set limits and motivate them to respect them.
- Students should know the behaviours expected of them and have a teacher who enables them to choose, and then manage, their behaviours.

The teacher is expected to be assertive (i.e. confident, clear and consistent) in applying these rules. If the teacher is not assertive (i.e. tentative, unclear or inconsistent) then students can become anxious, frustrated, and even hostile. Positive feedback is essential for the student to recognize and appreciate their own positive behaviours.

✔ **Tip**

☐ This can work well with students (also colleagues, friends and family) if they like clear guidelines. However, for those who prefer PARTICIPATION to imposition, this is a red rag to a bull.

Assessment used to be largely summative (i.e. assessment *of* learning), where a snapshot of students' achievements was taken termly or annually. Then in 1998 the Assessment Reform Group concluded that there needed to be an acknowledgement of the power of formative assessment (i.e. assessment *for* learning) to raise attainment levels.

- *Summative Assessment* is a snapshot of each student's achievements, often undertaken termly and/or annually (or as SATS). It is often used for keeping parents informed of students' progress, and – when the student changes class or moves school – for informing their new teachers. It provides an indication of strengths and weaknesses, developmental patterns, and gaps in knowledge and understanding. It is similar to ACADEMIC MONITORING which is usually carried out once a year to review academic progress with the student and their parents.
- *Formative Assessment* is carried out by the teacher for each student on an ongoing basis. A teacher could, for example, focus on a fifth of their class each day so that every student receives this close focus on a weekly basis. The teacher records the evidence of the students' learning, plus any other factors such as interactions with parents. And then, vitally, suggested actions are noted, discussed with the student, and progressed. This not only helps the teacher to plan more effectively by monitoring progress more regularly, but also feeds into students' summative assessments.
- *Assessment for Learning* (AfL) is an evidence-based process of determining

  1 Where students are in their learning (assessed by, e.g. examination, observation or self-assessment).
  2 Where they need to be (e.g. in terms of agreed learning goals).
  3 How they might best get there (e.g. with an agreed action plan).

It is used to raise achievement with a clear plan of action, in order to reach agreed, achievable and desirable goals.

- *Criterion Referencing* assesses achievement in absolute terms (e.g. does the student know X?). It follows on from PERFORMANCE BASED INSTRUCTION, and contrasts with norm referencing.
- *Norm Referencing* assesses a student's achievement relative to a group, rather than in absolute terms (e.g. is this student in the top 75 per cent of this particular group of students? If so we will 'pass' them and if not we will 'fail' them).
- *Oral Assessment* is testing for learning and understanding, through face-to-face conversation and questioning rather than in writing. It is especially important

to use oral assessment for students with special needs and the very young. It relies less on the one-shot written answer, as the conversation can tease out information and evidence of skills over a period of time. Some exams still have an oral element to them but the difficulty with oral assessment is in having a standardized evaluation.

✓ Tips

☐ A practical and fun way to assess learning at the end of an activity or class is to ask them to classify themselves according to traffic light colours, as a prelude to further discussion:

   ▪ Red – I'm not really sure what that was all about, as I wasn't really paying attention, or didn't understand.
   ▪ Amber – I sort of get it.
   ▪ Green – I got it, and know I got it.

☐ You might then, as just one possibility, put the greens and reds together for two minutes and get them to sort it out for themselves, and focus yourself on the ambers' needs. (Bill Lucas, one of our Advisory Panel, brought this to our attention. It's also a great way of de-stigmatizing not knowing, and of forming instant ABILITY GROUPS.)

Assessment Centres can be

1   Educational establishments, training organisations or employers which an awarding body has approved for assessing and verifying qualifications.
2   Locations for assessing learning and other disabilities, so that future action and support can be agreed.
3   Where an organisation conducts PSYCHOMETRIC TESTS or work-related simulations for the selection of job applicants and/or to determine the development needs of staff.

Associated Examining Board *see* AQA.

Assumptions are what we make all the time. 'The bus will (or will not) be on time'. This is going to be a boring meeting. 'I am no good at X'. How we assume things will be, inevitably, conditions our expectations. We have heard of teachers who agreed with the statement 'Not all children have the potential to be creative'. Imagine what hard work their classes will be, for everyone.

✓ Tips

☐ Be aware of your assumptions of yourself and those around you: if you assume someone cannot do something, you're right. If you assume that they haven't been able to, and it's your job to help them, you're right. And if you assume that no-one's found the way for them to do it yet and it'll just take some relaxed experimentation, you're right, again!
☐ Putting negative assumptions into the past tense is a very useful first step, before moving on, e.g. instead of 'I am no good at X' how about 'I have never been good at X. So what, if anything, would help me in the future?'.

AST Advanced Skills Teacher is an ideal role for experienced teachers who want to progress in grade, and therefore salary, but who do not want to leave the classroom for a more administrative or managerial role. ASTs are often heads of year or department in larger schools. The 'advanced skills' are the teacher's, and not the skills they are teaching to students. They typically help other teachers (and teachers in other schools) by sharing their knowledge and experience.

ASVCE Advanced Subsidiary Vocational Certificate of Education is the vocational equivalent of A/S levels and is at level 3 on the NQF National Qualifications Framework.

ATL Association Of Teachers And Lecturers.

Attachment Theory was developed by John BOWLBY who defined attachment as an affection between two people, beginning with the bond between the child and its mother, and then using this bond as a model for other relationships.

In their first year of life the child learns to trust. If they are hungry, for example, their signals are picked up and they are fed. And after many 'healthy attachment cycles' of this pattern, they learn to trust (i.e. bond with) their primary caregiver (normally their mother). As the child's 'needs' become more adventurous and they get better at communicating their needs (e.g. ice cream, toys) the second year then needs to bring 'secure attachment cycles'. Here they begin to experience the caregiver's limits (e.g. no more ice cream) and – as long as the caregiver is consistent, fair and clear – the child will develop trust in authority, and boundaries.

When all goes well, patterns of bonding and attachment are attained by age three, and the child's social development progresses successfully. When all does not go well, at its worst the child's distrust of adults grows into an inability to form relationships, and Reactive Attachment Disorder may be diagnosed.

✓ *Tip*

□ A child who is over-attached to you as teacher, may reflect a lack of attachment with their own care-giver. While flattering, it can become burdensome (at its extreme, think stalkers!). Bring other adults that you trust into the situation, so the child gradually, hopefully, learns to trust by modelling your own trust. But, above all, get help and support for both your sakes.

Attendance Centres are where young people who might be tempted by criminal or other anti-social activities can spend, or be ordered to spend, their Saturdays. Activities are intended to be inviting and absorbing, such as web design and sports training.

★ **Attention Span** is the length of time, without a break, that a student (or teacher) can concentrate on a task, before becoming ineffective. If a student has reached their limit then attempting to pour more into them will be ineffective, like water off a duck's back.

✓ *Tips*

□ Since we are talking of animals, we are reminded of the expression *Never Try To Teach A Pig To Fly*. Why? There are three reasons:

1 You won't succeed.
2 It'll be really hard work.
3 You'll really annoy the pig!

□ One rule of thumb for estimating a student's attention span in minutes is to add one to their age. So a 3-year-old could be expected to concentrate for up to four minutes. A 10-year-old may focus for up to eleven minutes, and an 18-year-old for up to 19 minutes at a time.

□ Another is to double their age and add three. So a 3-year-old could be expected to concentrate for up to nine minutes. A 10-year-old for up to 23 minutes, and an 18-year-old for up to 39 minutes. (And by the time we retire in our sixties, we would theoretically have a 'stickability' of over two hours).

□ Strong influences on lengthening attention span are the student's LEARNING STYLE and your TEACHING STYLE. For example, if a student needs an element of the KINAESTHETIC in order to learn, then if you endeavour to teach simply by engaging their AUDITORY sense (e.g. by reading to them or talking to them) their attention span could be a matter of seconds. Any teaching style with a strong bias towards a single sense will disengage those without that bias.

Teaching is about how much students retain and not how much you present to them. For example, it is thought that people can only assimilate a maximum of seven pieces of information at any given time. (Try remembering an international telephone number, rather than a UK phone number? Or a whole shopping list rather than a handful of items?) Until we have fully integrated a manageable 'batch' of information or instructions, we cannot handle any more.

✓ *Tips*

☐ Between periods of attention, it is important to have breaks, for distracting and refreshing the brain so that it is ready for more. Breaks should be as different from the task as possible, e.g. something physical if the task is static; or something logical if the task is creative. In most cases, fresh air and drinking water are also beneficial. If in doubt, ask – e.g. shall we take a break now or do you want to finish the task? how long do you need? what do you need, to come back refreshed in a few minutes?

☐ You can give yourself a five-second refresher by taking a deep breath – out! This will expel the old, and then 'in with the new' will happen naturally. (Breathing *in* stresses the chest and increases tension – ask any half-decent singer or actor).

Auditory is

1 One of the five senses – hearing.
2 Broader than just hearing, covering all words and sounds, e.g. listening, talking, reading aloud, reading silently, talking to yourself, and writing.

Auditory Sequential Memory *see* ASM.

★ **Authenticity** is one of the best ways to build respect, support and a relationship with your students, and colleagues. Authenticity is being genuine and the real you. It is being both true to yourself and completely 'there' for your students. If you are giving anything less than your all, they will know. If you hold a belief that 'near enough' is good enough then that will come through in the way you teach and you will likely receive a similar level of inauthenticity back from your students. Do the best you can as often as you can with the most positive attitude you can.

✓ *Tip*

☐ Being authentic involves talking from the heart at times and using personal anecdotes. If you use personal experiences to reinforce a learning point then make sure you are not rambling self-indulgently; make sure what you are saying is pertinent to the subject and to the learning experience at hand.

✗ *Trap*

☐ You can be authentic and yet careful about what you divulge. You can be both present and prudent. Be careful with how much and what you tell students about yourself. Even with authenticity, there are boundaries and the need to look after *you*. And that is exactly what being authentic to yourself is about, too.

Authorized Absence is where permission from a teacher or another authorized representative of the school has been given because of, e.g. illness, special leave. Parents are expected to make every effort to ensure medical and dental appointments are outside school time. In special circumstances authorized absence may be given for a holiday but this is vigorously discouraged. Unauthorized absence is known as TRUANCY.

✓ *Tip*

☐ Frequent requests for absence may indicate an underlying situation that needs addressing. For example, if a student is taking time off because they need to translate for a parent at the doctors, another solution could be found that enables the student's education to be interrupted less.

★ **Authority and Power** usually come together, and as a teacher you have – believe it or not – potentially unlimited amounts of both. This can be both daunting and reassuring.

There are several types of authority and power:

■ *Structural*: this is the authority that comes from your position and status within an organization. A head teacher has more structural power than a teacher, for example.
■ *Reward or punishment*: is when you are in a position to give someone something they want or take away something they want to hang onto. Detention is taking away freedom. Extra tuition is giving them an improved education.
■ *Physical*: is where one person is bigger or holds a weapon and could damage another. This is a danger area with the increasing use of blades and guns within gang fights and territorial conflicts. A gun is instantaneous power which is hard to handle for those not used to feeling powerful.
■ *Emotional blackmail*: is where someone is in a position to negatively or positively influence someone else's emotional state. Comply with my wishes or I'll make you feel bad about what you have done to me or made me do.
■ *Expertise, information, and knowledge*: this is power that comes from what you know, that others want to learn or share. If you are the only one who knows how to operate the computer, you have power over those who want to use it.
■ *Personal power*: this is about you as a person, your personality, your charismatic qualities, your interest in and helpfulness to others, your enjoyment of life and work, your confidence and self-esteem.

✓ *Tips*

☐ Notice which source(s) of authority you use most and consider if they best suit your objectives.
☐ Notice how others, especially students, respond to the type of authority you use.
☐ Never abuse power in any way; never take advantage or manipulate or bully: the abuse of power may gain you short-term compliance but it can also generate long-term resentment.
☐ As a teacher try to major on knowledge and personal power if you want to stimulate and inspire students to learn from and with you.
☐ Remember – all authority and power can be used to good effect, or to damage others.

✗ *Traps*

☐ Do not confuse authority with responsibility – if you are made responsible for something, ensure that you are also given the authority to enforce it. And ensure that everyone else involved knows this.
☐ Similarly, if you make students responsible for something, discuss with them the authority they have, and don't have.

Autism *see* ASD (AUTISTIC SPECTRUM DISORDERS).

Autistic Spectrum Disorders *see* ASD.

AVCE Advanced VOCATIONAL CERTIFICATE OF EDUCATION is the vocational equivalent of 'A' levels, at level 3 on the NQF (NATIONAL QUALIFICATIONS FRAMEWORK).

AVQ Accredited Vocational Qualifications, e.g. VCE (VOCATIONAL CERTIFICATE OF EDUCATION) and AVCE (ADVANCED VOCATIONAL CERTIFICATE OF EDUCATION).

Awarding Bodies (AB) are organizations that offer and award QCA-accredited courses and qualifications (*see* QCA QUALIFICATIONS AND CURRICULUM AUTHORITY). There are over one hundred in the UK. Many also offer their own awards, for example City & Guilds and EDEXCEL.

B.Ed Bachelor of Education is the most usual degree route to qualify as a teacher, lasting typically 3 years. It covers both teacher training and subject knowledge (e.g. for secondary teachers).

B.Teach Bachelor of Teaching is the Australian and New Zealand equivalent of the UK's B.Ed (Bachelor of Education). Some universities there also offer a Bachelor of Teaching and Learning.

BA/BSc with QTS courses combine Bachelor of Arts/ Bachelor of Science degrees with teacher training, leading to QUALIFIED TEACHER STATUS and – like the B.Ed – are for teaching specialized subjects (e.g. modern languages, science) at secondary school level. Broadly speaking, these are for students who want to concentrate on their subject 'with added teaching', whereas the B.Ed is more for those who want to study to be a teacher, 'with an added subject'.

Baccalaureate (Bacc for short) is a confusing term (literally 'of a bachelor') since it refers to several different awards:

1 An undergraduate degree, i.e. a bachelor's degree (US).
2 A farewell sermon at graduation ceremonies (US).
3 The international broader-based equivalent to A levels where students take six subjects plus:

  ■ A 4,000 word essay, requiring primary research.
  ■ Theory of knowledge.
  ■ One hundred and fifty hours of supervised CAS (creativity, action, service) time.

4 The Welsh pilot of an international-style baccalaureate to replace A levels. Sixth-form students continue to study for GCSES, A/S and A LEVELS, BTECS and NVQS in addition to:

  ■ Key skills – communication, numeracy, information technology, working with others and problem-solving.
  ■ Contemporary Welsh life, Europe and the world, and a language.
  ■ Personal, social and work-related community-based programmes.

Baker Days *see* INSET.

Banding was a much derided form of selection by schools, where they were forced to admit set percentages of lower-performing students as well as higher-performing students. It's now being advocated again as a way of forcing high-performing schools to be more available to all students in their community.

Bandura, Albert (b 1925 Canada) is a psychologist best known for his SOCIAL LEARNING THEORY.

BAS British Ability Scales are reading, spelling and numeracy tests.

Baseline Assessment was introduced in the mid-1990s when a student left FOUNDATION STAGE (ages 3–5). Since there were nearly 100 different tests being used, a single FOUNDATION STAGE Profile superseded it in 2002/3.

Basic Skills are those considered to be the bare minimum necessary to live in modern society. Reading, writing and arithmetic used to be the main three, with the ability to understand and reason being implicit within them. Adults who missed learning these skills through poor or no schooling are encouraged to learn them through the BASIC SKILLS AGENCY.

The terms KEY SKILLS and Basic Skills are often used interchangeably (and confusingly) and the three basic skills are currently

- Communication.
- Application of Number.
- IT.

For adults, Adult Literacy is added into Communication, and Adult Numeracy is added into Application of Number.

Basic Skills Agency aims to enable all children and adults in England and Wales to have at least adequate BASIC SKILLS. It was originally the Adult Literacy Resource Agency (ALRA), then the Adult Literacy Unit (ALU) and then the Adult Literacy and Basic Skills Unit (ALBSU).

Beacon Schools were intended to help raise standards through sharing good practice with other schools in, e.g. specific curriculum subjects, school management, parental involvement or anti-bullying strategies. It was part of the Eic (Excellence in Cities) strategy. Each Beacon had on average nine partner schools, and around half were involved in ITT (INITIAL TEACHER TRAINING). The intention was that schools with lower achievements followed the methods, approaches and systems set by these beacon schools in order to model excellence. The LEADING EDGE PARTNERSHIP programme will replace it from 2005 in secondary schools, and plans are being discussed for replacing it in other school sectors.

BEC Business Education Council was established in 1974 to prepare learners for the world of work and improve the work relevance of vocational education in FE (Further Education) and HE (Higher Education).

BECTA British Educational Communications and Technology Agency is the Government's lead agency for the use of ICT in education, to raise standards, widen access, improve skills and encourage effective management. It was responsible, for example, for the Government's Laptops for Teachers initiative in June 2002.

Behaviour Management can take a lot of a teacher's time and attention. Let's be honest, if a student is mis-behaving then their attention is elsewhere. This article deals with recognizing and managing inappropriate behaviours which affect the learning of the student, or those around them, or both. In all cases, however, dealing with the individual student's needs is key.

Anyway, let's look at three different levels of behaviour – largely intended to describe students, but teachers and others can also display these:

1 *Appropriate* behaviour is where an observer would agree that how the person behaves is appropriate to the task, e.g.

- Sitting quietly in a written test.
- Listening and talking respectfully in discussions.
- Giving encouragement as a sports spectator.

Appropriate behaviour signals that the person's attention is engaged in the task, e.g. in the examples above:

- Writing on the test paper; or looking thoughtfully for inspiration.
- Bringing other people into a discussion, or asking for time out to reflect.
- Shouting loudly on the sports field when the action is distant, or keeping quiet when players need to concentrate.

2 *Mildly inappropriate behaviour* signals that the person's attention is distracted, and that they might disengage themselves from the task, but that is not yet a problem, e.g.

■ Remembering something you want to buy, in the middle of a test.
■ Feeling out of your depth in a discussion, and planning your weekend.
■ Talking to other sports spectators about unrelated matters.

3 *Grossly inappropriate behaviour* not only signals the person's disengagement with the task, but a preference for engaging with a task of their own choosing, and with a disruptive effect on others, e.g.

■ Singing loudly during a test.
■ Hitting someone they disagree with.
■ Throwing things at sports participants.

Sometimes, inappropriate behaviour can lead to disaster, but there are four stages leading to disaster, and the first three are your early-warning signs:

1 Distraction.
2 Disengagement.
3 Disruption.
4 Disaster.

✓ *Tips*

☐ Engage students at the very beginning by letting them feel motivated by the task and by the appropriate behaviours for the task.
☐ Re-engage them (and yourself) periodically with e.g. a break, or a different mini-task. This also gives you breathing space to work out what to do next.
☐ Develop the habit of being available to go to a student to answer their questions one-on-one, so no student needs to feel embarrassed to ask.
☐ Notice that if several people are asking questions, or having problems, your set-up or explanation has almost certainly missed the mark. Rather than answer each in turn, think about how you can re-explain and thereby re-engage everyone with the task.
☐ If you are asked to explain something again, don't! They didn't understand it the first time, so explain it *differently* after you've first asked what it was that they didn't understand.

Doesn't this mean that the teacher takes responsibility for the student's 'bad' behaviour? No, because it's the student's choice. And yes, because it's the teacher's job to get and to keep the students sufficiently engaged to prevent disruptive disengagement, with specialist help if necessary. Of course you are not responsible for the disengagement of a student who's angry with the whole world, or has learning difficulties, or 'problems' at home, for example. But you are responsible for engaging that student, somehow.

Example

We knew a 'disruptive' student who always had an opinion, a joke, a challenge, a disagreement – you name it – on every single point. 'He's always like this with everyone.' people said, resignedly. At a break the teacher quietly and privately said 'It's obvious that you're not very interested in what we're doing here. Is it me, personally? Is it the subject matter? What exactly can I do to make this better for you?'. The student immediately looked as though the wind had been taken out of his sails. With relief in his voice he explained that a close relative had been ill for a long, long time and was close to death. He had asked to be excused from the class, but this was denied. He'd much rather be at the hospice. It was not the teacher, nor the subject. It was just the wrong place for him to be right now. Realistically, there is little chance of engaging someone who has something so powerful on their mind. So the teacher explored some tasks that might take his mind off the situation, to enable him to feel more comfortable, but agreed that he was free to leave if he needed to, and how about they both went to OK this with the head?

In reality, by exploring the situation, it changed the teacher's expectations of the student, and enabled everyone else to feel more comfortable. And they changed his seating position so he could tuck himself away at the 'back'. No-one could have addressed this by guessing. Only by asking.

Some More Tips

☐   There are typically three mindsets in any group:

   ■   *Learners* who are here to learn, and you just need to ensure that they remain motivated and engaged.
   ■   *Holidaymakers* who don't really want to be here, but while they're here, they might as well find ways of enjoying themselves. Your job is to find out, for each individual, how to engage them, to turn them into learners.
   ■   *Prisoners* who are here under sufferance and don't want to be here at all. Your job is to find out, for each individual, how to engage them and give them reason(s) to become learners, or at least help them to become holidaymakers (so they find some ways of enjoying their 'sentence' rather than having to endure it).

☐   Save your major interventions for destructive or disruptive behaviours, rather than students who are just staring out of the window distractedly, otherwise all your time will be taken up unproductively. (And if you do want to address a particular student's habit of staring out of the window, because you suspect it's too task-unrelated, check it out with them privately, e.g. I notice that you spend time staring out of the window: what can I do to help your thinking? We all need time-out to reflect, think, visualize.) After all, no-one's ATTENTION SPAN will be more than a few minutes, without a change of focus, pace or activity.

☐   Sometimes you might state out loud what's obvious to everyone, e.g. 'I've clearly not made this very interesting for you, so let me ask you…(and then ask the Magic Questions, e.g. What do you need? or What are you missing? or What will make this easier/ more achievable/ more enjoyable for you?). You're not 'losing face' – you're demonstrating learning. How can you possibly know in advance what will engage every single student? You have to find out, and asking questions is the best way to do so. Another way is to put yourself in the students' shoes. Here's a strategy ('Changing Places') that many teachers use:

1   Imagine teaching a group of students. Then imagine sitting as one of your students, being taught by you. In this position get a feel for what is working well for you, the student, and what is not yet working well for you? What do you need, to make learning and engaging easier for you? Now imagine sitting as each student in turn. What specific needs does each one have, for this lesson to be a success? What introduction to the topic stands the best chance of engaging them all? Maybe you need two or three options, to hook everyone back in (e.g. 'In this statistics lesson, we're going to look at great chat-up lines. We're going to find out what really works for you, and what turns you off. We're going to research how they work on other people, and which are likely to be the most successful. And which are likely to work the worst. All based on solid statistics. Now, is anyone NOT interested in this?!')

2   Now imagine you're a fly on the wall observing the lesson, you, and your students. What can you see from here that would make the lesson go even better?

3   And, in your own shoes, what do you yourself need to make this go better for you?

Behaviour Policy should be clearly understood in every school, covering

- The standards of behaviour expected of students.
- How these standards are determined.
- How to address behaviour that does not meet these agreed standards.

These are vital guidelines for your use and protection, as it means that you are not alone with a problem. It also enables *patterns* of behaviour to be addressed, as well as each incident in isolation.

Behaviourism is a huge and much discussed field of study that was a dominant theory of learning in the 1970s, based on the idea that it was possible to change behaviours by offering rewards. You could spend many a happy (?) hour on the internet getting embroiled in the discussions. Essentially it is the study of how, by changing what we do, we can change what we achieve.

Examples

- By stopping doing what doesn't work for us, we achieve more.
- By promising ourselves a treat on completing a task, we can finish tasks we weren't even motivated to start.

✗ Trap

☐   Using food as treats has contributed significantly to current obesity levels.

See also SKINNER (the 'father' of behaviourism), GAGNÉ, and OPERANT BEHAVIOUR.

Benchmarking is making comparisons with others, in order to assess your own levels of achievement. By measuring yourself, your students or your school against others, you are able to gain information on:

- Areas where your performance can improve.
- Areas where you are already performing well, i.e. strengths upon which you can build.

Benchmarking, however, can also apply the pressure to improve, without identifying the ways in which to improve. Also, when benchmarking is used primarily as a means of negative comparison, the measurement is not always fair: league tables have only recently been making allowance for the potential of the students, e.g. with the VALUE ADDED measure. Also, if benchmarking is used in a negative way, teachers and students alike may start to perform in order to avoid criticism, rather than to maximize achievement.

✓ Tips

☐   Recognize benchmarking for the benefits it can bring.

☐   Benchmark yourself against the best in order to be inspired and to aspire.

☐   Ensure there is a level playing field, and compare the inputs as well as the outputs.

BESD Behavioural, Emotional and Social Difficulty/Difficulties.

Best Value is a way of judging different suppliers, in order to place an order for goods or services. Local authorities used to be expected to apply 'lowest cost' principles, until they found that this often resulted in 'lowest quality' practices. The guidelines to best value are called the four Cs:

- *Challenge:* ask probing questions about why, how and by whom the purchases will be used and whether they are needed at all.
- *Compare:* find out what other parts of the school and other schools have done, and the results they achieved.
- *Consult:* talk to all stakeholders to test and evaluate the intended action.
- *Compete:* use competition to secure efficient and effective services as opposed to the cheapest.

Bias when obvious, e.g. racism or sexism, is relatively easy to deal with. Hidden biases are the subtle, sometimes unnoticed, mostly unintentional messages that not everybody is equal – and are less easy to spot, and therefore to deal with. Even those of us with a commitment to equality and the absence of prejudice have to be aware of these pitfalls. Of course, bias, prejudice and stereotyping exist in society. You need only go back one generation to see television programmes based on racial discrimination. So how can you design school uniforms, or discuss differences in gender, learning styles, and levels of achievement, without recognizing your own biases? If you need to move furniture, do you ask the males to do it because they are physically stronger (usually)? Do you talk about football results and expect only the males to be interested?

✓ **Tips**

- ☐ Acknowledge differences without putting any values on them.
- ☐ Getting rid of bias is a continuous task that requires observation and self examination. What might seem unimportant or insignificant to one person can often offend another.
- ☐ Many welcomed the 'black'board becoming the 'chalkboard' – but seemed strangely, to us, not to have a problem with the WHITEBOARD – but equality is likely to come about by these small steps rather than by massive changes.

See EQUAL OPPORTUNITIES and PC.

Binet, Alfred (1859–1911) was a French psychologist who was interested in the workings of the normal mind, and who developed the first IQ test in 1905 as a special needs diagnostic tool.

BIP Behaviour Improvement Programme or Behaviour Intervention Plan, both of which address problem behaviours, normally with parental involvement.

Bitesize Learning (or Distributed Learning) breaks learning down into manageable parts. It recognizes the importance of remembering and integrating knowledge step-by-step as opposed to being inundated by information. Bitesize learning is useful for longer-term revision, as it discourages students from 'cramming' at the last minute and encourages them to see revision as an ongoing process that can be planned.

Blended Learning involves multiple media – e.g. a combination of classroom teaching with independent E-LEARNING.

Bloom's Taxonomy of the Cognitive Domain was published in 1956 by a group of educators led by Benjamin Bloom. It is a commonly-used hierarchy of THINKING SKILLS and learning abilities, starting with the 'easiest' and finishing with the most cognitively demanding, or 'higher-order' skills. (Incidentally, it also illuminated (in 2004) why Mike hated his university education (in the 1970s) as the teaching never progressed beyond the first level. His brain, therefore, lay dormant for the whole three years!)

1 *Knowledge* – re-calling information and facts from memory, e.g. dates, times, events, safety instructions. This is normally assessed by asking questions beginning with

- inform me, describe, tell me, list, define, who, when, where, etc.

2 *Comprehension* – understanding the meaning of their knowledge, e.g. explaining in their own words, or understanding the implications. This is normally assessed by asking questions beginning with

   ■ explain how or why, tell me in your own words, compare x with y, discuss, etc.

3 *Application* – putting a concept to use in a new situation, e.g. solving new problems with existing knowledge. This is normally assessed by asking questions beginning with

   ■ apply, solve, experiment, discover, etc.

4 *Analysis* – seeing the parts, and patterns of parts, that make up a totality, e.g. troubleshooting a situation, finding a bottleneck in a process. This is normally assessed by asking questions beginning with

   ■ analyse, find, identify, sort out, deconstruct, etc.

5 *Synthesis* – constructing something new from existing parts, e.g. designing something that achieves specific objectives, rearranging what already exists in order to satisfy new needs. This is normally assessed by asking questions beginning with

   ■ synthesize, create, design, invent, devise, what if?, etc.

6 *Evaluation* – making decisions about the value of different items, e.g. select the most appropriate solution, decide who is best able to do that. This is normally assessed by asking questions beginning with

   ■ evaluate, judge, compare, select, etc.

See another of Bloom *et al.*'s Taxonomies under AFFECTIVE LEARNING.

★ **Body Language** is how we communicate non-verbally (e.g. a frown, a shrug, a raised eyebrow, the tone of our voice) whether we intend to or not. Every part of our body can give non-verbal signals.

It is generally recognized that most of what we communicate is non-verbal, and the actual words play a relatively small part. Think of someone hissing 'Yes Of Course I'm Happy To See You' through clenched teeth. Or people who have said 'this is a wonderful piece of work' or 'I'm so pleased to be here today,' but you were absolutely certain that they didn't mean it. Even children not old enough to speak or understand words will know what is going on around them by listening to voice qualities and watching body language. They recognize patterns and know when patterns are disturbed. Your students will, therefore, be paying attention to your voice qualities and body language as well as to the words you use. You as a teacher will also read the messages that a class or individual student is giving to you from the way they act. When checking for understanding, you need to be seeing it quietly demonstrated in their body language as well as by using oral questions and answers.

✓ *Tips*

□ Ensure that you are giving out the right non-verbal signals by preparing your internal state and frame of mind. Key factors in this are preparation, practice, clarity of objective, knowing your subject and feeling good about yourself.

□ Find a way of standing that makes you feel good, positive or any of the other qualities you want to bring to teaching. Practise standing this way. When you're at the front of a class, adopt this positive physical state to trigger the positive frame of mind that accompanies it. It's easy, with practice, to stand in a way that makes you feel how you want to feel.

□ EYE CONTACT is a key piece of non-verbal communication. Maintain eye contact and become curious if someone will not maintain eye contact with you.

□ Observe other people – watch television documentaries or news programmes with the sound off and work out what is happening through visual observation alone.

☐ When talking on the phone, pay special attention to the other person's voice qualities and identify if the words they use match their tone.

☐ Some body language is supposed to apply to everybody. For example, touching your mouth or nose when talking is supposed to denote lies, but other people say it's a sign of being thoughtful. Crossing your arms is meant to be defensive by putting up barriers, although some people just find it comfortable! Always check how you interpret what you see by questioning more deeply, or by further observation. We often ask something like 'you say X but your body seems to be saying the opposite – can you help me out here, please?'.

☐ And, finally, if someone's voice tonality and body language give different messages to the words they use, trust the non-verbal signals. Only a truly accomplished actor can fake these.

Booster Classes in literacy and numeracy began in 1999, to provide extra support for targeted students in Year 6. These students had not had the benefit of LITERACY and NUMERACY HOURS in their primary schooling, and were thought unlikely to achieve Level 4 at the end of Key Stage 2. The number of students achieving Level 4 rose from two-thirds to three-quarters, and has since levelled off. (Some teachers are against booster classes, feeling that they are discriminatory against the non-targeted students.)

★ **Boring** is one of the worst insults a student can throw at a teacher. How do we know if we are boring? How can we avoid being boring? How do we handle the insult? Well, let's face it, students do struggle to learn if the teacher is boring. No matter how motivated a student is, if the teacher does not inspire them and keep them engaged then they will not learn as much as they could. If a student has to fight to learn, then there is something wrong with the teaching style. If you want your students to perform, and turn up for your classes and speak well of you, then 'boring' is probably the most important quality to avoid.

1   *How to avoid being boring?* Boring is about sameness and predictability. If your voice never varies its speed, tone, intonation and volume then your speech is likely to sound boring. If your movement is static, lacks energy, or if you sit behind a desk all the time then you are likely to be boring visually. If the way you structure your lessons and put across learning points is the same and predictable then your teaching style is likely to be boring.

2   *How to handle accusations of being boring?* Ask how you have bored them, and how they need you to behave differently, and take any feedback as a contribution to your improvement and growth. Imagine yourself sitting in one of your lessons – would you be bored? Be objective about the way you teach.

3   *How can you tell if you're being boring?* Let's use our senses to recognize the evidence that shows if we are being boring or not. If you see the students' body language showing a lack of energy, slumping, yawning, looking around, rubbing their eyes, then this is likely to be as much to do with you as to their lifestyle or lack of sleep. If you feel you have to push them or supply all the energy to the lesson, this could be another sign. An enthusiastic class will provide you with energy. Obviously if someone tells you that you are boring this is a clear auditory sign of you being boring. But another sign would be a lack of questions or responses to your questions.

✓ *Tips*

☐ It is part of British culture to be modest in the way we behave, and being modest is potentially close to being dull. So if you want to be an engaging teacher, bring variety,

vitality and surprise to your teaching – whatever you feel comfortable with. And, if necessary, get some help with some ideas.
- Don't take it personally: no-one *is* boring, but we all can *do* boring. It's something specific that we can change, once we know what to change.

Bowlby, John (1907–1990) was a British psychoanalyst and psychologist who developed ATTACHMENT THEORY in 1969 and was a pioneer in working with children regarding loss and grief.

Brain Gym® is a programme of physical exercises devised by Drs Paul and Gail Dennison to prepare the person physically for learning. The exercises are simple like the old 'game' of head, shoulders, knees and toes where the teacher names the part of the body and the students touch that part of the body. The different exercises help people to feel, for example, focused, calm, clear-headed, co-ordinated or centred. Even though these are physical exercises, they are said to enhance academic skills such as reading, writing and maths as well as listening, co-ordination, attention and communication skills. It is also known as educational kinesiology (the study of anatomy, physiology and movement, and their effect on learning) and Edu-K.

Brain Structure It is said that over 80 per cent of what we know about the workings of the human brain has been learnt during the last 20 years, and yet we are still in the dark about 95 per cent of the brain's workings. So, how does the brain affect learning? A simple description comes from the triune (three-part) model:

1 *Reptilian* – this area at the base of the brain is thought to control survival instincts if we are under threat, and all routine bodily functions. When a student is feeling under threat, this sector dominates all others, and learning (and everything else) takes second place to survival.
2 *Limbic system* – is in the middle of the brain and is thought to involve emotions and long-term memory. Positive emotions are thought to speed up overall transmission in the brain and so facilitate learning. From a teacher's point of view, the more positive you are in the way you teach, and the more positive the student feels, the easier they will learn.
3 *Neo-cortex* – is at the top of the brain, and is thought to be the cognitive or thinking area where problem-solving and pattern-seeking happen.

Another model describes the two distinct hemispheres of the neo-cortex as if they were individual brains:

- Left hemisphere/brain – was thought to be the verbal and analytical side of the brain, controlling facts and language and logic.
- Right hemisphere/brain – was thought to be the creative and non-verbal side, controlling imagination, intuition and movement.

But, and this is a big 'but', MRI scanning of the brain is beginning to shed more light on what parts are actually involved in performing tasks and is casting doubt on models such as 'left brain' and 'right brain' thinking.

✓ *Tip*

- Some techniques, e.g. BRAIN GYM®, aim to get all areas of the brain working together, to enhance learning.

Brainstorming describes a variety of two-stage processes for solving problems.

- *Stage One* is generating lots of possibilities in response to a specific brief (*see also* DIVERGENT THINKING and POSSIBILITY THINKING).

- *Stage Two* is choosing the solution, from those possibilities (also known as convergent thinking).

It was developed by Alex Osborn, of the BBDO advertising agency, from Hindu teachers' techniques used in India for more than 400 years. (The Indian term for this technique means 'questioning outside yourself'.)

The four basic rules that Osborn stipulated for brainstorming are:

1   Criticism is not allowed during the process, as it inhibits ideas.
2   The wilder the idea, the better; as it is easier to tame down than to think up.
3   The greater the number of ideas, the more likely are there to be useful ideas.
4   Participants can also suggest how others' ideas can be improved upon.

✗ Trap

☐   This term is now arguably not POLITICALLY CORRECT in some circles because of its associations with epileptic episodes.

Broadband is a computer connection that uses coaxial cable (like a TV aerial) which can carry much more data (e.g. to and from the internet) than a simple telephone wire can. It is always 'on' so you don't need to 'dial-up' each time you need a connection.

Bruner (often mis-spelled Brunner), **Jerome** (b. 1915) is an influential US psychologist who developed CONSTRUCTIVIST THEORY, DISCOVERY LEARNING, and a Theory of Instruction that suggests that instruction needs to consider

1   The students' *predisposition* to learning, including their social and cultural contexts.
2   How knowledge might be *presented*, to be most easily understood.
3   The most effective *sequence* in which to present material, for step-by-step learning.
4   The best nature and pacing of *rewards* and *punishment*.

Bubble Time *see* CIRCLE TIME.

 Bullying is where one or more people abuse their AUTHORITY AND POWER and systematically persecute or intimidate others, physically, mentally, or both. Maybe it is part of human nature, jostling for position, but whatever its causes, it has no place in schools – whether of students or staff, or parents or anyone else, come to that. Fortunately, bullying is no longer thought of as inevitable when children are together, and the heat is now on the bullies. Every school should have a policy on bullying, so that instances can be dealt with consistently, and so teachers are not left alone with problem situations.

It is a priority that students are turned away from bullying because the evidence is that people who bully as children, and gain results from bullying, continue to do so throughout their lives. (And, at last, bullying at work is now being taken as seriously as bullying at school.) Bullies tend to bully others into supporting them and therefore form GANGS. The values and rules within these gangs can be as strong as in underworld gangs, and as hard to control. And those who are bullied can suffer tragic consequences.

Bullies themselves tend to be suffering, or have suffered, abuse or bullying at home and tend to have very low SELF-ESTEEM. They hit out at others because they cannot hit out at themselves, and the only way they can feel 'big' is by belittling others. Bullying can be both a natural trait or a learnt behaviour copied from seeing others bullying and being bullied. In some homes, this is the main means of communicating for children to model.

Many schools now use older students to act as bullying mentors for younger students so that the younger ones know they have someone safe to talk to. Unfortunately, many students who are bullied do not tell their parents because of the fear of the parent taking action, the bully being reprimanded and then the bully taking retribution for having been identified.

✓ *Tips*

☐ Although statistics are not concrete on the matter, it is believed that bullying is less common where general discipline is higher in schools.

☐ You need to be alert to signs of bullying and act early. It does not go away. It escalates.

☐ Never make light of bullying behaviour in any form. No matter what form the bullying takes, if a person *feels* bullied, then they have been bullied. That's the only test. Their main need in the short-term is to be heard, believed and supported – i.e. no longer alone with the situation.

☐ If bullying persists then professional help should be sought through the head teacher.

☐ Television drama and soaps depend on conflict and behaviour that constitutes bullying to form their plots. You can use these examples in general conversation to show how that behaviour will eventually work against the bully, and is not acceptable.

☐ It is said that 'sticks and stones may break my bones, but words can never hurt me'. This is nonsense. We can all recall being called something that wounded us so deeply, we can still remember it even now. Mental bullying can often have longer lasting effects than physical bullying. *See* APPEARANCE BULLYING.

☐ A technique called 'fogging' is often useful, if someone is called something hurtful (and let's face it, bullies manage to find our tender spot to hurt). It moves the attack from the personal to the practical, e.g., 'Fat face!' could get the response 'And your point is what, exactly?'.

☐ RESTORATIVE JUSTICE approaches are useful in addressing bullying behaviours.

☐ And remember, all of this applies just as much to you, if you yourself are feeling bullied. Don't keep it to yourself. Get help. Consider approaching your union representative.

Campaign for Learning is a charity that aims to stimulate learning that will sustain people for life, by working for an inclusive society in which learning is understood, valued and accessible to everyone as of right. *See also* LEARNING AT WORK DAY, FAMILY LEARNING WEEK, LEARNING TO LEARN IN SCHOOLS.

Catchment Area of a school is the geographic area that is the primary source of their students. Even though a family lives within a particular catchment area, they must still apply to the school for a place for their child. (CLASS SIZE limits any guarantees of a place.) If a parent wants to apply for a place in a school outside their catchment area they may do so, but whether or not they are granted a place depends on factors such as capacity, and having a sibling at the school.

Causality, Law of has been at the heart of scientific enquiry since it was defined by Socrates around 400 BCE. It observes an event and is then curious about understanding the reason for it – and is commonly known as the law of 'cause and effect'.

CCEA (Northern Ireland) Council for the Curriculum Examinations and Assessment gives advice on, and support for, what is taught and assessed in schools and colleges in Northern Ireland.

CE Citizenship Education became a statutory part of the NATIONAL CURRICULUM for Secondary Schools from September 2002 at Key Stages 3 and 4. It builds on the Primary School initiative of Citizenship Framework in Key Stages 1 and 2. Citizenship was triggered by a sense that young people were becoming increasingly alienated from society. Increased crime levels, unemployment levels, drug-taking, under-age drinking and a reluctance to vote, were taken as a wake-up call. Citizenship was seen as a way of instilling society-based values that would increase the quality of life for all, and empower students to make a positive difference to their communities as adults. The National Curriculum for Citizenship at Key Stages 3 and 4 states that students should be taught about

- The work of parliament, government and courts in making and shaping the law.
- The importance of playing an active part in democratic and electoral processes.
- The opportunities for individuals and voluntary groups to bring about social change locally, nationally, in Europe and internationally.
- The legal and human rights and responsibilities underpinning society, and how they relate to citizens, including the role and operation of the criminal and civil justice systems.

The 'how' of citizenship is left to the individual school to organize but it is hoped that citizenship will become part of the school fabric and way of life – the lessons of citizenship should be demonstrated in issues such as bullying, fundraising and local community initiatives. It can also be woven into other subjects. And, as a result of citizenship education, it is hoped that students will

- Know their rights and responsibilities.
- Analyse and discuss significant issues.
- Understand how society works.
- Play an active role in society.

- Understand the importance of human rights.
- Understand religious, ethnic and national diversity.
- Know how political systems work and why they should vote within a democracy.
- Recognize global responsibilities.
- Understand ecological issues and sustainable development.
- Understand consumer, employers' and employees' rights.

✓ *Tip*

☐ All staff should be a walking demonstration of the values of citizenship, not just relying upon the specific lessons.

CEDC *see* CONTINYOU.

★ **Celebrating Achievement** and giving praise is a way of building on positives with a view to encouraging students to want more success. It installs the habit of achieving and being successful. When you show you are pleased then the student will feel uplifted and want to be more successful to get that uplifting feeling. It is a virtuous circle.

The celebration of success can take many forms. Praising them in front of fellow students is often enough. Announcements in front of the class or whole school are even stronger, although some might find it embarrassing.

Certificates of achievements are useful because they last a lifetime, and are an ever present reminder of success and can form part of a CV. (*See also* MOTIVATION.)

✓ *Tips*

☐ Before publicly celebrating success make sure you will not cause embarrassment or the student to lose credibility with their peers. Some success is best celebrated covertly.
☐ If you have established a class culture where success is celebrated make sure nobody is missed out. Find a way of celebrating everyone's achievements over time.
☐ Extreme as though this might sound, avoid using sweets or food as rewards so you do not fuel the trend towards child obesity.

Centres of Vocational Excellence *see* COVES.

Certificates (1) can be awarded by anyone to anyone for anything. They certify only what they claim to certify (2) are normally taken part-time by people in employment, recognizing the knowledge and skills gained at work whereas DIPLOMAS are normally taken by full-time students.

Chalkface is a term meaning in the classroom (literally, at the chalkboard, chalk in hand). It's intended to mirror the term 'coalface' where miners work, hands-on.

Chess Although computer games have their own attractions (including computer chess, naturally), chess has a lot to offer when it comes to learning:

- *Eye to hand co-ordination*, placing pieces without knocking over others or disturbing the layout of the board.
- *Forward planning moves*, thinking through ramifications and responses, and contingency planning if what you expect to happen does not happen.
- *Conceptual and strategic thinking* – are you going to attack, defend or evaluate your opponent before you decide?
- *Spatial awareness* – looking both at the whole board, and the possible interactions within it.
- *Building* the different pieces, with their different capabilities, and limitations, into a team that works together and shares a goal.

- *Having a clear outcome* and a way of measuring if that outcome has been achieved.
- *Working out how your opponent thinks*, and how they evaluate you.
- *Winning and losing* with dignity.
- And it's relatively inexpensive, portable and needs no batteries.

✓ **Tip**

☐ Many games go in and out of fashion. If you introduce chess into an after-school club, you might just start a fashion.

Child-centred Learning is putting the child (learner) first, starting with their needs, abilities and preferences, and building a skills-based curriculum for them, rather than expect them to fit into a pre-determined system or curriculum. It is more of a philosophical approach, than a defined methodology, and the role of the teacher is, therefore, as a skilled FACILITATOR. The concept probably started with Henri ROUSSEAU in 1762 and was taken forward by thinkers and practitioners alike, who realized that individuals had their own needs and ways of learning.

✓ **Tip**

☐ You will hear people complain 'if only we had the luxury of the time to do this' and they mean this in a truly heartfelt way. However, the time and energy that's spent in 'trying' to get people to do what they can't, won't, don't want, or don't need to do, is enormous and never satisfying. We know many teachers who have invested time in building a one-to-one RELATIONSHIP with all their students, and who reap the dividends from their investment on a daily basis.

✗ **Trap**

☐ You may not succeed at this with every student (or colleague) but you will at least get respect for trying (even if they don't admit it to your face).

Top Tips from Debbie Prior

- Remember what it was like to be a child.
- Use the children's interests to lead your teaching.
- Don't use just stickers for rewards, use your imagination.

Child Development is a huge field of study with models and theories galore. For example, Freud proposed five stages – oral, anal, phallic, latent and genital (but this is probably of little use in the classroom). We suggest that you see our pieces on BOWLBY and PIAGET, and then you research the actual age group you are teaching.

✓ **Tips**

☐ Your students will represent a wide spectrum of abilities and most of them could cause you concern if you compared their abilities to what any one model or theory tells you.

☐ Focus on what your students *are* able to do rather than on what you might consider to be any developmental or learning difficulties. (Many studies show that building upon strengths not only reinforces the strengths, but improves performance in other areas as well, thanks to feelings of motivation and success, whereas focusing on areas of weakness can drag down performance in previously strong areas.)

☐ Consult, consult, consult – with colleagues who have experience of your students' age group, and with your SENCO if necessary.

Circle Time is often thought only to be where students (as well as teachers and assistants) sit in a circle to express their feelings about events, whether celebratory, concerning or just neutral. Certainly it can help students build self-esteem and confidence, as it provides a forum for better understanding others, and how to be respectful when others express themselves. It can also be a useful way of having younger students express what is happening in some of the more social aspects of school, such as break times, friendship failure, and bullying. Circle time can provide a structured way for issues to be dealt with.

✓ *Tips*

□   With very young students you could have a 'talking-stick' type of object, that designates who has a turn to speak, without interruption.

□   With younger students, teachers often use hand puppets, because the students will often talk to a puppet whereas they may feel intimidated by an adult or their peers.

✗ *Trap*

□   Jenny Mosley, who developed circle time, does *not* advocate the above processes in isolation. She describes a 'whole school quality circle time model' which incorporates a complete behaviour management system of social and personal education, for all students and staff. It includes:

  ■   *Bubble time*, or talk time, which is time for one-on-one listening, rather than group listening in the circle.
  ■   *Incentives* to reinforce appropriate behaviours.
  ■   *Sanctions*, mainly the loss of incentives, to reinforce the value of the incentives.
  ■   *Golden rules* or codes of conduct, which are formulated in the circle, and reinforced by the circle.

✓ *Tip*

□   The classic 'quality circle time' structure is

  1   *Meeting up* – with a game or warm-up activity.
  2   *Warming up* – by going around the circle and giving everyone the chance to speak on the chosen topic (e.g. I find I can play best at break time when…).
  3   *Opening up* – the open forum for airing problems or setting goals (e.g. I need help with X, because…) and getting feedforward (e.g. maybe you could…? or 'would it help if I…?).
  4   *Cheering up* – celebrating successes.
  5   *Calming down* – a game, perhaps, to get a sense of closure, and to lead appropriately into the next part of the day.

Citizenship Education *see* CE.

City and Guilds of London Institute (CGLI) known as City & Guilds, is the biggest awarding body for vocational qualifications such as NVQs and apprenticeships.

Class Size in KEY STAGE 1 is supposed to be thirty students or less. If this figure is to be exceeded it needs to be cleared by the LEA who will assess the extenuating circumstances. For other key stages class size often seems to be controlled by the physical area of the classroom available. Some teachers feel that 25 is an absolute maximum for key stage 1, or that 20 is an absolute maximum for A level classes. However, to look on the positive side, the more students there are in a class, the more choice a teacher has in grouping similar-ability students together. Then, with or without a teaching assistant, the teacher's job is simply to manage, say, six groups of five students, rather than thirty individuals. Naturally each student will require attention at times, but the groups can be largely self-managing if the tasks are motivating and clearly briefed.

IRRELEVANT FACT

In round numbers, in the public sector, there are 9 million school students and 0.5 million teachers in the UK, giving an average class size of 18. But then again, who's average?

Classics is an umbrella term covering the study of Greek and Roman literature.

Classroom Assistants *see* TEACHING ASSISTANTS.

Classroom Stagecraft is essential. Great emphasis is rightly put on the information that teachers present to students. You receive excellent guidance on teaching techniques and how these relate to learning theories. Not so much is taught about the stagecraft or delivery techniques that will more effectively engage your students. And so here are some ideas:

 Tips

☐ Be enthusiastic, passionate and excited by what you are teaching. If you are not then the students won't be.
☐ Experiment with your physiology, the way you stand. The essence of body language is that the way you feel inside shows itself in the way you hold your body – and visa versa. So if you're feeling unresourceful, that will show in the way you stand and the students will read your frame of mind from your body language. Find the way you stand when you're feeling great and then stand that way every time you're in front of a class.
☐ When you talk, imagine your voice coming from your belly and see what it does to your voice quality. Projection is not volume – it is the force within the voice that projects. Use your whole body as a sound source, and you can whisper and still be heard.
☐ Get used to being quiet when in front of class. They will wait for you to speak and your composure will intrigue them.
☐ Move around the classroom to alter their point of attention.
☐ Practise making more use of movement. Allow your arms, hands and body to move with the words. Movement gains attention.

Cognition means knowing or thinking.

Cognitive Development is how our thinking skills develop as we grow. There are many theories and models but BRUNER, PIAGET and VYGOTSKY were key early influences.

Piaget found that cognitive development can't be taught or forced – it has to be allowed to happen. The two stages he suggested are

1   *Egocentric* – the whole world revolves around the child, e.g. mother is *mine*. That ice-cream is *mine*.
2   *Away from* – where other possibilities can be entertained, such as moving away from the centre of our universe and imagining what it would be like to be in someone else's shoes (some people never reach this stage).

Another key influence is known as MAP (aka Marion A Perlmutter) who has been Professor of the Department of Psychology of the University of Michigan, at Ann Arbor (US) since 1985.

Cognitive Structures are patterns (i.e. structures) of thinking. *See* PIAGET.

Co-Learners *see* STUDY BUDDIES.

Collective Worship is compulsory in maintained schools in England and Wales although parents may withdraw their children if they choose to. (Students may not withdraw themselves.)

Common Entrance Examination *see* PUBLIC SCHOOLS.

Community Schools and Colleges offer services not only to their school-age and college-age students, but also to others in the community, e.g. sports facilities, meeting rooms, classes for adults, inviting adults into students' classes, coffee-shop facilities, or learning centre access.

★ **Completion** is essential and satisfying to all of us. Completing the circle and not leaving unfinished business creates a sense of well being. It is a principle used in many art forms. For example, a novelist might start a book in the present moment and then go to the beginning of the story in order to take the reader through events to arrive back in the present. Many movies have a similar structure, showing the viewer where the film will end and then taking them through the events that will bring about that ending. Comedians often start with a joke that they come back to in a slightly different form at the end of their act. There is something in us that enjoys coming 'full circle', with a sense of completion. How can we apply this principle to learning? Start your lesson with an overview of what will be covered and then, at the end, summarize and reflect back in a way that makes a clear connection to the outcomes and objectives set at the beginning. This process of reflection, and connecting back to the introduction, provides a sense of achievement, builds a positive attitude and completes the circle. It also enables students (and teachers) to move on to the next topic with no unfinished business.

Comprehension is not just having knowledge, but understanding the meaning of that knowledge, e.g. being able to explain in your own words, or understand the implications, rather than just repeat facts and information, parrot-fashion.

✔ *Tip*

☐ To find out what students have comprehended (i.e. understood), ask questions beginning with, e.g. explain how or why; tell me in your own words; compare x with y; discuss. (*See* BLOOM'S TAXONOMY OF THE COGNITIVE DOMAIN.)

Comprehensive Schools were intended to be non-selective, and became government policy from the 1960s. However, because there are still around 200 GRAMMAR SCHOOLS, some comprehensive schools in those areas are in reality little different from the secondary modern schools which they were intended to replace. Others, although denied the most academically able students, still thrive as wide-ability schools. SPECIALIST SCHOOLS are, however, taking over rapidly.

★ **Confidentiality** is a responsibility we all have, if things have been told to us privately. (If we betray a confidence, we might get a reputation for being untrustworthy, or a gossip, or both.) We all, however, also have a responsibility to report any situation where we feel that someone may be at risk. How do we balance these two responsibilities?

✗ *Traps*

☐ Do not agree to keep anything confidential unless you know what you're letting yourself in for.

☐ Go step-by-step and say that you'll listen to what they have to say before you can promise complete confidentiality. Tell them you'll let them know if at any stage you feel uncomfortable, and *you* need to discuss your feelings further (or words to that effect).

They'll respect your honesty, as only a fool promises blindly and then lets the person down by having to break their promise.

✓ *Tips*

- ☐ Ensure that your school or college has a policy on confidentiality so you all have clear boundaries.
- ☐ Go easy on promising that you'll never tell anyone something told to you in confidence. Ask the teller who *you* may discuss this with if you feel a need to off-load.
- ☐ If you feel someone else needs to know, tell the teller first, and discuss together how to move the situation forward.
- ☐ If in doubt, consult, without betraying any confidential information, about the principles involved.

★ **Conflict Resolution** is no longer a case of teachers hitting students and scaring them into apparent submission, nor of senior teachers hitting junior teachers verbally.

No matter if the conflict is among students, groups or gangs of students, or among staff, or between staff and students, or parents, your priority is to help those involved to find the resources to resolve their conflict themselves. Sometimes they might want or welcome an expert facilitator. Alternatively, they might be enjoying the conflict, and not want to resolve it. (Some people only feel 'alive' when angry, and don't (yet) know how else to get that 'buzz' from other activities.) Your school might well have a policy on this, or might benefit from one. Just as they would benefit from policies on BULLYING, RESTORATIVE JUSTICE, PARTICIPATION and GANGS. These policies, if drawn up by all involved, are essential for having ways of dealing with conflict, rather than having to deal with each case on a reactive basis.

✓ *Tips*

- ☐ The best way to resolve conflict is to avoid it in the first place – if something is bothering someone, encourage them to talk about it, in a FEEDFORWARD way perhaps, and to decide what resources they need to be able to do this.
- ☐ You may not be the best person to resolve all the conflicts around you – always consult: that's what managers are for!
- ☐ But if your problem is with your manager, there should be procedures within the school for talking with someone else. However uncomfortable you might feel about 'going above their head' if there's a situation that needs addressing, you are entitled to do something about it. Especially with all the legislation now on human rights, workplace bullying and discrimination.
- ☐ As we said before, the best way to resolve conflict is to avoid it in the first place or talk about a situation informally before it grows into a situation that needs to be handled formally.

★ **Confusion** is an essential part of the learning process. People often think of it as an undesirable state to be in, and get frustrated. But confusion is a very natural process. It is when we are trying to make sense of new information or experiences, in light of what we know already. We are trying to fit together the pieces of a jigsaw puzzle, whilst incorporating new pieces, and making sense of it all! No wonder it feels like hard work, and it is – genuinely – confusing.

✓ *Tips*

- ☐ If a student tells you they are confused, ask them 'about what, exactly? what are you *clear* about, and what do you still need some help with?'
- ☐ Ask the student if they are happy to stay confused for a while, and see how the pieces settle.

Connexions is the government's support service for young people in England aged 13–19 (up to 25 with learning difficulties and disabilities). They can get advice and guidance for making decisions and for getting help in achieving their goals. By 2004 every young person should either have a personal adviser or access via a drop-in centre, telephone or internet, to get help with education, careers, training, housing, health, money, leisure, voluntary work etc. The Connexions Card is available to all 16–19-year-olds (up to 25 with learning difficulties and disabilities) in England, whether in learning or not. Points are awarded for regular attendance at a place of learning or for achieving specified personal goals, and can be redeemed for a wide range of rewards.

Constructivist Learning is step-by-step learning, building on previous learning. It typically uses problem-solving and research rather than traditional teaching and lectures. Groupwork is key, as the teacher facilitates the students to discover their own knowledge and learnings. DIRECTED LEARNING, by comparison, typically teaches specific knowledge and skills, and the teacher is expected to be the expert source of the knowledge and skills.

Constructivist Theory/Constructivism developed by Jerome BRUNER from the work of Jean PIAGET sees learning as a process where the learner constructs new ideas or concepts based upon their experiences and knowledge. By using the way they have mentally organized their existing experience and knowledge, they are able to extend this, with new learnings, to construct something new for themselves.

The teacher's role is to facilitate the learners to discover *principles*.

Example

A student who learns how to bake both a chocolate cake and a syrup pudding might be able to construct an approach to baking a chocolate pudding.

 Trap

☐ Constructivism is the term applied to a mass of concepts both broad and narrow, not only within psychology but in philosophy, science and languages. When talking about any of the above, specify that it's Bruner's constructivism that you're talking about!

Continuing Education *see* CPD CONTINUING PROFESSIONAL DEVELOPMENT.

ContinYou is a charity whose projects and training aim to make learning a part of everyone's everyday life, especially those who have not taken up learning opportunities in the past. It grew from a merger in 2003 of CEDC Community Education Development Centre (community-based learning approaches with hard-to-reach groups, in education, public health and community regeneration) and Education Extra (out-of-school-hours learning).

Contract, Home-School (HSC) *see* AGREEMENT, HOME-SCHOOL.

Convergent Thinking *see* DIVERGENT THINKING.

Convincer Strategy *see* LEARNING STYLES.

Co-operative Learning is where students work in pairs or small groups, and with gentle facilitation if needed, can learn, negotiate and problem-solve together. This also helps their social and teamworking skills.

Corporal Punishment was made illegal as recently as 1986 and at the time there was an outcry by some who did not believe control could be maintained without this.

There are many reasons why corporal punishment was banned:

- Students could be punished without being able to defend themselves either verbally or physically.
- It condoned the abuse of power over those who are weaker.
- It gave permission by example for students to strike other students.
- It could cause physical harm, sometimes permanent.
- It was used by some teachers as a personal form of gratification.

Teachers are still allowed to use physical restraint in exceptional circumstances but there is no longer one law for society and another for schools. Your school should have a clear policy on necessary restraint.

Correspondence Course is distance learning, conducted by post or by email. It enables students who can't get to a college to study in their own time and at a pace that suits them. Assignments are sent by the tutor, completed and returned by the student, and then marked. Correspondence courses may have residential elements to enable students to ask questions face-to-face, and to check that the work completed at home is genuinely of the same standard as that achieved in a class in front of a supervising tutor. Distance learning is a method used, and largely pioneered at degree level, very successfully by the OPEN UNIVERSITY.

Coursework is what the student does during the course of a term, rather than in examinations. In the past, a student's level of attainment was measured by examinations, and their future was influenced by ASSESSMENT of their competence in these one-off exams. No consideration was given to the fact that

- They might have been under the weather, but not ill enough to qualify for exemption.
- They might have had a bad day.
- They might have suffered from exam nerves.
- They might not work well under pressure.
- Their exam skills might not be as developed as their subject skills.
- The exam might not have been in a style they found easy. (*See* DIFFERENTIATION.)

Since no account was taken of the work they had produced over the rest of the year, it was agreed to allocate a percentage of the overall marks to coursework. (The percentages are still under discussion: GCSE subjects can have 20–70 per cent of marks based on coursework and this could be adjusted from year to year.)

Coursework encourages greater application to studies during the year and reduces the likelihood that a student will take life easy and then cram for the exam. However, a counter-argument is that students can get higher grades with the help of teachers, parents or the internet, as it is impossible to ensure that the work is the student's own. Coursework has also been cited as overloading both students and teachers. It is also felt that part of the decline in males' academic performance (relative to females') is that females are typically better at the methodical skills needed for consistent coursework, while males perform better with the adrenaline rush of exams. There is a move currently towards implementing the IGCSE INTERNATIONAL GCSE and BACCALAUREATE exams, with minimal coursework content, as universities feel that performance under exam conditions are better predictors of students' abilities.

CoVEs Centres of Vocational Excellence were set up to promote VOCATIONAL EDUCATION to level 3 in the NQF (NATIONAL QUALIFICATIONS FRAMEWORK) for students in schools and in further education. They are typically local partnerships of training providers, such as colleges and employers. They focus on enhancing the skills of those already in work, as well as new entrants to the labour market.

CPD Continuing Professional Development is where, once qualified, you keep your knowledge and skills up to date. In some professions this is mandatory (e.g. law, accountancy). Teachers have INSET days for this.

CPS (1) *see* CREATIVE PROBLEM-SOLVING (2) Crown Prosecution Service.

Creative Problem-Solving (CPS) Model is based on the work of Alex Osborn (of the BBDO advertising agency) in the 1950s and suggests that the creative process has five stages:

1 Fact-finding.
2 Problem-finding.
3 Idea-finding.
4 Solution-finding.
5 Acceptance-finding.

Creativity is a well-researched field of study, sometimes linked with intelligence. It can be defined, simply, as using existing knowledge and experiences in new ways, to produce something of value to the individual or to a wider audience.

So, it is not learning by rote, but coming up with original ideas, which may be new to the world at large, or to the individual concerned. It is, therefore, ideally suited for problem-solving.

✓ *Tips*

☐ We always try to achieve a task by being creative in *how* we can achieve it. (The 'what' is normally fixed – that's the task.) Thinking *how* we can achieve it, opens up limitless possibilities that take account of the time and preferences and needs of all concerned. As an example, if we're asked to do a task in an impossible time – say 3pm today – we'll think about two things: what we *can* do by then, and what else we could do. And we'll offer the options:

  ▪ We can do it by 3pm if someone can take the rest of our workload for two hours.
  ▪ We can do a topline by 3pm with a full rationale by 3pm tomorrow.
  ▪ We can give you a thought-through answer by 3pm tomorrow, or a rough guesstimate today.
  ▪ And then we always ask 'Which would you prefer?' and leave the decision to the person that briefed us!

☐ Encourage little 'c' creativity (LCC), also known as lifewide creativity. This ensures that students (and others) experience small-step-by-small-step successes in identifying and solving problems in *all* tasks, not just those labelled 'Creative' or arts-related. (LCC and lifewide creativity are concepts developed by Anna Craft, one of our Advisory Panel.)
☐ Remember that there is enormous scope for fostering students' creativity right across the curriculum, in the way you teach, in the thinking you encourage, and in the links and partnerships you make with others. So long as you achieve *what* is required, the *how* is the fun bit.
☐ Along the way, facilitating student creativity, there is plenty of scope for creative teaching i.e. for you yourself to be creative.
☐ Choose carefully when you need to intervene, and when to hold back, to enable your students to explore their creativity.

Criterion Referencing *see* ASSESSMENT.

Critical Thinking (also known as logical or analytical thinking) is the process of weighing up, and making choices or value judgements.

Criticism can be dressed up as feedback, guidance, or help. But if it hurts the recipient, it's not useful. *See* more under FEEDBACK and FEEDFORWARD.

Cross-age tutoring is where older students teach younger students.

CSV Community Service Volunteers is the UK organization founded by the same people (Mora and Alec Dickson) and on the same principles as VSO Voluntary Service Overseas, for people who want to make a difference in their own community.

Day Release is when an organization allows an employee to study for one or two days a week at a college or adult education centre. The employee can then gain qualifications they missed at school, or qualifications of a specialist nature. It is an effective form of development and learning for people who want to combine work and study. It works well for people who did not, or could not, make the most of their school days. (Unrelated, it also refers to people in prison who are no longer considered to be a risk to society, and are allowed out during the day.)

DCM Dynamic Causal Models look at cause and effect. For example, neurological disabilities (e.g. brain damage) may result in cognitive disabilities (e.g. memory impairment) which may therefore result in behavioural disabilities (e.g. forgetfulness).

Dearing Report 'Higher Education In The Learning Society' was produced in 1997 by the National Committee of Inquiry into Higher Education, chaired by Sir Ron Dearing. It has already proved to be enormously influential in recommending how higher education should develop in the UK over the next 20 years.

The many specific recommendations include:

- A focus on LIFELONG LEARNING for a flexible workforce.
- Work-based National Traineeships modelled on Modern Apprenticeships (called simply APPRENTICESHIPS from 2004) but focused on achieving NVQ Level 2.
- Increased opportunities for higher education at e.g. sub-degree level.
- A single framework for higher education qualifications (*see* FHEQ).

Degree is the qualification awarded by a higher education institute as, typically, a 2-year foundation degree, a 3-year degree or honours degree, or a post-graduate masters degree. In Scotland and the US a degree typically takes four years. In mainland Europe, it can often take more than four years.

Delegation in its truest form is giving the responsibility for a task to another person. For an effective model

1. Explain exactly what is required and by when.
2. Ask the person to explain in their own words what exactly they understand you have asked them to do.
3. Ask them to consider how they might do this.
4. What resources they are going to need.
5. What support they'd like.
6. Any other questions (after they've had time to think about it).
7. How they'll be reporting back.
8. Any interim reviews they'd like, and with whom.
9. Then agree with them who you are going to tell about this delegation.

✓ **Tips**

- ☐ Ensure, when delegating, that other people know that you've given responsibility and authority to this person, e.g. to make specific decisions, or to spend up to £X.
- ☐ Sometimes 'delegation' is simply 'dumping' – where the person just dumps something on you without ensuring that you are willing and able.

- [ ] If you feel dumped on, try something like 'In order to get this exactly right for you, first time, I need to make sure I understand exactly what's expected of me, so can I just ask you...'
- [ ] If you get fobbed off with 'I haven't got time right now' try asking 'so when *will* you have five (or whatever) minutes for me to have a clear briefing, please?'
- [ ] If you get fobbed off with 'Oh surely you know how to do this, just get on with it' try something like 'In order to get this exactly right for you, first time, I need to make sure I understand exactly what's expected of me, so can I just ask you...' and maybe even add '...to avoid us having to redo it like the last few times because we didn't make time for a clear briefing in the first place'.
- [ ] Some people delegate to you and then interfere – when this happens ask them if they want the job back: they've told you *what* to do, and it's down to you *how* you do it.
- [ ] Never accept a delegation without the necessary authority.

DENI Department of Education for Northern Ireland.

Deputy Head The essence of the role is to deputize for the head teacher when they are unavailable. The deputy needs to have all the responsibility and authority of the head's post, if they are to be effective and not undermined. If they don't, then they need to have clear boundaries, e.g. while the head is away, you can do everything needed, without consulting the board of governors, except 'hire or fire' staff. It is essential preparation for teachers wanting to apply for head teacher posts.

Detention is keeping students in class as a punishment during breaks or after school. They may be set work to do, or just sit and ponder the reasons for the punishment. (The sitting and pondering is notoriously unsuccessful: our prison system was built on the Victorian principle that prisoners left alone in their cell would have nothing else to do but (1) think and then (2) repent. It doesn't work in the vast majority of cases.) If a student is kept behind after school then parents must be given a full day's notice and be told the reasons for the punishment. It is also advisable to make sure that the student has a safe way of getting home especially if they normally travel in a group or with their own or other students' parents. Obviously, in winter, early darkness is also a factor.

✓ *Tips*

- [ ] Detention is an area where knowledge of the Human Rights Act is advised, and therefore a school should have a clear policy.
- [ ] Nip the problem in the bud, rather than having to 'detain', because the problem has blossomed.

Dewey, John (1859–1952 US) was a highly influential philosopher, educational theorist and commentator on contemporary issues. He believed that

- Curriculum should arise from students' interests, and not be imposed.
- Subjects could be integrated rather than separated.
- Education occurs through connection with life.
- Learning should be hands-on.

He was also at the forefront of EPISTEMOLOGY (the study of thinking, although he preferred to define it as the 'theory of inquiry').

DfE Department for Education which became the Department for Education and Employment (DfEE) in 1995 which, in turn, became the Department for Education and Skills (DfES) in 2002.

DfEE Department for Education and Employment, formed in 1995, it became the Department for Education and Skills in 2002.

DfES Department for Education and Skills was set up in 2002.

Dial-Up is the original way of accessing the internet, by dialling up using a telephone line. Now ISDN, ADSL and BROADBAND offer faster always-on connections, without blocking the phone line.

Didactic Instruction is the 'chalk and talk' method of teaching and learning, where the teacher has a body of knowledge to convey and the students are expected to learn by watching and/or listening.

★ **Diet, Water and Oxygen** A student will be unable to learn effectively if their basic physiological needs are not met. Unfortunately, many students do not take care of their own needs. Many are dependent on their parents and expect the teacher to take over that role while they are at school. The amount the teacher can do to ensure the students' well-being is limited but here are some pointers.

- *Diet*: The debate on sugar intake is hotly debated. Many television companies using children in an active audience will ply them with chocolate (high in caffeine and sugar), colas (ditto), fruity drinks (with sugar and colorants that are known to promote hyperactivity) and crisps (high carbohydrate, and salty to make children thirsty for more of the above). These make the children more active and energetic while the programme is being recorded. It is unfortunately common to see students arrive at school with the same sugary drink, crisps and chocolate, in place of breakfast, which makes it very hard for them to concentrate. And the day can only get worse if this dietary pattern continues. That is why many schools now offer breakfast as well as lunch, to overcome students coming to school without proper nutrition. As a teacher you are unlikely to be able to alter a student's diet. What you can do is to be aware of the energetic times of day, and the sluggish times, caused by poor diet and adapt your teaching to suit. You can also hope that the vested business interests of the 'junk' food manufacturers, the education authorities and medical advisers will come together and form a food strategy for the good of the students.
- *Water*: Even slight dehydration can impair the workings of the brain. The best drink for students to improve their health and learning capabilities is water. The body needs as much as eight glasses of water a day. Sugary soft drinks with caffeine can often dehydrate rather than re-hydrate. When a student is physically active, or the temperature is hot, their need for water is higher. Ensure that drinking water is freely available. When taking a break, remind students to take a drink of water.
- *Oxygen*: A room with restricted ventilation, air conditioning or central heating can rapidly become depleted of oxygen with thirty or more people breathing in it. Even in summer with the windows open, oxygen levels may drop. This depletion is unlikely to drop to dangerous levels but even a slight drop can limit attention, concentration and, therefore, learning. Make sure the room is as ventilated as possible, at a comfortable temperature and, if possible, that students are not seated by closed windows with direct sunlight coming through. If necessary, take breaks in 'fresh' air.

 Tip

☐ All this advice applies to teachers as well!

Differentiation acknowledges that students are different – they have different learning abilities, methods of working, learning styles, etc. – and aims to ensure that students are treated fairly. Do you use the same test for all Ability Groups, for example, or test them appropriately? or do you ensure that each student is sufficiently stimulated – not too much nor too little though? Those of similar ability (e.g. aptitude for the task, support needed, resources needed or outcomes expected) are best grouped together in class for work to be tailored to their needs.

The groups are sometime called differently-abled which should not be confused with the same US term for dis-abled.

Dip. Ed. is a post-graduate Diploma in Education or Educational Studies, taken not only by teachers and lecturers, but increasingly by parents, school governors, and others interested in education.

Dip. HE Diploma in Higher Education lasts for two years full-time and is broadly equivalent to the first two years of a degree. It is especially suitable for mature students who do not meet traditional entry requirements. It can lead to entry, possibly directly, onto the final (= third) year, of a degree course.

Dip. Teach. is a postgraduate Diploma in Teaching similar to a DIP. ED.

Diplomas are normally taken by full-time students (whereas certificates are normally taken part-time by people in employment, recognizing the knowledge and skills gained at work).

Directed Learning is where the student is told what to do. It contrasts with SELF-DIRECTED LEARNING where the student decides what and how to learn. Directed learning typically teaches specific knowledge and skills, with the teacher expected to be the expert source of the knowledge and skills. All students are expected to learn the same material, irrespective of their motivations. For example, multiplication tables could well be learned by rote in this way. It is sometimes called the Jug and Empty Vessel method – where the teacher (= jug) is full of information that they have to pour into the empty vessels (= students). To ensure that the water (= knowledge) has been effectively transferred, they will examine this knowledge to ensure that nothing has been spilled, leaked, lost or, indeed, added. There is little room in this model for original thinking.

★ **Discipline** is

1   An old-fashioned military/power term demanding that everyone should do as they are told.
2   The opposite of disorder, where quiet obedience prevails (as in exam conditions).
3   Punishment – *see* PUNISHING APPROPRIATELY.

✓ *Tip*

☐   When disciplining, choose your timing carefully – a teacher always needs to decide whether

   ▪   To discipline on the spot (but avoiding disrupting other students).
   ▪   Not to discipline at all (inevitably signalling that you accept this type of behaviour).
   ▪   To discipline later (when you can address the overall pattern coolly and privately, rather than confront a single example of the pattern when it's still 'hot').

Discovery Learning and Discovery Activities are where learnings will be independently discovered by the student, rather than told to the student, thus encouraging the student to be an active participant in the learning. (This contrasts with Application Learning and APPLICATION ACTIVITIES where the student is told what they will find, and then set out to prove this for themselves.)

A quote we like:

'All who wander are not lost' (JRR Tolkien).

See also EXPERIENTIAL LEARNING, and BRUNER who developed this theory.

Discovery Project is funded by Portsmouth City Education Department to develop the **Emotional Intelligence** of school students in order to enhance their academic and soft skills.

Distance Learning was originally just CORRESPONDENCE COURSES. Now it covers all learning where the student and teacher are not in the same room, e.g. video, internet, email, television, text messaging.

Distributed Learning *see* BITESIZE LEARNING.

Divergent Thinking is the ability to create many possible answers. As a teacher you might want to stimulate divergent thinking to help students to be more creative, problem-solve or learn by experimentation. The sort of question you could ask is 'how could it be if you were the Prime Minster?' or 'suppose Shakespeare was still alive, what could he be writing today?'.

Convergent Thinking is the ability to select the best, or only, answer to a problem. It focuses on decisions and facts.

Everyone has a natural bias towards one or other of these forms of thinking but as a teacher you need to be clear which you are expecting from your students. *See* BRAINSTORMING for a technique that includes both types.

DLHE Destination of Leavers from Higher Education survey is compiled annually by the Higher Education Statistics Agency. This survey replaced the First Destination Survey from 2003/4.

Down's Syndrome is a genetic abnormality and the most common cause of learning disability, affecting around 1 in 1,000 babies. (It was once known as mongolism because people with the syndrome have flatter facial features, like those of native Mongolians.) Many people with Down's syndrome also have other health issues, such as heart defects, hearing and vision problems. There is a growing tendency to integrate Down's syndrome students into ordinary schools.

DRB Designated Recommending Bodies each handle a minimum of ten graduate teacher trainees per year – around 85 per cent of all GTP places. Most DRBs are partnerships of schools, Local Education Authorities and initial teacher training (ITT) providers.

Dropout (US) is a student who drops out of college or university (college dropout, university dropout) without completing the course. A high-school dropout is a truant, who should be in school until age 18/twelfth grade. (A dropout in many states is in limbo – since they are in violation of compulsory school attendance laws they cannot work legally as they cannot get a work permit.)

DSM-IV Diagnostic and Statistical Manual, 4th Edition is the American Psychiatric Association's 'directory' of psychiatric disorders. It is a standard work in the US and is increasingly used to diagnose cognitive disorders in students for special needs assessments.

Dual Task Measures are indicative of a student's attention capabilities. They test the ability to combine two types of task that they have already practised individually.

Dunn & Dunn *see* LEARNING STYLES.

Dyslexia is a complex learning disability primarily affecting spelling and reading, although difficulty with writing and numbers can also occur. It often runs in families and affects more males than females. Many go through life without having their dyslexia diagnosed, having found their own coping strategies. Many experience a huge sense of relief when they are diagnosed, as they had previously been labelled as 'thick', 'stupid', 'backward' or 'lazy' – all of which can cause intense frustration as, no matter how hard they tried, they were still branded as failures. It is not linked to intelligence or ability and many successful people have dyslexia, channelling their energy and capabilities into areas where they can excel – such as business, art, music and theatre.

The following are common symptoms that, if in evidence, should alert the teacher to contact the SPECIAL EDUCATIONAL NEEDS CO-ORDINATOR (SENCO) for professional diagnosis and support:

- *Sequencing:* numbers, the alphabet, the letters that spell a word, months in the year, days of the week, songs and columns of letters may all throw them into confusion.
- *Speech:* might well be highly skilled but written spelling may be unexpectedly poor – often phonetically 'correct' but not literally correct
- *Late in learning:* they may be slow to learn speech, tell the time, tie shoelaces, and may be confused between east and west, right and left, up and down. They may also have difficulty with motor skills such as catching, throwing, skipping and jumping.
- *Reading:* they may be slow when reading, complaining of letters and words being jumbled, and may experience uncomfortable physical reactions to reading. Their performance may be inconsistent and inaccurate with spelling, e.g. mistaking b's for d's and vice versa. Their difficulties with the written and printed word can be persistent and severe, irrespective of the quality and quantity of the teaching input.
- *Concentration and memory:* a student may have difficulty concentrating for as long as their peers. Their short-term memory may also be poorer than their peers'. They may struggle with long words, miss out syllables or pronounce syllables out of order. They may be slow to complete many tasks or have to give up without finishing.
- *Achievement:* almost invariably they will achieve below the expectations of those who know their true abilities from more relaxed home or social settings.

✓ Tips

☐ Always

1 Tell them in headline terms what you are about to teach them.
2 Check their understanding of what you've told them.
3 Teach them.
4 Tell them in summary what you have taught them.
5 Ask them what they've understood, and praise, reinforce and correct where necessary.
6 Ask them what they've not yet understood, and act as appropriate – either on the spot or at a later date.

☐ People with dyslexia should not be referred to as dyslexics – the disorder should not be used to label their whole identity!
☐ They need quiet in order to concentrate. This applies to homework as well as the classroom.
☐ Because activities such as reading can be such a struggle, they can tire quickly and need regular breaks, and sufficient sleep. Parental support is important in these areas.
☐ Most people with dyslexia, when identified, can learn within a normal class with support from the teacher, or others.
☐ Marking their work can be adjusted to take account of dyslexic problems and will help to develop a positive attitude to their work, and an improved self-image. This adjustment can apply to all tests and examinations as long as advance permission is obtained.

(For example, the student might be allowed extra time, or someone to read aloud the question to them, or write down their answers for them.)

☐ They often benefit from using MIND MAPS®.

☐ They generally benefit from repetition of instructions, repeated practice and patient teachers.

☐ Be aware that some parents resist the notion that there is anything wrong with their child – so discuss dyslexia in a factual way, as something their child has, like having one leg shorter than the other – it's a fact, and life can go on, with minor adjustments. It's not a personality defect, or a stain on their character as parents.

☐ If you adopt a positive attitude towards dyslexia it will encourage the student to follow suit. Avoid words such as 'overcoming', 'problem' 'disability', 'handicap' or 'drawback'.

☐ Encourage students to find their own strategies for coping and thriving with dyslexia.

☐ In order not to give them a sense of overload, use the principle of 'little and often' to help them learn, and build up to larger learnings.

☐ Give students the opportunity to demonstrate their strengths and capabilities as often as possible, to create a sense of achievement.

☐ Discuss and praise positive role models who have dyslexia.

☐ Always write down homework, and other, instructions rather than expect the student to remember.

☐ They will probably welcome help with organizing and structuring their work. (*See* SCAFFOLDING and WRITING FRAMES.)

✗ Traps

☐ Many people with mild symptoms may 'get by' without being diagnosed as having dyslexia.

☐ Mild dyslexia is often not noticed by the parent, student or teacher – the student is just put into lower competency groups.

☐ They may be comfortable with words, reading or spelling but experience dyslexia in numbers.

☐ Never force them to read aloud to the class in the hope that you'll give them encouragement.

☐ Don't ask them to read a form, or sign something, on the spot – let them take the papers with them, to read at their own speed, and with whatever help they need.

☐ Dyslexia is an easy label to place upon other disorders. Some non-dyslexic students may try to use dyslexia as an excuse for lack of application.

Example

We knew a student with dyslexia who was good at chemistry even though he and his teacher had little rapport. He moved to a new teacher whom he liked a lot, and his performance strangely became very poor, and he started to become disruptive because this situation was so frustrating. But it was easily fixed. It appears that the new teacher spent the first third of a lesson writing instructions on the board for the students to copy. The second third was spent explaining what to do with this information. And the final third was for doing the experiment previously explained. But our student has dyslexia, so the first third, copying from the board, was a nightmare. The second third was even worse – trying to listen to the instructions whilst struggling to fill in the missing words. And the nightmare came true in the final third when the teacher said 'Right, so you all know what to do, then?' Our student was in such a panic by this point, he couldn't even ask for help. We worked with him, and recognized the above pattern of how exactly he was failing in chemistry class. And we then generated some.

FEEDFORWARD ideas for addressing the situation – both *what* lesson structure would work better for him, and *how* he might broach this to the teacher. In the event, all worked out well. The teacher was upset that she hadn't been communicating appropriately for this student's needs, and – more importantly – that she hadn't noticed his difficulties. The teacher gratefully seized upon several of the ideas (e.g. give written handouts to save this student copying from the board; give written handouts to save *all* students copying from the board; asking a useful open QUESTION to ensure that any problems could be voiced, e.g. 'what is not clear yet?' or 'what other information do you need?' rather than a closed front-loaded question like 'So you all know what to do, then?').

Dysphasia is a language disorder that used to be referred to as word-blindness. The person has difficulty

■ Expressing themselves, because they have difficulty in finding the words.

   and/or

■ Understanding others, due to the difficulty of understanding written or spoken words.

Dyspraxia is a co-ordination disorder that can be interpreted as clumsiness or difficulty with organizing thoughts and movements. The person may have difficulty with

■ *Fine motor skills* such as handwriting or using a computer mouse.
■ *Gross motor skills* such as catching a ball, or keeping their balance.
■ *Sequencing movements* in dancing, or imitating other people's actions.
■ *Sequencing thoughts* and getting themselves organized.

It is thought that signals from the brain are not correctly received by the parts of the body that need to action the signals, and it often is found in people who also have DYSLEXIA.

✓ *Tips*

□ As with all potential learning difficulties, the first port of call is the Special Educational Needs Co-ordinator (*see* SENCO).
□ Because of the nature of the disorder, other students may mock dyspraxic behaviours. Needless to say, this form of BULLYING should be addressed.

E

e2e Entry To Employment is a programme for people who are not yet ready for full-time employment. It is tailored to each person's needs with e.g. work experience, basic skills tutoring, and/or personal development life skills.

EAL English as an Additional Language.

Early Literacy Support (ELS) is a twelve-week daily INTERVENTION PROGRAMME for year 1 students who are behind in their literacy skills. It is designed to prevent them being left behind at this critical early stage. They are selected for this programme by testing their ability to listen and understand, how they contribute to literacy lessons, and their apparent knowledge and confidence with words. (It is not designed for students with special needs.) There are normally only six students in the group, and each lesson lasts half an hour. If a student makes sufficient progress there are opt-out points after four and eight weeks and, if needed, there is an additional eight-week programme. It enables students to build words with PHONICS (sounds), to break down the construction of simple words, to practise spelling and reading, and to gain confidence with words. A puppet is sometimes used to allow the students to notice the mistakes the puppet is making and thereby give permission for them to make their own mistakes, and learn from them. The emphasis is on interactive fun so that literacy is perceived as enjoyable and rewarding.

Early Years are from ages 3 to 6, from nursery to the end of the FOUNDATION STAGE. Learning for the early years is covered by curriculum guidance which is broken down into six areas of age-appropriate learning that lead towards the learning goals to be achieved by the end of the foundation stage. A student's early years experience should build on what they already know and can do. It should also encourage a positive attitude and disposition to learn, and aim to prevent a mentality of failure at the start of a school career.

Early Years Action is for a child who makes little or no progress even when attempts have been made to improve their educational, behavioural or emotional difficulties. Together with the SENCO and parents, additional activities and strategies will be agreed, and targets set to allow progress to be measured.

If this is ineffective then EARLY YEARS ACTION PLUS can be considered. This can also involve external support services with more specialist assessments, advice and support, e.g. from a specialist teacher or speech therapist or other health professional.

EBD Emotional & Behavioural Difficulties.

ECDL European Computer Driving Licence is a basic qualification for computer skills.

Edexcel is one of three unitary examining and Awarding Bodies for GCSEs, GCE A and A/S levels, GNVQs, NVQs and BTEC Higher National Certificates and Diplomas. It was formed in 1996 by the merger of the Business & Technology Education Council (BTEC) – the provider of vocational qualifications – and London Exams (University of London Examinations & Assessment Council – ULEAC) – an exam board for GCSEs and A levels. It was the first awarding body to offer both academic and vocational qualifications. On 1 June 2003, it was taken over by Pearson to form London Qualifications but continues to operate as Edexcel.

★ **Education** is a systematic process of training, teaching, instructing and developing the academic, intellectual, physical and moral capabilities of a student. (Well, that's about as realistic a definition as we could put together.) Hence the education 'system'. But, frankly, we are doubtful about the effectiveness of any child having to fit into a 'system' or be treated as the object of an education, as opposed to finding out what their interests and capabilities are, and helping them to take charge of getting what they really want in life. The origins of the word 'educate' are in the Latin for 'bring out' or 'lead out'.

Education Action Zones are geographic areas deemed to need special attention and support. They are now incorporated in the EIC EXCELLENCE IN CITIES programme.

Education Acts and other key events give a (highly selective!) feel for how we got to where we are today:

1870 established the principle that elementary schools should be free, and the responsibility of the state, instead of religious bodies. This enabled local people to be elected onto school boards to run local schools and enforce attendance of children under 13 years.

1902 as a response to the variable standards brought about by the above, local school boards were abolished and LOCAL EDUCATION AUTHORITIES (LEAS) established in borough and county councils.

1918 increased the school-leaving age to 14 and introduced services such as medical inspection and special needs schools.

1944 raised the school-leaving age to 15 (as from 1947) and provided for free secondary schooling in grammar, secondary modern and technical schools, based on the 11 Plus examination.

1960s saw the growth of non-selective comprehensive schools.

1962 growth in further education as local authorities were obliged (from 1964) to cover living costs and tuition fees for full-time first degrees, Diplomas in Higher Education (Dip. HE), Higher National Diplomas (HND) and teacher training.

1973 school leaving age raised to 16 years.

1988 the Education Reform Act introduced the National Curriculum for all 5–16-year-olds in England and Wales (from 1992). Parents could now vote a school out of local authority control.

1990 'Top-up' loans introduced for HE students.

1992 FEFC Further Education Funding Council established and 6th Form and FE Colleges removed from local authority control.

1996 consolidated all schools legislation since 1944.

1997 'Investing in Young People' aiming to reduce drop-out at age 16 by improving the relevance and quality of post-16 training to at least NVQ Level 2 standard. Also DEARING REPORT ('Higher Education In The Learning Society').

1999 Learning To Succeed DfEE White Paper on post-16 learning was published.

Education and Youth Transitions is a major study to review education and training provision in the United Kingdom which will report back in 2005. It is funded by the Economic and Social Research Council, and carried out by the Centre for Educational Sociology at the University of Edinburgh.

Education Extra *see* CONTINYOU.

Educational Kinesiology is the study of anatomy, physiology and movement and their effect on learning – *see also* BRAIN GYM®.

Educational Psychologists in the public sector are often employed by the LEA (LOCAL EDUCATION AUTHORITY) or contract their services via the LEA. Students requiring an assessment by an educational psychologist will first be assessed by a SENCO.

Educational Studies covers not only the principles and practices of learning but also special interest areas such as political intervention in education, and community participation in learning. Degrees in educational studies span from the theoretical (e.g. the history, sociology, philosophy and psychology of education) to the practical (e.g. bullying, equal opportunities) and, ideally, the interaction of all aspects.

Edu-K *see* EDUCATIONAL KINESIOLOGY.

★ **Efficiency** means doing something effectively by using your time, energy and other resources as sparingly as possible. It means working smarter rather than harder.

✓ *Tips*

☐ If you're short of time or energy, find someone else, maybe by asking for a volunteer or group of volunteers, who has time to do parts of the job, and then DELEGATE.

☐ We often ask ourselves 'how would someone who is really good at this do it?' or 'what could I leave out that would not matter or be noticed, and allow more space to do the rest of the job better?'

☐ Always make the task fit the time available. Ask yourself how you can best do something in ten minutes (or thirty, or whatever) rather than attempt perfection (whatever that is!) while hoping that extra time will magically appear.

See also TIME MANAGEMENT.

EFL English as a Foreign Language.

Egocentric *see* COGNITIVE DEVELOPMENT.

EiC Excellence in Cities is a programme launched in 2000 that aims to improve standards in inner-city areas. Projects include Learning MENTORS (especially for children who have been bullied or have truanted), Learning Support Units, extended opportunities for gifted and talented students, Learning Centres, more Specialist Schools and Action Zones. These follow on from EDUCATION ACTION ZONES and are local partnerships which are encouraged to develop innovative solutions to raise educational standards, typically focused on a single secondary school with its associated primary schools.

E-Learning is learning using electronic (hence the E) media such as DVDs, CD-ROMs, Internet, Intranet, mobile phones, email, calculators, video, computers and TV. It can stimulate students more than books and boards, by using the media that they are more familiar with.

Electives (US) are optional courses chosen by students as part of their studies.

Elementary Schools (US) or grade schools are the equivalent (approximately) of UK primary schools for GRADES 1–6 or 1–8, and can sometimes include Junior High Schools (grades 7–8).

Eleven Plus Exams were used at the beginning of year 6 (age 11) to select students for GRAMMAR SCHOOLS, TECHNICAL SCHOOLS or SECONDARY MODERN SCHOOLS, prior to the advent of comprehensive education. They no longer exist universally, except as GRAMMAR SCHOOL entrance exams, as Key Stage 2. SATS tests are taken at the same age.

ELS *see* EARLY LITERACY SUPPORT.

ELSIN European Learning Styles Network.

EMA Education Maintenance Allowance is being phased in for 16–19-year-olds in England who can get up to £30 a week, depending on parental income. It is intended to encourage students to complete their full-time education rather than be attracted by the earnings of a job.

Emotional Intelligence was proposed by US psychologist Daniel Goleman in 1995, although there is some debate as to whether it is truly an 'intelligence', or a set of skills. It can be defined as how people manage

- their own state of mind and body, through self-awareness, and particularly being aware of, and controlling, impulses
- relationships with other people.

It overlaps with two of Howard Gardner's MULTIPLE INTELLIGENCES (intra-personal and inter-personal intelligences).

Emotional Literacy is literally, how we read our emotions, feelings, and body sensations (such as 'butterflies in our tummy', or 'I've got a funny feeling about this' or 'I feel angry') as a prelude to acting on them appropriately.

✓ *Tip*

☐ The alternatives to acting on our emotions include bottling them up into stress, or exploding when the last straw breaks the camel's back.

Empirical evidence or information describes first-hand information based on what has actually been experienced i.e. seen, heard, felt, tasted or smelled, e.g. I actually saw you succeeding this time, so I don't have to rely on second-hand information.

EMS Extra-Mural Studies are literally 'outside the walls' of the school, and maybe in the community, e.g. museums or field trips.

★ **Energy Levels** We can all be high-energy at times, or low-energy at other times, depending on our mood. We normally avoid irritating others by instinctively noticing their mood and then moving our own energy level a little towards theirs. Think of someone with whom you slow down a bit? Think of someone else with whom you speed up a bit? It all helps us to be on their wavelength.

✓ *Tips*

☐ It's essential to notice the energy level of colleagues or students. If they're very energetic, for example, there's no point trying to de-energize a whole group: it'll be hard work, and it won't succeed. You might as well raise your own energy level a little, go towards where they're at on the energy spectrum, and gradually try to move them to where they need to be for the task. If you don't succeed, substitute a task that's better suited to their mood.
☐ The next time you raise your energy level, notice how you do it. This is your strategy for energy level control: maybe you think of something that energizes you, or you change your physiology in some way? The next time you need more energy you can then do it consciously rather than wait for your subconscious strategy to kick into place.

Engagement *see* PARTICIPATION.

Enneagram is a way of categorizing people. It is over 2,000 years old, and is both practical and predictive. Each of the nine categories, which have names such as perfectionist, performer or observer is predictable in terms of how behaviour changes when under stress, or when relaxed. This helps a teacher, for example, to spot when students or colleagues are particularly stressed, and to address the situation before it becomes a problem. It's also helpful to know one's own early-warning stress signals!

⭐ **Environment, School** gives subliminal messages about the value we put on school and learning. Poor decoration, disrepair and hard tarmac grounds reduce aspirations, as they show so very clearly that the school doesn't think they are worth investing in. Obviously students have inventive ways of making their environment arguably worse, through graffiti and other disfigurements, but with the conditions some of them find, it is hard to be too critical. Unfortunately many of the grassed sports areas were sold off for housing. This was obviously a short-term financial policy with long-term negative ramifications. Teachers can only do so much with decoration – work pinned to the walls – and maintaining positive attitudes.

✓ *Tips*

☐ Another way to literally broaden students' horizons is through school trips to interesting and attractive places.
☐ Making students aware of litter, taking care of property and taking pride in their own appearance are vital lessons to show how they can rise above such disadvantages and distractions.
☐ Check out ideas from LEARNING THROUGH LANDSCAPES.

Epistemology is the study of knowledge i.e. how we think about what we think about, or how we know what we know. (Genetic epistemology is the study of how knowledge develops in humans over time.)

EQ Emotional Quotient is a measure of EMOTIONAL INTELLIGENCE, intended to parallel IQ, and often confusingly used to mean emotional intelligence.

⭐ **Equal Opportunities** means making the same provision accessible and available for all students (and colleagues, friends and family) regardless of gender, race, religion, ability, size or any other factor. It does not mean treating everyone the same or ignoring difference. For instance, where English is not a student's first language, equal opportunities can mean making appropriate provision. *See also* DIFFERENTIATION.

✓ *Tips*

☐ Avoid discriminatory words like 'special', 'normal' or 'positive discrimination' (which is just as discriminatory as 'negative discrimination' – maybe try 'positive action' or 'appropriate action' or 'necessary action'?).
☐ Put yourself in others' shoes to avoid giving offence.
☐ When you get it wrong, as we all do at times, it's quick and easy to apologize and then ask how they would prefer you to behave in future.

ESOL English for Speakers of Other Languages.

European Computer Driving Licence (ECDL) is a basic qualification for computer skills, available from many awarding bodies.

Evaluation is the process of judging the value of different items, e.g. select the most appropriate solution, decide who is best able to do this.

✓ *Tip*

☐ To find out how able someone is at evaluating something, ask questions beginning with evaluate, judge, compare, select, etc. (*See* BLOOM'S TAXONOMY.)

Exam(-ining, -ination) Boards *see* AWARDING BODIES.

Examinations *see* TESTS.

Examiners are the people who set tests and exams, and may sometimes mark them too. They are often teachers, but increasingly computers are being employed with multiple choice questions.

Examining and Awarding Bodies *see* AWARDING BODIES.

Exclusion is the barring of a student from attendance at school either permanently or for a fixed time not exceeding 15 days. Permanent exclusion used to be called expulsion, and may be a consequence of persistent bullying, carrying weapons, violence, sexual misconduct, possession or dealing in drugs, for example. Those excluded permanently may be expected to attend a PUPIL REFERRAL UNIT (PRU) where their education should be tailored to their individual needs. Permanent exclusion can have a positive effect on the remaining students and staff, since the anti-social behaviours will have been eliminated, but it can also be an attractive proposition for students who are not happy at school, and encourage them to mis-behave.

✓ *Tips*

☐   If a student is excluded it doesn't mean you have failed as a teacher, but identifying anything you could have done differently will help you to deal with similar situations in the future.

☐   You can only do your best – being a teacher doesn't mean you have the responsibility to make every student's life work, even though, of course, you will do what you can. *(See* FIFTEEN PER CENT.)

Expectations Many studies show that if you have low expectations of someone (students, colleagues, or oneself) then the performance will tend to be correspondingly low. High expectations tend to breed high achievement.

✓ *Tips*

☐   Expect everyone to be able to do a task, in their own way, and if motivated. This is at the heart of your job as a teacher – finding out:

  ■   How to get people motivated.
  ■   How to get them to motivate themselves.
  ■   How to find their own ways of doing things.

☐   Be realistic though – expecting someone in their sixties who has never run a mile to run a three-minute mile may be unrealistic.

☐   Negotiate the expectation with the person(s) concerned – do you think we/you/I can achieve this? what questions or doubts or concerns do we need to explore, before we decide? what resources do we think we'll need? what support do we think we'd like?

Experiential Learning is where students learn through experience, experimentation and discovery. Many feel that this is a stronger form of learning, than from books or formal educational methods, because the student discovers and learns what is most relevant to them and what excites them. The levels of retention, and ownership of the lessons learnt, are also believed by many to be higher than in traditional education. The student tends to drive the process rather than the teacher or the curriculum, and so it can be difficult to measure, as it is so very individual. But that's where SELF-ASSESSMENT comes in. There are many students – the more curious, adventurous or entrepreneurial – for whom experiential learning is by far the most suitable way to learn. Even with a NATIONAL CURRICULUM, learning this way through DISCOVERY has a very important place.

Extended Schools are a fast-growing sector that provide services and activities way beyond those historically associated with schools, to support students, parents and the community. For example, there are schools that house healthcare, childcare, and parenting support facilities – often extending beyond the 'normal' school day. The intention is that these schools will become the focal point for joined-up services for their local community.

Extra-Curricular Activities are voluntary (for both staff and students) and outside school hours, rather than part of the core school curriculum. They encompass a wide range of activities from art and music to sports and hobbies as well as academic activities such as homework clubs. Since students select the activities they want to participate in, the level of motivation tends to be high, and discipline and attendance are good. This tends to create a better all-round attitude to school as

- Everyone responds best when participating in 'want to' rather than 'have to' activities. (The challenge is to make the core curriculum feel as attractive.)
- Any passion or interest will create a positive attitude to life and improve self-image.
- Any energy channelled into something positive will displace energy channelled into negative activities.
- The careers that students follow are often stimulated by extra-curricular activities.
- Students will form friendships within these groups that they might not normally form, often because of the smaller group size: a shared interest is a strong bond.
- Teachers can gain respect from students when facilitating these groups and investing their own time in sharing students' interests.

✓ **Tip**

☐ Where there is a significant need identified among your students then you can select attractive subjects to address these needs, indirectly but in a fun way. For example, where there is extensive low self-esteem, then teaching stand-up comedy enables participants also to learn skills such as assertiveness, confidence and dealing with conflict (=heckling!).

Extra Mural Studies *see* EMS.

★ **Eye Contact** is better thought of as I-contact. If you want to work with, and be with, other people – students and colleagues, friends and family – there are some useful basics.

- *Rule One – if I look at you, you look at me*
  - ☐ Looking at everyone in a group all the time is impossible. Start with a couple of people at the far left, and a couple at the far right, to draw them in. This will also draw others in with them. Add in the others as you feel comfortable. Return to people from time to time as you speak. (Think of how excluding and boring it was when you were in a group and no one paid enough attention to you?)
  - ☐ To avoid a staring competition if facing people, try looking between their eyes, or at the top of their nose, or – if a bit further away – at their mouth. They won't know that you're not looking at their eyes. And it gives you a bit of movement.
  - ☐ With a group, notice that you can appear to look straight ahead, but if you relax and soften your eyes, you can see, with a little practice, about 190 degrees around you, so out of the corner of your eye(s) you can see if there's any inattention or problem that needs to be addressed.

■ *Rule Two – if I look at Some Thing, then you look at Some Thing*

    □ There's a lot of nonsense about 'never looking away from a group'. It's perfectly possible to turn sideways and look at something on the wall or board, and draw the group's attention to it, because you are MODELLING that attention yourself.

EYT Early Years Teacher (or Team, which can include nurses and teaching assistants) – *see* EARLY YEARS.

4MAT® System *see* LEARNING STYLES.

★ **Facilitation** is literally making something easy, and in our case that's learning. It's probably the most important skill for a teacher to have and to use.

✓ *Tips*

☐ Always ask yourself how you can make learning easier, for your students and for yourself.

☐ Always ask your students, too. They'll also come up with great ideas on how you can make your own work easier, so long as you don't expect one-off immediate answers. Allow for regular enquiry on this.

☐ A facilitator moves around and rarely stands in front of a class. Relatively little whole-class teaching takes place – rather there is extensive use of ABILITY GROUPS peer tutoring and individual and group projects.

☐ A facilitator will stretch those students who are well-supported, and support those who are already stretched (whether in school or outside).

Faith Schools *see* RELIGIOUS OR FAITH SCHOOLS.

Family Learning Network is a forum for family learning professionals to discuss issues and share good practice. It is co-ordinated by the Campaign for Learning in partnership with NIACE and ContinYou.

Family Learning Week is a national event each autumn, co-ordinated by the Campaign for Learning.

Fast Track is an intensive training scheme for teachers and trainee teachers with the potential to build careers as leaders in education.

★ **Favouritism** is inevitable. You'll like some of your students more than others unless you are truly remarkable and objective (and have no emotions whatsoever!). Many parents have favourites among their children so why should teachers be different? Favouritism towards particular students will be based on a number of factors:

■ They might be similar to how you were when you were a child.
■ They gain your sympathy, as you want to help them overcome some disadvantage.
■ They remind you of a childhood friend.
■ They demonstrate values and beliefs that are like your own and you can relate to.
■ They maybe value education as you do.
■ They show a willingness to support you.
■ They have an innocence that appeals to your protective nature.

On the other hand, sometimes we dislike a student for reasons we do not fully understand. They may have the opposite of the list above. They could be like someone we didn't like in the past. Or maybe they come from a family we do not like.

By having a favourite you alienate the rest of the students – you cannot have a favourite and keep it a secret. And the fact of having a favourite will lower your esteem within a class and may make the favourite vulnerable to rejection and bullying.

Top Tips from Dr Michael Waters

1   Get students in the right mind–body state for whatever you want them to do
If you need them to focus calmly on a task, then it's no good their being in an
excited state. They need to be in a calm state. If you need them to be really alert,
then they need to be in an alert state, not in, say, a state of torpidity. This is all
very obvious, really, except that very few teachers have ever been trained in the
specific skills of student state management (unless they've been on one of my
courses!). To my mind, these are just about the most important skills a teacher
can have and crucial to good behaviour management as well as to learning.

2   Be a model learner rather than a model teacher
Your students need to know how to be excellent learners much more than they
need to know how to be excellent teachers. They may not be exposed to models
of excellent learning in their homes or in their local communities. Some of their
other teachers may not even be models of effective and passionate learning, so
you need to be. When they look and listen to you, they need to know what a
really good learner looks and sounds like. What do they look like when they are
curious, for example? What do they sound like when they are working something out?

3   Assume (validly) that few if any of your students learn exactly as you do
Then get very, very interested in exactly how they do learn. It is helpful to know
about learning styles and preferences – sensory-based, and otherwise – though
a lot that is written and spoken about them is simplistic and misleading. (Very
few students can ever securely be labelled 'visual learners', for example, as
though this simple tag somehow summed them up.) What's most important is
that you notice what particular students do when they are working and learning.
You might notice, for example, that one student seems to learn best when he is
standing up, and another when she is able to talk out loud to herself. Above all,
know your own preferences and peculiarities; understand that you may not share
them with the majority of your students, and be aware of the need to teach in
ways that are better suited to learning styles other than your own.

Ask your students frequently 'Am I teaching this in the ways that are right for
you?' and then ask 'And if not, what could I do differently – or allow you to do –
that would make the topic (say) more engaging and easier to understand?'.

4   You can teach your students but you can't do their learning for them
The essential point to add is – so don't even try. A lot of teachers do try, and
often end up providing support that is more disabling than enabling. Of course,
you can do all kinds of things to facilitate learning and make it more likely that
your students will learn (like teach to a variety of learning preferences and
involve students in active activities that really engage them). But don't spoon-
feed, or answer your own questions or any of the many other things that try to
secure learning by proxy. It doesn't do your students any favours in the long run.

*5   Make 'getting students to learn' and 'turning students onto learning' your
    absolutely essential default settings*
In busy demanding classrooms, it is so very easy to get distracted into other
concerns which can (often unwittingly) become your default modes – like getting students to be compliant, keeping them quiet and occupied, and 'getting
through' the topic or scheme of work. These things may be necessary and
even important but, ultimately, they're not what either you or your students are
there for.

✓ *Tips*

☐ Even if you feel a liking for one student, you must give all students equal opportunities, equal time and you must have an equal desire to see them do well.

☐ Your role is to educate at the levels of behaviour, skills and capabilities and help your students to form beliefs and values that will serve them well, not to like or dislike them or their identity (*see* LOGICAL LEVELS).

☐ If your favourite is always the student to answer questions, organize the students so that everyone has a chance to answer.

☐ Be equal with your praise and celebration of achievement.

☐ Check out from the list above, or other insights you have, why exactly you have this favouritism. Once you have analysed exactly why this is, it will be less dominant.

FBA Functional Behavioural Analysis is typically in three parts

1 By observing the nature and context of a child's behavioural problems.
2 By trying to understand why the behaviours are occurring.
3 And then developing strategies for managing them.

FDS First Destination Survey now the Destination of Leavers of Higher Education Survey (DLHE).

FE Further Education is post-16 (colleges, etc.) education but the category excludes Higher Education (universities).

FEDA was the Further Education Development Agency (now Learning and Skills Development Agency). It was established in 1995 from a merger of the Further Education Unit (a policy body founded in 1977) and the Staff College (a training and professional development institute), and it became the pre-eminent development agency for colleges.

★ **Feedback** is

1 Howling from a loudspeaker when a microphone is too close.

   or

2 Giving a critical opinion or observation about what has happened in the past.

FEEDFORWARD (see later) is, however, constructive rather than destructive – making suggestions about what might happen in the future rather than criticism of the past.

Both FEEDBACK and FEEDFORWARD are important when giving directions for improvement to a student. They need to understand what has already taken place, and what needs to happen next time.

✓ *Tips*

☐ Criticize in private but praise in public.

☐ Explain what exactly you are not happy with, where exactly (you think) the student has gone 'wrong', and the behaviour that could replace the unwanted behaviour.

☐ Explain the drawbacks for the student and other people if 'improvement' doesn't take place and the positive consequences if it does.

☐ Criticize only the behaviour or the quality of work in terms of what specifically happened (e.g. you did X and it had the effect of Y).

☐ *Never* criticize someone as a person (i.e. using the model of LOGICAL LEVELS, at the levels of their beliefs, values or identity), e.g. you are hopeless, you don't care.

☐ Always use the past tense for negative criticism (e.g. you got that wrong) and never the present (e.g. you always get that wrong).

☐ Always immediately follow feedback with 'feedforward' as to what could happen in the future (Feedforward is simply offering suggestions, with soft phrases such as 'maybe next time you could…' or 'perhaps you might…' so the ultimate choice stays with the student.).

☐ Similarly, if someone tells you what you 'should' do, take the advice as information ('maybe I could…' or 'perhaps I might…'), and reach your own conclusions.

☐ When receiving criticism yourself, search for the learning that could help you, rather than rush to defend yourself.

☐ If you have been criticized, fairly or unfairly, respond with the facts of what happened, and ask what they would prefer or suggest in future, and thank them for their opinion, which you'll consider.

☐ Use feedforward wherever possible, as there are none of the adverse side-effects that come with the alternatives, e.g. you should, you must, you ought to, you have to, you mustn't.

✗ Trap

☐ The 'feedback sandwich' is now believed not to work (and maybe it never really did?) because students recognize the pattern and therefore discount the positives as they're only used as wrapping for the criticism:

1 Give three positives about the student's work.
2 Give the criticism.
3 Give more positives, about the future.

This model leaves many people feeling manipulated and undermined.

★ **Feedforward** is simply offering suggestions for future action, with soft phrases such as 'maybe next time you could…' or 'perhaps you might…' so the ultimate choice stays with the student. *See also* FEEDBACK.

✓ Tips

☐ Always offer at least five possibilities (including some that are wacky and some that you yourself would not recommend) so that you don't implant your own preferences.

☐ This will also act as a model to stimulate your students (or colleagues, family members, friends?) to generate their own possibilities too.

FEFC Further Education Funding Council is now merged into the Learning & Skills Council. It was formed in 1992 when the Further and Higher Education Act removed FE and 6th Form Colleges from local authority control.

FHEQ Framework for Higher Education Qualifications for England, Wales and Northern Ireland is similar to the Scottish framework, but still in development, especially where existing qualifications (e.g. Higher National Certificates) cannot easily be placed at a single level. We have simplified the table, therefore, leaving out level numbers which are rarely used and overlap inconsistently with the NQF NATIONAL QUALIFICATIONS FRAMEWORK – which does *not* cover further and higher education!

■ *C Level* (Certificate), e.g. Certificates of Higher Education.
■ *I Level* (Intermediate), e.g. Foundation degrees, ordinary Bachelor degrees, Diplomas of Higher Education and other higher diplomas, e.g. Higher National Diploma (HND).
■ *H Level* (Honours), e.g. Bachelor degrees with Honours, Graduate Certificates and Graduate Diplomas.
■ *M Level* (Masters), e.g. Masters degrees, Postgraduate Certificates and Postgraduate Diplomas.
■ *D Level* (Doctoral), e.g. Doctorates.

★ **Fifteen Per cent** of a student's waking hours are spent at school in classes compared, therefore, to 85 per cent of their time spent outside school:

- 52 weeks in the year = 8,760 hours
- minus 13 weeks holidays
- minus (say) 4 INSET days and 1 bank holiday (outside normal holidays)
- is 38 weeks × 23 hours lesson time, average, per week
- equals 874 hours a year lesson time
- and assuming 365 × 8 hours sleep a night (!) (= 2920 hours)
- gives us 874 ÷ (8760 − 2920)
- which is 14.966 per cent of their waking time.

✓ *Tips*

☐ Accommodating outside influences on your students is, therefore, essential.
☐ Equipping them for the 85 per cent of their waking hours spent outside classrooms is also essential.
☐ Pointing out this percentage to parents who blame you for all their child's behaviours might also be useful (gently, though!).

See also SCHOOL DAY.

★ **Flexibility** means being sensitive to circumstances, and the demands of a class, and altering your own behaviour to best suit the needs of the moment. The purpose of being flexible is to maximize the value that can be derived from the time and resources available. It is like being in a canoe going down rapids – you follow the path the water takes rather than forcing your own path. There used to be a time when a teacher could break from the set lesson and discuss current affairs or something of local interest. Experimentation, new methodologies and idiosyncrasies used to be the essence of creative teaching. With the increase in targets set for teachers, the tighter forms of measurement of their performance, the close scrutiny of regulatory bodies, the pressure to get through a fuller syllabus and the other pressures that seem to funnel teachers along an even tighter pathway, the concept of flexibility may seem not only alien and impractical, but somewhat ill-advised. Flexibility, or going with the flow, may also open the door for others to interpret your behaviour as being driven by a negative intention or objective. It can be seen as rebellious or lax, especially by people who need to stick rigidly to rules.

However, circumstances do change from day to day. How you feel, events outside school that may affect attitudes within the school, the time of year, the pressures of exams, the weather, all come together to create different learning attitudes and environments. Being rigid in your approach can be like swimming against the tide. The class wants to go one way and you have to fight to keep them going another way. In such circumstances it is essential to be flexible in your approach.

✓ *Tips*

☐ Always be clear about your lesson plan, your learning objectives and outcomes, and the way in which you and others will measure that these have been achieved.
☐ Always be in control of the content even when being flexible in the way you achieve that content i.e. you always know *what* you will achieve even when being flexible in *how* you will achieve it.
☐ Ensure that any flexibility meets the needs of the class and is not a statement about you and your independence.
☐ Be sensitive to how others outside the class may perceive your flexibility. Pre-advise them if necessary.
☐ Inspirational teachers are often rebellious or unconventional by nature. There is too little room in today's education system for those who step out of line, or appear to know

better than those setting the system: being seen to be too flexible may be a high risk strategy – unless you are in a school where creativity in achieving your goals is highly prized and praised.

Flexible Learning is where students enrol at a college (physically or otherwise) but instead of attending regular classes, they learn in their own time, at home, at work or indeed at college. Regular tutorials, workshops and group sessions also take place as appropriate. Courses can start and finish at any time of the year, and often work towards nationally recognized qualifications, such as NVQS & GCSES.

Flow is a sense of being totally absorbed in an activity when you and the activity feel 'as one' and the activity seems to have its own momentum. The flow state was described initially by Mihaly Csikszentmihalyi (pronounced Me-High-Eee Chick-Sendt-Me-High-Eee). It is a state of profound yet relaxed concentration, where ideas and performance just flow.

Flynn Effect In 1984 J.J. Flynn identified that norms become unreliable over time as there are improvements in the performance of the whole population overall – for example, the mean IQ of Americans showed massive gains from 1932 to 1978. This could be because their IQ increased massively. Or because their ability to do IQ tests increased massively.

✔ *Tip*

▫ Be sceptical of norms and averages. We have a friend who delights in pointing out, much to people's horror and indignation, that 'half the UK population has below-average intelligence!' (Clue: half of *any* population's *anything* is below average, just as half is above average – that's what average means!)

FMA Foundation level Modern APPRENTICESHIP.

Fogging is a technique to combat name-calling. (*See Tip* under APPEARANCE BULLYING)

Ford, Henry 1863–1947 (US carmaker)

■ 'Anyone who stops learning is old, whether at twenty or eighty. Anyone who keeps learning stays young. The greatest thing in life is to keep your mind young.' (Much quoted.)
■ 'I only want to employ people who don't use their brains from 9 to 5.' (Allegedly practised.)

Format see 4MAT® under LEARNING STYLES.

Foundation Degrees were launched in September 2001 as largely part-time work-based qualifications, e.g. teaching assistants, legal executives, laboratory and engineering technicians, at 'associate professional' and 'higher technician' levels.

They are the equivalent of 2 years full-time study, and are at Intermediate Level in the Framework for Higher Education Qualifications FHEQ and level 4 in the National Qualifications Framework NQF. Credits are given for relevant prior learning or experience, and individual learning programmes are designed to build on students' existing skills and knowledge. Students may also credit their foundation degree towards an honours degree at a later stage. It is expected that other Intermediate Level Qualifications such as HNDs will become foundation degree courses in time.

Foundation Schools are state schools, introduced in 2001, which, like the proposed Foundation Hospitals, will be managed by an independent foundation, rather than by an LEA.

Foundation Stage covers ages three to five and includes nursery, pre-school, play groups and the first year in school. There are QCA national standards that link with the

NATIONAL CURRICULUM early learning guidelines, which are measured in the *foundation stage profile*. This is compiled throughout a student's foundation stage and is not just a snapshot at any given moment. The curriculum covers six areas of learning:

- Personal, social and emotional development.
- Communication, language and literacy.
- Mathematical development.
- Physical development.
- Knowledge and understanding of the world.
- Creative development.

(These may sound daunting for such young students, but learning and assessment through play are recognized as vital for developing these skills.)

The profile is mainly compiled through observation, e.g. a student may be given a task for a specific skill area and then observed to assess their skill level. Unlike BASE-LINE ASSESSMENT (which it replaced in 2002) the foundation stage profile also reflects the contribution that parents make to the student's education, hoping that it will encourage parents to continue to be involved in their child's education in the long-term .

Fresh Start Schools are established after a school fails to improve after SPECIAL MEASURES are imposed following a negative Ofsted report. The school is closed and re-opened with a new name and a fresh injection of leadership and cash.

Fresher is a first-year university undergraduate.

Freshman (US) is a first-year undergraduate in the Fresher year.

Froebel, Friedrich (1782–1852) was an influential German educationalist who recognized the value of play as a coordinating and integrating mechanism in which the child makes sense of the world. He founded the first kindergartens (German = garden of children). He believed that children were self-motivating and thought it important that adults should not damage this.

FTE Full Time Equivalent, e.g. we have 12 staff who work half-days only, making six FTE staff.

Full-Service Schools offer facilities such as health, counselling, sports and youth activities in addition to the usual teaching. This enables non-teaching issues such as teenage pregnancy, substance abuse and mental health to be addressed in an integrated way for the young person.

Further Literacy Support is a pilot INTERVENTION PROGRAMME for students in year 5 who are not making the expected progress, and are still at level 3.

Gagné, Robert is an American behavioural psychologist whose Nine Events of Instruction offer a systematic approach to teaching, with a focus on the outcomes of learning (i.e. observable behaviours).

1 Attract students' attention.
2 Inform students of objectives.
3 Recall previous relevant learning, to build upon.
4 Present new material.
5 Provide 'learning guidance' (e.g. case studies, stories, examples) to facilitate understanding and assimilation of new material.
6 Allow student to use the new material, to explore it, question it, and integrate it into their learnings.
7 Provide feedback as guidance.
8 Assess performance to ensure new material is integrated.
9 Provide repetition to maximize retention, and facilitate real-life usage.

Gangs have probably always existed. They are groups of people with shared values (or in some people's judgement, lack of values) who identify with shared goals (e.g. eliminating rival groups, or personal gain). Some now have clear criminal backup and are not just part of natural childhood groupings. A gang's goals may range from bullying, through drug distribution, to robbery or worse. Forming gangs can no longer be seen as a phase that some children go through. Every school needs a policy on handling gangs, especially as weapons become more easily accessible. Any evidence of gang activity, regardless of the age of the students involved, needs to be monitored and addressed. The police and other specialist mediators have the expertise to deal with this situation, diverting gangs' energies into more productive activities.

Gap Year is when a student takes a year away from studying – typically between finishing school and starting college or university – to work or travel in order to gain some non-school experience before settling down to their studies again. They can apply for a college or university place and then ask to defer it for a year. Or they can postpone their application until they have had their gap year. There is no doubt that travel and work experience broaden the mind. The danger with gap years is that students can sometimes find more interesting things to do with the rest of their lives than continue studying!

Gardner, Howard (b. 1943) is the US psychologist perhaps best known for his work on MULTIPLE INTELLIGENCES. He also researches creativity, and 'good work' – which is what happens when, in various professions, excellence and ethics meet.

GCE General Certificate of Education was introduced in 1951 with Ordinary (O) levels at age 16 and Advanced (A) levels at age 18. They superseded School Certificate and Higher School Certificate, respectively. Ordinary (O) levels were replaced in 1988 by the GCSE General Certificate of Secondary Education. A LEVEL GCEs continue.

GCSE General Certificate of Secondary Education was introduced in 1988 as a replacement for GCE O levels.

Gender Differences in education are much discussed, and conclusions are often clouded by PC POLITICAL CORRECTNESS, arguments about NATURE AND NURTURE, and concerns about EQUAL OPPORTUNITIES. Even though female students achieve better exam results than male students in many subjects, there is no clear evidence that this is due to genetic differences. Here are some generalizations that many teachers hold to be true based on their experience and, as with all generalizations, there will be many exceptions. (You might also spot yourself in some of these and take appropriate action):

- A high percentage of teachers in infant and primary schools are female which leaves male students without male role models – this creates a teaching style and ambience more suited to female students, making males feel excluded.
- Many teachers have a leaning towards VISUAL and AUDITORY teaching styles which does not suit males who might have more KINAESTHETIC learning needs.
- Males tend to be more robust, competitive and aggressive in their play, whereas female students tend to be more sociable and tend more towards academic study, so female students tend to work harder than males in class.
- Male bullying tends to be more physical whereas female bullying tends to be more psychological and/or manipulative.
- Male students may have shorter ATTENTION SPANS than females especially where their kinaesthetic need is not being satisfied, so they are more likely to fidget and be disruptive, and need frequent breaks.
- Males tend to be more adept with spatial challenges whereas females tend to be more adept with verbal communication and building relationships.
- Many male strengths such as eye-to-hand co-ordination are not necessarily as valued in the classroom.
- Males develop motor skills through robust play as a substitute for less aggressive motor skills such as holding a pen and writing.

✓ *Tips*

- ☐ Recognize difference without putting a judgement on it.
- ☐ Use TEACHING STYLES to engage all LEARNING STYLES.
- ☐ Have high expectations of all students.

Glue Ear is a sticky fluid in the ear that mainly affects children under the age of 5. It is quite common especially in winter or after cold or flu. It may also be triggered by allergies and passive smoking. It affects hearing and balance, and causes dizziness and clumsiness. It might manifest itself with poor attention levels or a growth in 'whats?' or 'pardons?'. As with all conditions where the teacher has a concern about attention levels, your SENCO (SPECIAL EDUCATIONAL NEEDS CO-ORDINATOR) should be consulted.

GNVQs General National Vocational Qualifications (at Foundation and Intermediate Levels on the NQF) are being replaced by Vocational GCSEs in 2004 to put vocational and academic qualifications on an equal footing.

Golden Hellos are one-off payments made to FE lecturers at the beginning of their second year of teaching to enable colleges to recruit and retain teachers in designated shortage subject areas. This scheme was extended to school teachers of basic literacy, numeracy and ESOL from September 2003 and, from April 2004, LEAs and schools are due to fund Golden Hello payments from their own resources.

★ **Good** as in a 'good' teacher or a 'good' school, or indeed a 'good' student ? A parent sums this up better than we ever could:

> I'm reassured that we made the right choice with this school. The teachers and staff are highly responsive, and parents and students are taken very seriously. K is treated as a responsible person, as opposed to a troublesome child, and 'listened to'. Teachers encourage students to look for their own solutions and then discuss how

these can be put into practice; the curriculum caters for individual solutions both on the emotional and academic side. (For example, over the weekend the teachers rearranged the seating for the third time this term, to try out a different solution, and they're also going to play some role-reversal games this week so that the 'leaders' swap with those they insist on leading!) These kids, who are used to being good at stuff, are encouraged to break out of their comfort zone and achieve their potential and not to stop short of it in case they make mistakes. In fact, K has made more mistakes than ever before, and while this is frustrating for her to some extent, she's also learning that you don't have to be perfect all the time. They're whizzing through all sorts of stuff and exploring new things all the time; the focus is on keeping them motivated and wanting to learn, rather than dull them down with unnecessary repetitions. It takes a very special kind of teacher to have that self-drive and sincere interest in getting the best out of everyone, and I have a lot of respect for them being able to keep just that one step ahead!

Good Work is one of Howard GARDNER'S fields of study, which explores what happens when excellence and ethics meet in various professions.

Goodhart's Law states that (and we paraphrase here) when you measure something, the very act of measuring it disturbs what you are measuring, so making the measure useless. It is sometimes used to argue against league tables, targets etc, meaning that if you choose a measure as a target, then the measure is no longer a useful one. (Professor Charles Goodhart FBA was Chief Economic Adviser on Monetary Policy for the Bank of England from 1980 to 1985.)

Governors and Governing Bodies exist for every maintained school. The board of governors acts like a business board of directors to ensure high educational standards, take general responsibility for the conduct of the school's affairs, oversee the school budgets including personnel head count, oversee the curriculum, participate in senior staff appointments and respond to OFSTED reports where necessary. The board is made up of the head teacher, LEA appointees, support staff representatives, elected parents, elected teachers and others recruited by the board from the local community. They need to be available for meetings, often held in the evenings, and to read all relevant material and keep up to date with changes in educational practice. Student governors are common in the majority of colleges now. But younger school students, who do not have an elected student governor, will have their views represented by parents and staff.

Grade School (US) *see* ELEMENTARY SCHOOL (US).

Grades (or marks) are measures of quality or achievement denoted by letters or numbers, with A or 1 being the highest. The failure mark has traditionally been F but that has changed in some exams to N for nearly succeeded. 'Pass' normally means a satisfactory performance; 'Merit' means significantly better than 'pass'; and 'Distinction' normally means an outstanding performance. (In the US, Grade represents the class or year of school e.g. first grade is the year that students begin elementary school at age 6–7, second grade is age 7–8, up to twelfth grade age 17–18.)

Graduation (US) is the completion of e.g. high school (i.e. high school graduation), or college (i.e. college graduation), or even the end of a year, often marked by a ceremony of celebration (i.e. graduation ceremony). This is being adopted extensively in the UK as it offers a sense of CELEBRATING ACHIEVEMENT to participants and friends and family.

Grammar is the collection of linguistic rules which define a language.

- *Prescriptive* grammar is most often used in schools, with tried and tested 'rules' that must be obeyed, e.g. 'John Smith is the great man to whom I wrote'.

- *Descriptive* grammar reflects current usage and varies with peer groups e.g. 'John Smith is the gr8 man I wrote to'. (Prescriptive grammaticians would probably disagree both with the use of 'gr8' from texting, and the preposition 'to' at the end of the sentence.)
- *Universal* grammar recognises relationships between the brain and language, and you'll find more about this if you research Chomsky and Structuralism – two good names to drop!

Grammar Schools are secondary schools which select students on the basis of general ability in an examination at age eleven, provided either by the local education authority or by the school itself. (Many local authorities no longer have any grammar schools – there are around 200 in England and Northern Ireland, and none in Wales or Scotland.) Students are offered places related to their ranking in the examination results – no-one any longer 'passes' or 'fails'. (There are typically several hundred applications for each student place, hence the system of admission by examination.) In the class-conscious days after World War II, grammar school students were regarded as future managers and professionals. It was unlikely that you could go on to university education unless you went to a grammar school or PUBLIC SCHOOL. Working-class students winning a place at grammar school were often seen as 'getting above their station', and getting to university was an even greater achievement. Having recognized that age 11 was too early to put students into pigeon holes that would define their future careers, comprehensive education was introduced. The main arguments against grammar schools are

- SELECTION is unfair since some students develop later than others, and all students need to be in an environment where they can access a stimulating education;
- 'Creaming off' the allegedly more academic students has adverse effects on other schools locally. *See* BANDING.

Graphemes *see* PHONICS.

GRTP Graduate and Registered Teacher Programmes – *see* GTP and RTP.

Top Tips from Paul Pyzer

- The teacher should build up a great relationship with the learner.
- Make sure the learner is not only learning, but aware of what they are learning.
- Make sure the learner knows why they are doing each activity.
- Assessment is best done by the learners themselves – self-assessment.
- The teacher should be aware of what the learners already know and what to teach to bring them forward.
- Relate teaching to real life situations as much as possible, to make it more relevant to them.
- The teacher should use a mixture of visual, auditory and kinaesthetic activities.
- Where possible, do not stick rigidly to the syllabus but teach what would benefit the learners most.

GTC General Teaching Council for England was established in 2000 as an independent not-for-profit professional body for qualified teachers. It has statutory powers to advise the Secretary of State and others on matters of professional practice concerning standards of teaching and learning. All teachers (including part-time and supply) with QTS (QUALIFIED TEACHER STATUS) working in maintained schools, non-maintained special schools and pupil referral units are required, by law, to register with the GTC.

GTP Graduate Teacher Programme is normally a one year course, customized to individual needs, for UK graduates (age 24+) who want to become teachers in specific subjects. They may get a grant/salary during this year as it is largely school-based. It is a parallel qualification to the PGCE but with a focus on 'on the job' learning rather than academic study.

GTTR Graduate Teacher Training Registry processes applications for entry to Professional Certificate in Education (PGCE) courses on behalf of Initial Teacher Training (ITT) providers.

Guided Writing And Reading *see* LITERACY HOUR.

Guilford J.P. (1897–1988 US psychologist) working in intelligence and creativity. *See* SIT (STRUCTURE OF INTELLECT THEORY).

⭐ **Gurus** nowadays are any admired leaders in any walk of life. We are attracted to follow gurus when they do something to a high standard that we want to emulate or that we admire. We have fashion gurus, style gurus, music gurus, as well as the original spiritual teachers or guides. (Guru is a Sanskrit term meaning 'dispeller of darkness'.)

✓ *Tips*

☐ Be selective. Just because a guru is successful does not mean they get everything right. Don't hang onto their every word – choose the bits that work for you.

☐ A guru will operate in a particular context, lifestyle or environment. What may work for that guru within that context may not work for you within yours.

☐ It is the nature of many people to look for a powerful force to follow – they want something to believe in. Make sure you choose your gurus well. (*See* AUTHORITY AND POWER.)

☐ Many people find it flattering to be elevated to the role of guru. Some students, in search of a guru, may flatter you that way. Being a guru carries a heavy responsibility with it. Keep your feet on the ground and an objective view of yourself. (*See also* ROLE MODELS.)

Gustatory one of the five senses – taste.

Gymnasium, as well as an indoor place for exercise, is a German secondary school.

Handy, Charles is a UK writer and broadcaster specializing in the human impact of business, having worked in business, taught at university, and been a priest. One of his most influential models states that a leader (e.g. a teacher!) has three main objectives:

- Achieving the task.
- Managing the individuals and the team who achieve the task.
- Managing yourself.

It is only by addressing all three areas of responsibility that you can maximize long-term results.

Hart, Roger – *see* PARTICIPATION.

HE Higher Education, i.e. universities.

Head of Department is the person in charge of either one subject or group of subjects (e.g. humanities) throughout a school. Their function is to set a strategy and policy for the subject, ensure continuity and flow from one year to the next and to monitor results and progress. They must ensure that their subject is adequately represented within the curriculum and timetable. They need to drive their subject but within the larger framework of the school's overall objectives. This function is a useful grounding as preparation for headship. It will include managing staff, budgetary responsibility and accountability and team-building. Working more closely with the head teacher is also good development for the head of department, and more formal management training is becoming more consistently available.

Head of Year can be

1   Students who have a PREFECTorial role over their year-group.

    or

2   Teachers who have responsibility for overseeing the welfare and academic progress of all the students in a given year: as such they will liaise with heads of department, their head teacher, parents and outside bodies.

Head Teacher is the senior member of the teaching staff. The role has also been known as Principal, Head Master, Head Mistress and Head. The preference is for the title to be non gender specific. Although the NATIONAL CURRICULUM appears to take away much of the autonomy that schools used to enjoy, the role of head teacher is growing and becoming of greater importance. Their remuneration in comparison to other teachers is growing as the level of expectation and responsibility increases. Their primary role is to oversee the students' well being and education. To achieve this, the role necessitates leadership, and managing the performance of teachers. The head can create or change the culture within a school and can make a massive improvement (or collapse!) in attitude throughout the school. Many have responsibility not only for budgets but for fundraising for non-core activities. They need to be well-informed about the law relating to children, human rights, employment, education, and need to be able to deal with the media, local and national government, communities – oh, and staff and students. As with other organizations, the leadership role is probably one of the most important. A good head teacher can bring about massive improvement in overall performance. The National Professional Qualification for Headship became compulsory in 2004.

✓ *Tip*

☐ If you aspire to fulfil your potential as a teacher, if you want to work in a school that makes a positive contribution, if you want to learn and if you want a rewarding career then choose your head teacher with great care! (Being an excellent teacher doesn't mean they will automatically be a good head teacher.)

Headlamp is a training and support programme for new headteachers. *See* NATIONAL COLLEGE FOR SCHOOL LEADERSHIP.

Health and Safety is shorthand for all the legal requirements to ensure that all possible steps are taken so that no-one is avoidably put at risk. For example, ensuring that each person is appropriately supervised where there is a duty of care. Or making certain that areas are clear of dangerous objects before allowing play to commence. There are full guidelines available from the DfES that cover requirements inside schools, on visits, on overseas visits, sports activities, play areas and what to do in case of accidents. It is advised that not only do you read these through in depth but that you keep up to date with developments.

✓ *Tip*

☐ If in doubt, consult – your school should have its own policies in any case.

HEI Higher Education Institution, e.g. university.

HESA Higher Education Statistics Agency set up in 1993 for data collection and publication.

Heterodoxy is any 'unorthodox' position or point of view that differs from 'accepted' teaching (= orthodoxy).

✓ *Tips*

☐ You will need to follow precisely what is expected of you in your first few months or years of teaching, in order to qualify, fit in, and be seen in the 'right' light.
☐ Achieve 'what' is asked of you, by doing it 'how' best works for you and those around you. Remember, there's more than one way to skin a cat – or carrot, for vegetarians.

✗ *Trap*

☐ You will go mad if you're not able to express yourself by doing what you think is 'right'.

HI Hearing Impairment.

High Schools (US) are also known as Senior High Schools, Senior High, or High and are public secondary (= middle) schools usually offering grades 9 –12 (ages 15 –17), between an Elementary School and College.

High/Scope Curriculum originated in 1962 when David Weikart set up a project in response to the failure of high school students from poor neighbourhoods in Ypsilanti in Michigan (US). It is now in over twenty countries, and encourages students' active learning, decision-making and problem-solving in a stimulating environment supported by adults.

HNC/D Higher National Certificate/Diploma are vocational qualifications (with typically 180 credits needed for an HNC and a further 60 for an HND) introduced by the Technician Education Council in 1973 and now at Level 4 (Higher) of the NQF National Qualification Framework, alongside degrees.

Home Education About 1 per cent of UK students are educated at home. This can conjure up a picture of being stuck indoors all the time, but many parents group together to share expertise, with stimulating 'experts' or stimulating visits. Note that in the UK it is full-time education that is compulsory, not full-time schooling. Home education is an option open to victims of bullying, but social isolation needs to be avoided.

Home–School Agreement *see* AGREEMENT, HOME–SCHOOL.

Home-Start is a family support organization that provides trained volunteers to help any parent, with at least one child under five, who is finding it hard to cope. Some of your students may come from families who could benefit from this.

Homework is set to be completed out of school hours, typically at home. The amount set and the content will depend on the age and stage of the student. Those studying for A levels would be expected to have approximately two to three hours homework per day. When you add this homework time to the school day it is roughly the average working week for an adult. Not all students have the space or the support to study at home. Homework clubs allow students to stay behind at the end of the school day to study within supervised surroundings. Homework has a number of benefits:

- It instils a work ethic and a pattern of studying without supervision.
- It connects home with learning and the subliminal message is that learning is an all-life, all-time activity.
- It gives students the opportunity to consolidate classroom learning.
- It enables the teacher to keep in touch with how much is being understood and learned, and forms part of the FORMATIVE ASSESSMENT.
- It creates an opportunity for students who want to excel without any constraints that may exist within the classroom.

✓ *Tip*

☐ When allocating homework we need to remember that life is not just academic achievement. People who need counselling for work/life balance in later years often trace their workaholism back to excessive pressure around homework.

✗ *Trap*

☐ A recent survey found that three-quarters of school students are helped with homework, while a further one in ten have someone else do *all* of their homework for them. Remember that 'homework' only describes where the work was done, and not who actually did it. (*See also* COURSEWORK.)

Homework Clubs *see* OUT OF SCHOOL CLUBS.

Honey & Mumford *see* LEARNING STYLES.

Hot Seat is a technique that invites students into someone else's situation to imagine what it would really have been like for them. It is a form of role play that works well for subjects where people feature, such as history, geography, and religious education. It is best used after facts and information have been covered through discussion or reading. It elicits the feelings as well as the facts, thus reinforcing the learning.

Example

If you were teaching about Guy Fawkes and the gunpowder plot, you could designate the Hot Seat, a chair positioned at the front of the class, as Guy Fawkes' chair. One of the students would then sit in that chair and assume a posture they think Guy

Fawkes would use. You then have them 'become' Guy Fawkes, and ask questions about their motives, reasons for plotting, desired results, how they felt when they were caught and so on. Because this technique has the feel of a game and the students can be creative in how they respond, learning tends to be longer-lasting than in other methods. After the role play, a general discussion and summary of learning points should be made.

✓ *Tips*

☐ You could use this technique (carefully) in conflict situations and then trigger a discussion on the relationships and interactions between the various parties, and possible ways forward – actually trying them on for size in the hot seat.

☐ As well as the main character in the hot seat, you could have other chairs for other characters in the situation, exploring what it was like for each of them, and how it would be if one or more of them changed their stance on the issue. This is a good way of developing SYSTEMS THINKING skills.

★ **How To Say 'No'** is a skill we all need. There are different ways of saying 'no', and we need to choose the way that best suits us, our outcomes, our personality and the outcomes and personality of the person receiving the refusal. Otherwise we can get labelled 'negative' or 'unhelpful' or 'unlikeable'.

▪ *Direct 'no'* is the most simple but it depends for its fuller meaning on the way in which you say it – the intonation, the non-verbal messages and your eye contact. When giving a direct 'no' be sure you are in control of your frame of mind and clear about the message you want the other person to receive both by the word 'no' and the way in which you say it. Just saying 'no' will often lead to someone asking again and again.

▪ *'No' with explanation* states the downside of saying 'yes' as well as the benefit of saying 'no'. For example, 'no, I won't agree to you taking six weeks holiday because you would fall behind schedule, so by not taking that time you can make progress towards your exam preparation'. This is more palatable and more likely to get agreement. Another example: 'No, we won't do that because the school governors won't like it', could be inconclusive unless we explain the implications to the student, such as 'No, the school governors won't like it and that may affect the extra tuition they have agreed for you to receive'.

▪ *Exploring implications without actually using the word 'no' is* a way of creating greater ownership and responsibility as it gets the student to explore the implications for themselves. You can also use this method to have them consider their request from different perspectives. 'Of course we could, and how would you see the rest of the class fitting in with that?' or 'What would you see the consequences being if we did?' or 'I could agree to that if you could satisfy me how exactly you would benefit in the long-term, and what you might lose in the process?'.

▪ *Increasing choices* by asking for alternatives can encourage a broader view of events, e.g. 'Yes we could do that, but the downside from my perspective is X. What other ways could you think of that would achieve what you're looking to achieve, without the downside for me?'

▪ HOT SEATING by simply asking a student to step into your shoes and deal with their request from your standpoint, e.g. 'If you were me, would you agree to that? And why?'.

✓ *Tips*

☐ We ourselves almost never say 'no'. For example, if asked to do the impossible (again!) and produce some work to an impossible deadline, we might say 'yes, I can do that so long as I can offload other projects. OR (heavy emphasis here) I could give you a topline by 3pm and the full thing by the 9am you've asked for. OR I can do my best by 9am, or do a good job by 11am the day after. Which do you want? (and then we'd allow a complete silence here for the other person to think, and respond. We would never, repeat never, dig ourselves into a hole by filling the silence with 'oh, all right then (sigh) I suppose I'll be able to, somehow'.) Remember – *they* want it, you *can* do it, but you both need to agree on *how* and *when* you will do it.

☐ Avoid saying

 1 'Yes' and then (to yourself).
 2 'Why on earth did I say Yes to that?!'

 Try, instead, saying something like 'I'd love to, but let me get back to you once I check my diary/schedule'.

HSA *see* AGREEMENT, HOME-SCHOOL.

Humanities is the umbrella term for subjects related to human thought, relationships and achievements. Opinions vary, but these subjects are often covered: English, literature, languages, philosophy, classics, history, music, fine arts, theatre and religion.

★ **Humour and Laughter** are human traits that are easy to take for granted. Aristotle realised that 'laughter kills fear,' and being fearful is no frame of mind in which to learn. It is possible to be serious about something, wanting to do your best at it, without being solemn. It is possible to have fun, be amusing and still excel at what you are doing. Being humourless is not a sign that you are doing your best. Edward de Bono, the lateral thinker, said, 'humour is by far the most significant phenomenon in the human mind. It tells us to be aware of absolute dogmatism because suddenly something can be looked at in a different way'. Laughter has many health benefits. It releases endorphins, nature's pain killer; it reduces stress; it stimulates breathing and blood flow; it just makes us feel better. And we are designed to laugh. It's not that we are permitted by nature to laugh – laughter has evolved for a purpose. A baby laughs long before it crawls, speaks, eats solids or controls its bodily functions. As babies are built to survive, nature must have thought laughter was pretty important to have introduced it at such a young age. (Maybe a baby's laughter is a way to repay a parent's devotion and love at a time when their energy or temper is failing?) Laughter is a great leveller and it creates bonds. Used correctly, humour can greatly enhance the learning process. The only danger is how others view it.

✓ *Tips*

☐ Humour can create a good learning state in students because it relaxes them and makes them more receptive and involved.
☐ If you are teaching through the use of anecdotes, humour will make them more memorable (as they involve the body as well as the brain – whether the students laugh or groan at your attempts).
☐ Be aware of how people outside of the class will perceive the sound of laughter in your classroom – you do not want your motives to be misinterpreted.
☐ Humour is best when it is spontaneous and relevant to learning points.

✗ *Traps*

☐ Never be coarse, sexist, racist or in poor taste.
☐ Never make anyone the butt of your jokes.
☐ Never use humour to demean anyone or to be hurtful.

☐ Never force it or overdo it.

☐ You don't need to use humour if the class is already aroused and excited.

☐ If you are reprimanding a student they may try to make you laugh. If you laugh, your authority disappears until you quickly retrieve the situation, e.g. 'what you said was very funny, yes, but it's the seriousness of the situation I need you to focus on right now'.

IAG Information Advice and Guidance services, the provision of which are managed by the Learning & Skills Council (England).

IB *see* INTERNATIONAL BACCALAUREATE (the International Baccalaureate Diploma Programme).

IBP Individual Behavioural Programme is a course of action that might be taken following a special educational needs STATEMENT.

ICDL International Computer Driving Licence is a basic qualification for computer skills, available from many awarding bodies.

ICT Information and Communications Technology, e.g. computers, mobile phones, satellites, videoconferencing and accompanying software, and the use of them – known as IT (Information Technology) in the US.

IEP Individual Education Plan is often devised for early years students who need EARLY YEARS ACTION. It typically covers language, literacy, mathematics, behaviour and social skills and specifically focuses on

- What special help has been given.
- How often a child has received the help.
- Who has provided it.
- What the current targets are for the student.
- How and when their progress will be monitored.
- What help parents can give a child at home.
- What special help will be provided next, by whom, and how often.

The teacher will normally discuss the IEP with parents and the student, if possible.

✓ *Tip*

☐ A teacher should always be able to tell parents what progress their child is making, and how they are helping their child, whether or not an IEP has been formally developed.

IEP Individual Education Programme is a course of action following a special educational needs STATEMENT.

IGCSE International GCSE is an examination-only qualification launched by EDEXCEL in summer 2004 (initially in Maths). It is intended as a challenging two-year course after which students sit for examinations, with no COURSEWORK content. It is being adopted initially by independent schools who see it as giving their students an advantage in university applications. (State schools are currently obliged to offer GCSES.)

IiP Investors in People was established in 1993 as the national standard of good practice for training and development, for people to achieve their organization's goals. The number of schools participating is now around one in four who are fully recognized as meeting the IiP standard, with a further one in six in the process of recognition.

ILT is an Institute for Learning and Teaching (e.g. school, college, university).

Individual Behavioural Programme *see* IBP.

Individual Education Programme *see* IEP.

Induction Tutors are teachers charged with ensuring the smooth integration of new teachers, especially newly qualified teachers, and, increasingly, other non-teaching members of staff.

Inert Knowledge *see* SITUATED LEARNING.

Infant School used to be for students from 5–7 years, and is now supposedly replaced by the term Key Stage 1.

Informal Learning takes place outside a specific learning environment (such as a school, or training room) from everyday activities, e.g. watching someone use a coffee machine, and having them help you use it yourself.

INSET In-Service Training days (also PD Days – Personal Development Days) were introduced by the then education secretary Kenneth Baker (hence being also known as Baker Days) for headteachers to bring staff together for training and whole-school development planning. Usually they are timed to be at the beginning or end of the school holidays, as this often results in less disruption to teaching, but after-school sessions or instead-of-school sessions also take place. There can be up to five days in a year, or more by agreement. (Full-time teachers cannot be required to attend INSET outside their 195 days of directed time. Part-time staff cannot be required to attend INSET outside their normal teaching times.)

Inspiration In education today it is easy to feel constrained by league tables, inspections, the national curriculum and exams. Indeed, for reasons of self-preservation, our minds can become fixed on exam results and OFSTED. Let's not forget the most important people in the whole process of education, the students. How do they measure us? Certainly, they will measure us by how successful they have been in exams and the degree, maybe, which they get at university. In addition to qualifications, what they will remember most, and how they will measure us in the fullness of time, is how well we have *inspired* them to achieve, to fulfil their potential and to live their lives.

Many successful people trace their achievements back to a teacher, when they 'saw the light'; they felt as if something 'clicked', they were *inspired*. Young people, students in our schools, are in many ways like blank pieces of paper waiting to be inspired and to see their future written upon that blank page. Sometimes the day may seem bland, repetitive and heavy. Never forget that the moment for you to inspire someone may just be a moment away.

✓ *Tips*

- ☐ If you can inspire one student to excel and to make the most of their life then your time as a teacher will have been worthwhile.
- ☐ If you can do this for one student, you can do it – differently, of course – for each and every one.
- ☐ By inspiring a student you will inspire yourself.
- ☐ No matter what is going on around you, always remember that the student is the real customer, the person you are employed to educate and inspire.

Intelligence was originally defined as the ability to process and use information – but only in the brain rather than the whole body. Howard Gardner's work on MULTIPLE INTELLIGENCES and Daniel Goleman's work on EMOTIONAL INTELLIGENCE have, however, broadened the definition significantly. Who could argue nowadays, that a footballer's bodily instincts and excellence were any less 'intelligent' than a scientist's research? Who has never regretted ignoring their 'gut feel' or what their 'heart' was telling them?

Intelligence Tests were first developed by BINET in 1905, where children were expected to follow specific commands, copy patterns, name objects and put objects in order, for example. He also created norms based on his data so, for example, if 70 per cent of 8-year-olds could pass a specific test, then he defined success on the test as representative of the 8-year-old level of intelligence, or 'mental age'.

Binet and Théodore Simon developed the Binet–Simon tests from 1905 to 1908, and a major revision in 1916 was conducted after Binet's death by Lewis Ternam from Stanford University (US) to produce what became known as the Stanford–Binet tests. These also introduced the notion of the 'intelligence quotient' (IQ) as the ratio of mental age to chronological age, with 100 being the average. So, for example, an 8-year-old who passes a test for 16-year-olds would have an IQ of $16 \div 8 \times 100$, i.e. 200. (Binet always resisted scores that measured children's performance, preferring to think instead in terms of classifying their abilities.)

✗ Trap

- ☐ Any single-number measure may be extremely useful for specific purposes. However, when used as a good/bad or pass/fail measure (as it was, largely, in the 11 Plus exams) it can brand a person as a success/failure or clever/stupid for life.

Interdisciplinary, multidisciplinary or transdisciplinary studies are, as you would imagine, more holistic than, say, single subjects like physics or French. They typically give experiences to students, who then can study them using whatever disciplines are appropriate. For example, a nature walk (physical exercise) can involve drawing flowers (art) and learning to spell their names (literacy) and counting the different types of bird (numeracy and ornithology).

✓ Tips

- ☐ These are great buzzwords at the moment.
- ☐ Remember, these have been happening for years, especially with younger students who have a single class teacher, but have been hiding behind jargon such as 'nature walks'.

International Computer Driving Licence (ICDL) is a basic qualification for computer skills, available from many awarding bodies.

International English *see* STANDARD ENGLISH.

Internship (US) short-term relevant work experience where the college student earns academic credits.

Intervention Programmes are for students who need additional support in literacy and/or numeracy:

Literacy

- ■ EARLY LITERACY SUPPORT is for year 1 students needing extra help at the end of their first term.
- ■ ADDITIONAL LITERACY SUPPORT is for students in year 3 (and where necessary year 4) who attained 2C or under at the end of key stage 1.
- ■ FURTHER LITERACY SUPPORT is a pilot programme for students in year 5 who are at level 3.
- ■ Year 6 booster units address writing objectives for those not yet at level 4.

Numeracy

- ■ SPRINGBOARD 3 is for year 3 students who achieved level 2C at the end of key stage 1 and with extra help are likely to reach level 3 by the end of year 4.

- SPRINGBOARD 4 is for year 4 students who are likely to achieve level 3 by the end of the year with extra help.
- SPRINGBOARD 5 is for year 5 students who, without extra help, are likely to achieve level 3 in numeracy by the end of key stage 2.
- SPRINGBOARD 6 is for those in year 6 who with intensive targeted support can achieve level 4 in key stage 2 SATS.
- SPRINGBOARD 7 is a programme for year 7 students who achieved level 3 at the end of key stage 2 rather than the average, level 4.

Investors in Young People renamed CONNEXIONS from 2001.

Invigilators are the people who supervise candidates taking an examination. They check, for example, that there is no cheating, disturbance or deviation from the timing and conditions specified and that the welfare of all the candidates is respected.

IQ Intelligence Quotient *see* INTELLIGENCE TESTS.

Irlen Syndrome is also known as the scotopic sensitivity syndrome (SSS) and is a visual disorder where the printed or written page is seen differently, mainly in a distorted way. Helen Irlen, an educational psychologist working in California in the early 1980s, noted that some of her students read more easily when they covered the written page with a coloured overlay. The method she subsequently developed combines identification of the best coloured overlay (or lenses) with a broader look at all other factors impacting on the student's reading ability. This method should only be used by trained professionals, who can be accessed via your SENCO. It may bring about improvements where students demonstrate poor reading comprehension, misread words, miss words or lines, choose to read in dim light, experience strain when reading, have difficulty copying, experience headaches or nausea and are de-motivated to read. (It is not a syndrome where eyesight correction is appropriate, although that might be a separate intervention.)

ISDN Integrated Services Digital Network is an international communications standard that allows ordinary phone lines or optical fibres to transmit digital instead of analogue signals, allowing data (e.g. Internet and video) to be transmitted much faster than with a traditional modem.

Isolation exists in some schools where there is a room set aside for disruptive students where they must work alone, under supervision, for a specified period. It only occurs where it fits with the school's strategy for discipline, and works partly by separating the student from their peers/friends. It can also be counter-productive as it can be seen as 'cool' (or whatever today's word for 'cool' is).

IT Information Technology (US), e.g. computers, mobile phones, satellites, videoconferencing – more frequently known as ICT, Information and Communications Technology, in the UK.

ITE Initial Teacher Education (Scotland).

ITT Initial Teacher Training is an umbrella term for the many ways you can train to become a teacher. You will have colleagues who entered teaching through many different routes, which are listed separately. All lead, since September 2002, to QTS Qualified Teacher Status. Here are some of the ways, plus some of the jargon:

- *B.Ed* Bachelor of Education is the most usual degree route to qualify as a teacher, lasting typically 3 years. It covers both teacher training and chosen subject knowledge (e.g. for secondary teachers of physics, or French).

- *B. Teach* Bachelor of Teaching is the Australian and New Zealand equivalent of the UK's Bachelor of Education. Some universities there also offer a Bachelor of Teaching and Learning.
- *BA/BSc with QTS* courses combine Bachelor of Arts/ Bachelor of Science degrees with teacher training, leading to Qualified Teacher Status and, like the B.Ed., are for teaching specialized subjects (e.g. modern languages, science) at secondary school level. Broadly speaking, these are for students who want to concentrate on their subject 'with added teaching': the B.Ed. is more for those who want to study to be a teacher, 'with an added subject'.
- *Dip. HE* Diploma in Higher Education lasts for two years full-time and is broadly equivalent to the first two years of a degree. It is especially suitable for mature students who do not meet traditional entry requirements. It can lead to entry onto a degree course, possibly directly onto the final (= third) year.
- *Dip. Ed.* is a post-graduate Diploma in Education, or Educational Studies, taken not only by teachers and lecturers, but increasingly by parents, school governors, and others interested in education.
- *Dip. Teach.* is a postgraduate Diploma in Teaching similar to a *Dip. Ed.*
- *DRB* Designated Recommending Bodies each handle a minimum of ten graduate teacher trainees per year – around 85 per cent of all GTP places. Most DRBs are partnerships of schools, local education authorities and accredited initial teacher training providers.
- *Fast Track* is an intensive training scheme for teachers and trainee teachers with the potential to build careers as leaders in education.
- *GRTP* Graduate and Registered Teacher Programmes – *see* GTP and RTP.
- *GTC* General Teaching Council for England was established in 2000 as an independent not-for-profit professional body for qualified teachers. It has statutory powers to advise the Secretary of State and others on matters of professional practice concerning standards of teaching and learning. All teachers (including part-time and supply) with QTS (qualified teacher status) working in maintained schools, non-maintained special schools and pupil referral units are required, by law, to register with the GTC.
- *GTP* Graduate Teacher Programme, normally a one year course, is customized to individual needs for UK graduates (age 24+) who want to become teachers in specified subjects. They may get a grant/salary during this year as it's largely school-based. It's a parallel qualification to the *PGCE* but with a focus on 'on the job' learning rather than academic study.
- *GTTR* Graduate Teacher Training Registry processes applications for entry to Postgraduate Certificate in Education (PGCE) courses on behalf of Initial Teacher Training (ITT) providers.
- *OTTP* Overseas Trained Teachers Programme is for graduates with a teaching qualification from another country. Currently there is no training salary so you need to be employed by a school. Training is from a minimum of 'assessment only' to a maximum of 1 year.
- *PGCE Postgraduate Certificate of Education* courses, now renamed Professional Graduate Certificate of Education, are full-time one year, part academic, part practical, and lead to Qualified Teacher status. They are suitable for people who like putting theory into action (versus the GTP, for people who prefer learning on the job). Different courses allow students to specialize in, for example, Primary or Secondary education, with specific subjects to focus on. It is the most common entry route for teaching and can be taken in colleges, universities and schools. It is typically one-year full-time, but can be taken part-time, or extended to two years full-time if extra specialist subject-learning is needed. It typically involves classroom experience in at least two schools.

- *QTS* Qualified Teacher Status has been awarded to all trainee teachers since 2002 who have met all of the standards and requirements set by the Teacher Training Agency:

  - Professional values and practice – attitude, commitment, having a high expectation of students, and promoting positive values, attitudes and behaviour in students.
  - Knowledge and understanding of the subjects you are trained to teach.
  - Teaching skills – planning, monitoring, assessment, teaching and class management.
  - Literacy, numeracy, and information and communication technology skills.

- *RTP* Registered Teacher Programme is normally a two-year course, customized to individual needs, for people who have 2 years' higher education qualifications (e.g. DipHE, HND). They will be employed by a school as an unqualified teacher, and will need to study for, or complete, a degree. There are also specific GCSE/A level qualification requirements. A salary/training grant may be payable.

- *SCITT* School Centred Initial Teacher Training is a practical one year post-graduate course designed, led, run by, and based in schools, often in partnership with, e.g. higher education and local education authorities. The emphasis from the very start of the course is in real-life classroom environments with an established teacher acting as a mentor. Many teaching assistants find the SCITT course a suitable progression towards teaching because it is more school-based and provides experience in front of students. Core subject knowledge is delivered in lecture form. Each trainee has to complete both written assignments and school-based tasks. They are assessed by their tutors and by external examiners from an institute of higher education in order to receive their Professional Graduate Certificate of Education (PGCE). The trainee is paid a small sum while training and student grants may be available.

- *TACS* Teacher Associate Credit Scheme is a pilot programme for people who are interested in seeing if teaching is for them. It enables them to work in schools to build an experience-based portfolio if they are studying for a degree that does not lead to Qualified Teacher Status, and if they satisfy the ITT entry requirements.

- *UCET* The Universities Council for the Education of Teachers is the national forum for contributing to the formulation of policy relating to the education of teachers and to the study of education in the university sector. Its members are UK universities and colleges of higher education that are involved in teacher education.

- *UCS* Undergraduate Credit Scheme is a pilot scheme similar to TACS.

Ivy League (US) is a league of eight universities and colleges in the north eastern US with a reputation for academic achievement and social prestige. It is a similar concept to OXBRIDGE with supposedly ivy-covered old buildings rather than red brick or concrete and glass modernity. Yale and Harvard are probably the most well-known, and the others are Brown, Columbia, Cornell, Dartmouth, Penn and Princeton.

JCGQ Joint Council for General Qualifications was established in January 1999 and became the JCQ in 2004.

JCQ the Joint Council for Qualifications was formed in 2004 to represent the major AWARDING BODIES in England, Wales and Northern Ireland:

- AQA (the Assessment and Qualifications Alliance).
- Edexcel (incorporating BTEC and London Examinations).
- OCR (Oxford, Cambridge and RSA Examinations).
- CCEA (the Northern Ireland Council for the Curriculum, Examinations and Assessment).
- WJEC (the Welsh Joint Education Committee).
- City & Guilds.

It covers the following qualifications:

- GCSE.
- A Level.
- GNVQ.
- Certificate of Achievement.
- Key Skills.
- Advanced Extension Awards.

and exists to facilitate strategic debate amongst AWARDING BODIES, a means to express views jointly, and communication with teachers and others on educational issues.

Jug and Empty Vessel method *see* DIRECTED LEARNING.

Junior (Year) (US) third-year undergraduate (year).

Junior High School (US) are for GRADES 7–8.

K-ABC The Kaufman Assessment Battery for Children.

Kapp, Alexander was a teacher (in what is now Germany) who is credited with developing ANDRAGOGY in 1833.

KAS stands for three types of learning

- Knowledge (= Cognitive skills).
- Attitude (= Feeling and Emotions).
- Skills (= Manual or Physical Skills).

Keller, John *see* ARCS MODEL.

Key Skills is the term used for certain skills of people over 16 (and sometimes used interchangeably with BASIC SKILLS, and core skills in Scotland). The first three Key Skills were:

- Communication (e.g. how to take part in discussions, read and obtain information, write different types of documents).
- Application of Number (e.g. how to carry out calculations, interpret results and present findings).
- IT (e.g. how to find, explore, develop and present information including text, images and numbers).

Three further key skills were later added:

- Improving one's own learning and performance.
- Problem-solving.
- Working with others.

Key Skills Support Programme is to help training providers, schools and colleges to improve the quality of key skills provision for young people aged over 16. It is funded by the Department for Education and Skills. The Learning and Skills Development Agency manages the programme for schools and colleges, and Learning for Work manages the work-based programme.

Key Stage 3 National Strategy (more commonly known as the Key Stage 3 Strategy) was launched in 2001 to build on the national literacy and numeracy strategies in Key Stage 2 which led to improved results in English and mathematics for 11-year-olds. The intention is to raise standards for students age 11–14, by

- Smoothing their transition from Key Stage 2 to Key Stage 3.
- Establishing high expectations and challenging targets (for the students).
- Promoting more participative approaches to teaching and learning.
- Developing teachers' skills with a programme of professional development and support.

It covers English, mathematics, science, information and communication technology (ICT), and 'the foundation subjects' (*see* TLF) of Art and Design, Design and Technology, Geography, History, Modern Foreign Languages, Music, Physical Education and Religious Education.

Key Stages are age and year bands for students, introduced with the NATIONAL CURRICULUM in 1988. Key stages replaced categories such as infants, primary, junior, senior and secondary (but these terms still often exist):

	Student age (years)	Year groups
Key Stage 1	5–7	1–2
Key Stage 2	7–11	3–6
Key Stage 3	11–14	7–9
Key Stage 4	14–16	10–11

Kids' Clubs *see* OUT OF SCHOOL CLUBS.

Kinaesthetic/Kinesthetic is one of the three main ways we take in information, and express ourselves, embracing touch, movement, feelings and internal sensations. (The other two ways are VISUAL and AUDITORY.)

Kindergarten/Kindergarden is the first year of state-funded schools for 5–6-year-olds (US), prior to first grade (6–7-year-olds). The name was coined by Friedrich **Froebel** and means garden of children, in German.

Kinesiology is the study of anatomy, physiology and movement (*see* EDUCATIONAL KINESIOLOGY).

Knowledge is information that can be recalled from memory, e.g. dates, times, events, safety instructions.

 Tip

☐ To find out what someone 'knows', ask questions beginning with inform me, describe, tell me, list, define, who, when, where, etc. (*See also* BLOOM'S TAXONOMY.)

Knowledge Management is a term often used to describe very different philosophies, processes and policies. It is essentially the systematic management and use of the knowledge in an organization. So, for example, how do you know what your colleagues' and students' expertise is? Either you ask around for 'who knows anything about…?' Or there's a well-managed database. The purpose of knowledge management is to ensure that the wisdom and experience in an organization can be used by that organization, even if individuals are absent or leave.

Knowles, Malcolm (1913–1997, US) initiated adult learning theory developed from ANDRAGOGY.

Kolb's Learning Cycle *see* LEARNING STYLES.

Kraschen, Stephen is a controversial writer and activist on bilingual education and learning second languages. He hypothesized that people never learn more than they think they are going to need and 'proved' it in investigations with immigrants who were learning their new speech. He was chief architect of California's widely criticized bilingual education programme, which was abolished when it was found that students learned better when all the teaching was in one language (English), rather than in two languages.

KS *see* KEY STAGE.

KSA

1 Three types of learning

- Knowledge (Cognitive).
- Skills (Manual or Physical).
- Attitude (Feeling and Emotions).

2 Kingdom of Saudi Arabia.

Lancaster, Joseph (1778–1828) was arguably the founder of universal schooling in the UK. He became an enthusiastic teacher of poor boys ('poor' because their needs had been neglected, and 'boys' because a girl's place was in the home, back then) and opened his first school in 1798. Because he couldn't find suitable teachers, he developed the MONITORIAL system (with older students teaching and supervising the younger ones – mentors-cum-teaching-assistants, maybe?). And as many of his older students wanted to become teachers, he opened a teacher training college. In 1808 The Lancasterian Society was formed (renamed the 'British and Foreign School Society' (BFSS) in 1814) which set up schools and teacher training institutions on non-sectarian principles, providing both staff and support. The LANCASTERIAN SYSTEM aimed to provide a basic education for as many children as possible.

Lancasterian System of education (often misspelled Lancastrian) was pioneered by Joseph Lancaster in the late 1700s and was the forerunner of universal education (= education for all). Initially there was tiered seating and sloping floors in classrooms to help the teacher to supervise the class. (Often the 'teacher' was in fact an older student, or 'monitor'.) The classrooms were on a central corridor, to help the head teacher supervise the other teachers. This was clearly a model of control!

Lateral Thinking is the generation of new ideas by breaking out of the linear thought patterns (habits?) of old ideas. The term was coined by Edward de Bono in the 1960s, who showed how thinking can be learned rather than it being something we are born with. One of his early exercises gave rise to the expression 'thinking outside of the box, or the square'. Liberation from old ideas and the stimulation of new ones are two aspects of lateral thinking.

LCC little 'c' creativity *see* CREATIVITY *Tip*.

LCCI/LCCIEB London Chamber of Commerce and Industry Examinations Board is a worldwide awarding body (*see* AB) of business-related qualifications.

LEA Local Education Authority (UK) Local Education Agency. (US – we prefer this to 'Authority'!)

Leading Edge Partnership programme will replace the BEACON SCHOOLS programme from 2005 in secondary schools.

League Tables or school performance tables are based on students' attainment in SATS, GCSEs and A Levels. The better the results, the higher up the league table the schools are placed. They were originally intended to offer guidance for parents to make choices about the school their children should attend. But the amount of choice parents have can vary enormously. Some only have the choice to express a preference, and CATCHMENT AREAS often override choice. In extreme cases league tables do little more than confirm that the school a parent is forced to send their children to is a 'poor' performer.

Recently a VALUE ADDED component has been introduced that shows how the school has improved the performance of its students, in order to counter the criticisms that schools with more academically inclined students will score higher automatically. (Note that Scotland, Wales and Northern Ireland have recently abolished league tables, although they still publish individual schools' results.)

learndirect is

1   The provider of government-sponsored courses (online and through a network of learning centres) for people aged 16+ to learn and upgrade skills, mainly in

■   Skills for life (literacy, numeracy and ESOL).
■   Business and management.
■   IT skills.

2   The national helpline for information advice and guidance on learning and work opportunities.

★ **Learning** is (and there are *many* possible definitions)

■   Acquiring information, knowledge and skills and processing them into under-standing.
■   Growing by making new connections inside us.
■   Committing new information to memory and new skills to muscle memory. (Schools and universities have been predominantly academic for centuries, but practical vocational learning is now taking its rightful place alongside.)
■   What happens to you and your body when you know something, whether or not you know it at the time: awareness is not just in the mind – we feel it as well.

☐   Some people feel it physically as an aha! feeling, or something just 'clicked'.
☐   Others experience a physiological shift and say 'oh, now I get it,' as if cognition was something they could take in their hands.
☐   Others 'just see' it, or have a light coming on.

As a teacher it is worth recognizing how students know when they know something. When you recognize how a student responds physically to knowing something you then have a useful way of observing if your teaching is truly facilitating learning.

✓ *Tips*

☐   Learning is a two way street. Teaching is one of the most effective ways of learning and every student you meet will have something from which you yourself can learn.
☐   Learning is an unpredictable process that can lead to growth and excitement when it works, and disillusionment and disappointment when it doesn't.
☐   If we're not learning, we may think we're standing still, but in fact we're falling behind.

Learning Organizations are where a group of people are continually encouraged to increase their capabilities as individuals and as an organization. This is achieved with an ethos of open-mindedness and flexibility. (The concept grew out of Peter Senge's vision of team learning.) *See also* KNOWLEDGE MANAGEMENT.

Learning and Skills Council *see* LSC.

Learning Styles vary enormously from individual to individual – whether student or teacher. We each collect information through our five senses in different ways. We each process the information differently. We can no longer expect a class to sit and absorb in the style of the teacher. It simply doesn't work.

Example

■   Think of the PIN number for your cashcard. Ask other people (maybe not with strangers, though!) how they think of theirs. Without divulging the actual number, you'll be amazed how many different ways people use. We've come across hundreds, including

☐   I see it printed on the slip from the bank, in my mind's eye.
☐   I hear my partner's voice saying 'when will you remember that it's shout, shout, shout shout' (with the actual numbers shouted).

☐   I see the pattern on the keypad.

☐   I don't know – my finger remembers, not me.

Learning is also as varied as this, and the best way of helping someone to learn is to find out from them how they do it most, and least, easily. Then you can learn from them how you can best help them. The more we facilitate these personal strategies and needs, the more a student will learn.

Here are some thought-starters:

■   Some students need all the details first, before the big picture, whereas others need the big picture first so they know what to do with the detail.

■   Some prefer to see a lesson within a context, whereas others might be confused and prefer it as a piece of work standing alone.

■   Some need to sit quietly and work things out internally, whereas others need to discover things in discussion with others.

■   Some need to see a clear motivation or benefit to understand why they need to learn or do something, whereas others will take it on trust.

✓ *Tips*

☐   Be generous with your flexibility as you explore different TEACHING STYLES to connect with students' different learning styles.

☐   Share your learning on this subject with your students, so they can develop their range of learning styles as you develop your range of teaching styles.

There are literally hundreds of different learning style models, theories, definitions and products. Here are some of the common ones.

Sensory Preferences describe the three key ways we have of taking in information, and expressing ourselves – VISUAL, AUDITORY and KINAESTHETIC, i.e. what we see, hear and feel. We all have preferences – for example we know someone who simultaneously listens to the radio while reading not only the subtitles on the TV but a newspaper or magazine. Auditory, or what?! Have a look (visual) at the example above about how people remember PIN numbers, and see (visual) what you get (kinaesthetic) from each one.

Convincer Strategy is a number – the number of times something has to happen before you're convinced. We have a friend who'll only go to see a film when at least five people have recommended it. Another friend just hears a film title once, and wants to see it. We know someone who screamed at their child 'How many times do I have to tell you to tidy your room?!' and got the calmest of replies, 'Four, Daddy'. He realized that the child was right, and needed telling everything four times before there seemed to be a connection – getting into the car, coming to eat a meal, everything. So he started asking calmly four times, knowing that the first three just wouldn't somehow connect. No more screaming.

✓ *Tip*

☐   Knowing the convincer strategies of your self, your colleagues, and your students may save a lot of screaming, and it'll be fun to find out and then discuss the implications.

Myers–Briggs Type Indicator (MBTI) is based on Jungian psychology and is widely used in recruitment, matching people's 'type' to job specifications. It can also give useful learning style indicators. Personal characteristics are identified in terms of four preferences:

1   EI   Extraversion (outgoing) vs. Introversion (think things through internally).

2   SN   Sensing (needing factual external information) vs. iNtuiting (needing an internal 'feel').

3   TF   Thinking (judging logically) vs. Feeling (judging emotionally).
4   JP   Judging (seeking closure) vs. Perceiving. (preferring reaching conclusions to information-collection).

A learner could be any one of 16 types, combining the four scales above, which would define their preferences (but only preferences, not absolute characteristics).

Example

■   Expecting an INFP (Intravert, iNtuitive, Feeler, Perceiver) to go out and collect opinions from other people, organize them logically, judge the relative merits of them, and then recommend a course of action would be like pushing water uphill. They certainly *could* do this, but it would be going (fourfold) against type.
■   They would, however, be an excellent choice for deciding what unmet needs they think the class has, getting a feel for how they could be satisfied, deciding which priorities they would like to assign, and then make a presentation of the options.

Kolb (David) in 1984 described a cycle of four stages for fully effective experiential learning, which can start with any stage:

■   Concrete experience (CE) – hands-on personal experience.
■   Reflective observation (RO) – looking at experience from many perspectives, and forming ideas.
■   Abstract conceptualization (AC) – shaping ideas and knowledge into concepts.
■   Active experimentation (AE) – using concepts practically.

Honey & Mumford (Peter & Alan) developed these into four different types of learners:

■   Activists – are learners with concrete learning preferences, who really need to explore and discover for themselves. The teacher is most effective as a FACILITATOR who provides the material for the learner, and then keeps out of their way. (Students frequently ask WHAT IF?)
■   Reflectors – are thoughtful, reflective learners who question, and need explanations and reasons. A major role for the teacher is to MOTIVATE them and create reasons. (Students frequently ask Why?)
■   Theorists – are analytical thinkers who love playing with ideas. The teacher needs to be a source of ideas and information to keep them stimulated, and to ensure they have enough time and space. (Students frequently ask What?)
■   Pragmatists – learn well through hands-on trial and error, applying practical, common sense. The teacher is an essential coach, giving guidance, support and feedback. (Students frequently ask How?)

(Descriptions of Kolb and Honey & Mumford are often muddled, so we checked the two entries above directly with Peter Honey. Thanks, Peter.)

4MAT® System (Bernice McCarthy) offers a framework for designing learning and also offers four learning styles: innovative, analytic, common sense and dynamic. (Unlike MBTI, Kolb, and Honey & Mumford there is no assessment tool here since it advocates ensuring that each task in each lesson engages all four styles).

Dunn & Dunn Learning-Style Model designed by Drs Rita and Kenneth Dunn proposes five areas that affect a student's ability in the learning environment:

■   *Environmental* – i.e. noise, light, temperature and seating (e.g. some prefer background music in a cool room with lots of people, others prefer to work quietly in their warm bedroom).
■   *Emotional* – i.e. motivation, persistence, responsibility and structure (e.g. some need to have several projects at once, some need to persist on one project at a time).

- *Sociological* – i.e. presence of other people (e.g. some people work best when left alone, some need to be upervised, some like working with peers, some like working alone).
- *Physiological* – i.e. food, drink, movement, time (e.g. some people like eating or drinking while working, some like pacing up and down, some people are 'morning' people).
- *Psychological* – i.e. impulsive vs. reflective (e.g. some people just begin to work without thinking, whereas others scope and plan in advance, hemispheric domination) and global vs. analytic.
  - *Global* learners tend to question what's being done and why, and prefer to work in an informal environment with soft lighting, frequent breaks, and sound and movement (preferred style of many younger students).
  - *Analytic* learners prefer to work in a brightly lit, formally arranged environment with few or no interruptions (preferred style of many Victorian classrooms). They need more precise instructions of what to do and how to do it.

✓ *Tips*

- How on earth can a teacher bear all this in mind, successfully? Well, by ensuring that you are aware of your own preferences, and then having checklists to enable you to provide multi-sensory experiences as much of the time as possible (*see* MULTIPLE INTELLIGENCES for a useful list of seven).
- Look to your students for *exceptions* – if only a few are not engaged, go quietly to each of them and ask them what they need to be more engaged.
- Look to your colleagues or mentors if you have not been engaging the majority of your students – find a way for them to observe you in action and give you some FEEDFORWARD.
- If you know a task is, say, very auditory, say so! Explain what you mean, and tell them what they can look (visual!) forward to doing (kinaesthetic!) next.

Learning Support Assistant (LSA) *see* TEACHING ASSISTANTS.

Learning Support Units tackle disruptive behaviour through intensive support for the students concerned, as an alternative to exclusion, and provide short-term teaching and support programmes tailored to the needs of any students needing learning support. They are school-based, though they might be shared between schools, particularly at primary level. They are a positive preventative strategy and should be portrayed as such, not as 'sin bins'. Other punishment areas may also be referred to as 'sin bins', but this trivializes the importance of the corrective action being taken. (The term comes from sport where, if a player commits a foul that doesn't warrant being sent off, they are sent for a short period into the sin bin.)

Learning Theories *see* LEARNING STYLES.

Learning through Landscapes is a national charity that works with schools (and other organizations and individuals) to help them improve their grounds for outdoor play, socializing, exercise, and the appreciation of nature.

Learning to Learn in Schools is a Campaign for Learning action-research project that is investigating what happens when students are taught *how* they learn, in parallel with their learning. Learning to learn involves students becoming aware of

- How they prefer to learn.
- How they can motivate themselves and have the confidence to succeed.
- How sleep, nutrition, water and their environment affect their learning.
- Specific strategies and habits to help their learning.

See also RS, THE FIVE.

Lecturer is a teacher in a Further or Higher Education establishment.

LEP Leading Edge Partnership programme is intended to share good practice in secondary schools, taking over from the Beacon Schools programme which is being phased out by 2005. (Primary schools can become partner schools of participating secondary schools.)

Levels of Learning is a simple model based on the work of William Howell, that demonstrates the stages of learning:

1   *Unconscious incompetence* (=naivety): is not knowing something and not knowing that you do not know it. For instance, a baby doesn't know that it cannot drive a car.
2   *Conscious incompetence* (=frustration, leading to either determination or demotivation): is knowing that something can be done or understood, and knowing that you yourself cannot do it. A toddler will try to turn a car's steering wheel and get frustrated that the car doesn't drive properly. They might then decide never to learn, ever, or to learn to drive as soon as they possibly can.
3   *Conscious competence* (=self-conscious awkwardness): is being able to do something and being very aware of what you are doing. It's like your first solo drive after passing the driving test.
4   *Unconscious competence* (=elegance): is doing something without needing to think about it. Experienced drivers rarely think about the process of driving a car.
5   *Conscious unconscious-competence* (=mastery): is the ability to do something without thinking about it, yet being aware in parallel of how exactly you are doing it. This level of competence is ideal for a teacher.

✓ *Tips*

☐   Place yourself as a teacher within this model. If you are newly qualified you might be at the conscious competence (awkward) stage in some skills, so be aware that practice and familiarity will take you towards elegance and mastery.
☐   Many students are at level 2 and need determination, not demotivation.
☐   If we aim to have our students pass exams comfortably, level 3 is not enough as they need to be sufficiently practised to be at level 4.
☐   Once you are at level 4, occasionally go back to level 3 and consciously do a skills check to make sure you haven't developed bad habits through complacency or oversight. (This is what Ofsted does, so you or a colleague might want to get in first!)
☐   Be aware that many people who are good at something cannot teach it. Why? Because they just do it and don't know how they do it. Here's an example we like:

Laurence Olivier was in Shakespeare's Othello at the Old Vic Theatre in London, and was even more brilliant than usual. It was as if he had been born to play this role. One night he excelled even his own brilliant performance. Everyone was watching him in open-mouthed admiration. At the end of the performance, the audience went wild. Olivier briefly acknowledged the applause, stomped past the cast and stage crew, slammed into his dressing room, and then in a howling rage began smashing the furniture. Everyone was puzzled. Eventually a young stage manager peered around the door and asked, 'Sir Laurence? You were absolutely amazing tonight, so why are you ...?' He interrupted her. 'I *know*!' he howled. 'But I don't know *how* I did it'.

Licensed Teacher used to be an unqualified teacher who was allowed to teach in school but this scheme has now been replaced by the GTP GRADUATE TEACHER PROGRAMME and RTP REGISTERED TEACHER PROGRAMME.

Lifelong Learning takes place throughout life as opposed to at specific venues (e.g. schools) and at specific times. The term 'lifelong learning' is designed for adults to see learning as part of life, not something unpleasant that you gratefully leave behind when you leave school, either at the end of the school day OR at the end of your schooling. And since school students only spend FIFTEEN PER CENT of their waking hours at school, the importance of their learning outside school cannot be underestimated. If the joy and stimulation of abundant learning is properly grasped while at school, most people can continue to see learning as life-enhancing for life.

Link Learning Mentors *see* MENTORS.

Literacy Hour is part of the literacy strategy (now part of the PRIMARY NATIONAL STRATEGY) for all students in key stages 1 and 2. The objective is to establish their reading and writing skills, to stimulate creativity in writing through imagination and storytelling, and to promote a desire to read more and use their skills outside school, as well as inside. The NATIONAL CURRICULUM provides teachers with content, objectives and methodologies which include

- *Shared reading:* the teacher uses a text (e.g. a book, poetry, or poster) to stimulate ideas from the class, focusing on comprehension, spelling patterns, prediction (covering up a word so that students can predict what the word may be) and sentence structure;
- *Shared writing:* the teacher demonstrates and facilitates how a piece of writing is planned, so ideas can be sequenced and expressed;
- *Word and sentence work:* teaches PHONICS and spelling (for words), and grammar, punctuation and vocabulary (for sentences);
- *Guided reading:* the teacher hears a group of 4–6 students reading from a common text. Each has their own copy, and the teacher also discusses the text with them;
- *Guided writing:* the teacher works with a group and concentrates on a particular part of the writing process. Independent writing follows on from previous shared writing, e.g. when the rest of the class works on a task which has been explored under guidance previously;
- *Plenary:* this takes place with the whole class and is for discussing ideas, reflecting on achievement of objectives, presentation of work and a check on understanding.

Literacy Strategy is now part of the PRIMARY NATIONAL STRATEGY.

LMS (1) Local Management of Schools, introduced in the 1988 Education Reform Act, which transferred responsibility for most of the running of schools to the management team itself. (2) Learning Management System, e.g. to plan and manage specific aspects of learning and education processes.

Local Education Partnerships are where local education authorities partner a private sector company, or consortium, for a PFI (PRIVATE FINANCE INITIATIVE) such as investing in new school buildings.

★ **Logical Levels** (aka Neurological Levels) is a model that can give diagnostic insight into the relationship between self-esteem, upbringing, and a student's performance at school. It can help you to identify how best to help students improve more quickly and precisely. It will also help you to understand yourself and your performance better. And help you to give good feedback and feedforward, and not to take things personally. But we're getting ahead of ourselves here.

The Model

To introduce the model we use the five-word sentence *I can't do that here*. By placing emphasis on each of the words separately we convey five different meanings:

- 'I can't do that *here*' is about *where* you are (i.e. environment).
- 'I can't do *that* here' is about *what* you are to do (i.e. behaviours).

- 'I can't *do* that here' is about *how* you are able to do what you do, your (i.e. skills and knowledge).
- 'I *can't* do that here' is about *why* you do what you do (i.e. beliefs and values).
- '*I* can't do that here' is about *who* you are, or think you are (i.e. identity).

Example

- If you play a sport you can describe where you play and with whom (environment), what you actually do (behaviours), how high a standard you are (skills and knowledge), what you believe is true about this activity, why you do it and what is important to you about it (beliefs and values), and how you would describe yourself within this role (identity e.g. 'I am an expert', or 'I am a novice'). If you want to improve your performance, you can identify the level at which you could make the most improvement. For instance, it would be less useful to keep practising or repeating the *behaviours* if what was restricting you was the *environment* in which you were operating. Likewise, it would be less productive developing *skills* in an activity that wasn't very important (*values*) to you. If you are a student with a strong learning *identity* (I am a top student) and a positive set of *beliefs and values* around learning (I think learning is important, education creates a fuller life, learning is fun), then you are likely to develop the *skills* to learn, apply yourself to the *behaviours* necessary to learn, and create an *environment* in which to learn – by hanging out with other committed students and having a workplace at home.

Logical levels are a way of understanding some of our frustrations. We try to encourage or drive *behaviours* (please get your homework done, sit down and concentrate, pay attention, stop fighting) knowing that there is resistance to what we need the students to do. We are driving behaviours where the resistance or blockage may be at the level of identity or beliefs and values. Our frustration is compounded because we hold such strong, positive values about learning ourselves and we struggle to understand why others can't see the sense that we see.

Identity

- You will probably have identified that terms such as SELF-ESTEEM, self-worth and sense of self relate to the levels of identity, beliefs and values in this model. It would also be clear that learning, for someone who has a positive sense of themselves and holds positive beliefs and values around learning, is far easier than for someone who has little self-esteem and apparently thinks that school is a waste of time (by blaming their environment, not their identity). You may also notice that the levels of identity, beliefs and values often manifest themselves as 'attitude'.
- The levels of identity, and beliefs and values, are formed in a number of different ways. As people grow up they form their own sense of self and values based on their experiences. Negative comments like, 'you stupid child,' or 'university isn't for people like you,' or 'doing well at school is for wimps,' or 'you'll never make good,' all contribute to negative levels of identity, beliefs and values. Positive comments such as, 'learning is fun,' 'a good education sets you up in life,' 'you work very hard,' 'you're a dedicated student,' help shape the levels of identity, beliefs and values in a positive way. If a child has missed out on any of these, they may conclude, devastatingly, that they 'are' stupid, or worthless and make huge decisions about how to live their life, proving that they 'are' right in their conclusion. (Luckily it is relatively easy to point to inconsistencies in their conclusion e.g. you're not stupid in the way you handle a football, are you? What else are you not stupid at? maybe someone said you 'are' stupid, meaning you 'did' something stupidly? – and so on).

Identification with groups

- Children and adults with low self-esteem often compensate by joining with others, under a strong leader. They gain their identity from the group, GANG or cause. In order to be part of that group they need to share the values that unite the group, or appear to. That is why someone may act out of character, in order to be accepted and remain part of the group. This type of peer pressure can encourage normally placid people to act violently, and the reason that peer pressure can be so strong is that the individual might well be fighting to maintain their own sense of self. Without the group, they feel worth-less. And they are substituting a sense of identification (with the group) to compensate for their lack of a sense of identity.

Logical levels is a simple and effective model for understanding ourselves as teachers. It also enables us to be critical of negative behaviours without damaging a student's sense of who they are. It helps us to understand our own frustration when people do not share our values or beliefs. It can point us towards helping students to develop positive attitudes towards learning, so that the skills and behaviours come more automatically. This is best achieved by helping them gain self-respect and self-esteem by noticing what they do well (including when this isn't school-related) and giving examples of people who have lived successful lives irrespective of what they were 'called' as a child. It is much harder to try to change behaviours, than it is to stimulate self-esteem.

✓ *Tips*

□   If you have a student whose performance concerns you, follow the sports example above to decide the best Logical Level for an intervention.

□   If a student's performance is poor then give specific FEEDBACK on what they did, FEED-FORWARD on what they might do *differently*, and *never* relate it to who they *are*.

□   Avoid criticizing students at the level of identity (e.g. you are stupid, you are not going to succeed). Although you can have a massive immediate impact with personal criticism, you could be wounding them deeply, and making an enemy for life.

□   Many barriers to learning can be dealt with by identifying the level at which they exist, e.g.

   ▪   *Identity* I'm stupid.
   ▪   *Beliefs and values* Only nerds study.
   ▪   *Skills and Knowledge* I've got a block with numbers;
   ▪   *Behaviours* It's hard to concentrate when I'm sitting down.
   ▪   *Environment* It's difficult to concentrate when you're being abused at home.

□   You can find out the level at which a barrier to learning may exist either through observation or by asking questions. 'What's stopping you?' is a question that will usually give an indication of the right level. For example, 'what's stopping you applying yourself more?' – 'there's too much going on in the classroom,' shows clearly that the problem is one of environment. For that student to improve, either the environment needs to change or the student needs to learn how to cope with it differently. If the environment cannot be changed then shift to a different logical level. 'What else can you *do* (behaviours) that would make it possible for you to study?'

□   If someone lacks motivation, this is likely to be at the level of beliefs and values (what matters to them). You can address this at the same logical level by asking what is important to them in general life, and hope that education can in some way be linked to their beliefs and values e.g. if what they love doing is enjoying winning at football, maybe you can introduce the concept of 'winning' more often to motivate them? Or you could shift levels and say, e.g., 'do you want to be seen (identity) as someone who can stand out, positively, from the crowd?' and then link their response to better performance.

[This model has been attributed to both Gregory Bateson and Robert Dilts. It is considered by some people to be part of NLP NEURO-LINGUISTIC PROGRAMMING while others are adamant that it is not. We keep clear of the politics and concentrate on how it can usefully contribute to learning and teaching.]

Logical Thinking *see* CRITICAL THINKING.

London Qualifications is a joint venture announced in May 2003 between Pearson (75 per cent) and EDEXCEL (25 per cent) to modernize examination marking and processing in the UK.

Looked-after refers to those children who are 'in care', e.g. in foster homes or children's homes.

Lozanov, Georgi (b. 1926) is a Bulgarian physician, psychiatrist and psychotherapist – *see* SUGGESTOPEDIA.

LRE Least Restrictive Environment is the setting for a child with learning difficulties that allows them to be mainstreamed as far as is possible, with additional support if necessary.

LSA Learning Support Assistant *see* TEACHING ASSISTANTS.

LSC Learning & Skills Council is responsible for funding and planning over-16 education and training in England, e.g.

- Sixth forms and further education (except universities).
- Adult and community learning, and workforce development.
- Information, advice and guidance for adults.

It was formed in April 2001 by merging Training and Enterprise Councils and the Further Education Funding Council to work alongside the Employment Service, the Small Business Service, Connexions, National Training Organisations, colleges and community groups, to understand, define and then meet training and education needs. They have 47 local offices and a national office in Coventry.

Their vision is that 'by 2010, young people and adults in England will have the knowledge and productive skills matching the best in the world'. Their mission is 'to raise participation and attainment through high-quality education and training which puts learners first'.

LSDA Learning and Skills Development Agency was formed in November 2000 from the Further Education Development Agency. It is responsible for the development of policy and practice in post-16 education.

LSU *see* LEARNING SUPPORT UNITS.

Lycee/Lyceum (especially US, France) is a secondary school.

Maintained Schools are publicly-funded, or state schools. Maintained boarding schools are available within the state system for students who cannot attend day schools (e.g. if their parents work abroad). They only charge for boarding costs – tuition is free.

Major degrees in the US are typically structured to offer two years of more general study, and two years specialization in a major subject (e.g. I majored in sociology).

Major, Double (US) is a degree with two principal fields of study instead of one.

MAP (aka Marion A Perlmutter) *see* COGNITIVE DEVELOPMENT.

Marking is one of the most sensitive areas in education. Recent scandals over A level results and their re-marking have left students and the public uncertain about how accurate the marking process is, and whether marks are changed or fixed. There is, therefore, a move towards computer marking (only of multiple choice answers, naturally). No matter how rigid the guidelines for marking, the key and variable element in the whole process is the teacher marking the paper. Whether marking internal tests within your class, exam papers from inside your own school, or external papers for national exams, here are some

✓ *Tips*

☐ Take short breaks and drink lots of water to maintain your concentration.
☐ Stop when you are tired.
☐ Recognize that it will be tiring, so pace yourself and never expect to do too much at one sitting.
☐ If you feel your consistency and objectivity waning, stand up and stretch and remember that you are influencing a student's morale and/or future.
☐ Refuse to be part of any 'massaging' of results – always consult with your union representative, friend or head teacher.
☐ Never be influenced by the name on the paper. If the student is one you know well and you think they could have done better, mark the paper in front of you and not the one they could have completed on a better day.
☐ Plan to have a treat when you've finished your quota, or quota for the day, so even if the work is less than fascinating, at least you've got something to look forward to at the end.
☐ To aid your objectivity you might want to assume a different persona of, e.g. 'Jo(e) Objectivity' with all the behaviours and values that make Jo(e) perfect for the job.
☐ Remember, the purpose of marking for your own students is to give feedback to them on what they've done well, what could be improved, and how to improve it.

★ **Maslow, Abraham** (1908–1970) was a US psychologist, fascinated by how people function well. (Before his interest in what was to become humanistic psychology, most other psychology – Freudian and behaviourist – studied abnormalities rather than normality.) He saw human needs like a ladder, and his model of needs is also referred to as his 'hierarchy' or 'pyramid' of motivations or needs. There are many different versions as it developed over time. Here's one we like (because we've adapted it ourselves!):

1   Base level needs are *physiological*. These include food, drink, oxygen, warmth, rest, sex and other factors to sustain life. (People missing key items at this level are generally only concerned about staying alive. Sex may be the exception for most people, but not for all.)

2   The next level is *safety and security*. These include stability, a roof over our head, and protection from danger.

3   Next comes *belonging*. For example, our social and psychological needs, including love, being part of peer groups, having friends, and being part of a community and/or family.

4   Next is our need for *self-worth*. This comes in two forms, external recognition and internal self-esteem. Externally we need differing levels of respect from others, plus status, attention, and appreciation, e.g. being recognized for our contribution at work or at home. Internally we need to feel that we can like our self.

5   The fifth level is *self-actualization* – putting all the above into action, and fulfilling your potential. It is being who you want to be, being true to yourself and living the life you want to live. People at this level are 'givers' – they can contribute outwards because their inner needs are largely met. (And this is only being realistic – if someone's more basic needs are unmet, how can they be truly motivated to satisfy higher level needs?) At this level people feel more whole, more alive. (Maslow suggested that only 2 per cent of people actually reach this stage – and it's our job to get this much higher among our students, yes?)

The first four levels are sometimes called deficit needs. In other words if they are not satisfied we will be motivated to do something about them, in the order in which they are described. Once we have them, they cease to be motivating unless we lose them or are under threat of losing them.

✓ *Tips*

Here are some ways in which a teacher can address the needs, and therefore motivate students, at each level:

☐   *Physiological* Make available water, breaks, the right temperature, and be aware that a home life that does not satisfy the basic physiological needs will impact on a student's ability and motivation to learn.

☐   *Safety and security* Ensure there is a controlled classroom environment, an absence of bullying and physical attacks, no verbal abuse, well-planned lessons and an accepting and non-judgemental non-threatening attitude from the teacher.

☐   *Belonging* A teacher should get to know the students, be empathetic, supportive, a good listener, interested in individuals, interested in extra-curricular activities, encourage discussion, hold class meetings, and create a sense of a team with shared goals.

☐   *Self-worth* Create a positive and non-judgmental environment that allows students to explore their curiosity and make the most of their abilities. Recognize and celebrate their achievements, so that they, literally, can shine and grow.

☐   *Self-actualization* Expect and encourage students to do their best, and make learning meaningful for them and connect it to what they want to achieve. Talk about the future, about life plans, about self-fulfilment and achieving in a positive way. Be a model for them, especially if they have no other ROLE MODELS to look to. Expect them to be the best they can be. (And all of this applies to you too! Why should anyone settle for second-best?)

Matriculation ('Matric') was established in 1838 as the London Matriculation Examination to determine the admission of candidates for London University's degree courses. It was open to students over age 16 and became widely used as a school-leaving examination. (It literally means 'registration' at a college or university.)

Matriculation & School Examinations Council was established in 1930 to set matriculation requirements. It was superseded by The University Entrance & School Examinations Council in 1951 with the introduction of GSES.

MBTI *see* MYERS–BRIGGS TYPE INDICATOR, in LEARNING STYLES.

McCarthy, Bernice *see* 4MAT® SYSTEM in LEARNING STYLES.

Meditation is one of the most effective ways of relaxing and preventing stress. It will enable you to clear your mind, switch off from the stresses of the day, still your internal voices and prepare for the day ahead. The benefits of meditation happen quickly, and you do not need to be an expert or a Buddhist. You can meditate on you-own, when and where you want to, so that mediation fits in with your schedule and not the other way round. It is an essential component of many learning environments such as, for example, the DISCOVERY PROJECT and EMOTIONAL INTELLIGENCE programmes.

✔ *Tip*

☐ A common informal type of meditation includes 'sitting quietly', which can work for students and teachers alike!

★ **Memory** is an area where there is much debate about how it works, how much control we have of it, whether we can force ourselves to remember, which parts of the brain store or influence memory, or why some people are gifted with an exceptional memory. There is general agreement, however, that we have a short-term and a long-term memory. We use our short-term memory to store the beginning of a sentence in order to understand what the complete sentence means. The meaning of the sentence is later transferred to our long-term memory, until we re-call it. These two memories are similar to those of a computer. Random Access Memory (RAM) is for short-term workings, which we then may choose to store for long-term reference in the Read Only Memory (ROM). Needless to say, we want our students to put learning into their long-term memory so that they can re-call it when necessary.

✔ *Tips*

☐ We only remember what we have stored in the first place. Many people complain that they 'can't remember' things, when in fact they haven't stored them in the first place.
☐ Memory is influenced by relevance. Making learning relate to the aspirations of students enhances memory. (We filter out irrelevant information and do not consign it to long-term memory.)
☐ Many memories are encoded visually. Encourage students to make visual representations of learning and use visual metaphors to illustrate learning points.
☐ Many other memories have auditory encoding, so reading aloud doubles the potential for storage, compared to reading silently.
☐ Making written notes helps to store information in long-term memory, as it combines the auditory with the visual.

The memory seems to work best at the beginning of a lesson and at the end. This makes your opening frame and objectives, and the review at the end, of great importance (and if you can divide a lesson into two or more segments, this creates two or more beginnings and ends!).

Mental Age *see* INTELLIGENCE TESTS.

Mental Arithmetic is the ability to make calculations in your head. (It became unfashionable when calculators became widespread, but has come back into the arena as a necessary skill, largely stimulated by employers' needs.)

⭐ **Mental Rehearsal** is consciously creating pictures and sounds in our head in order to help us to get what we want. It's like a movie screen in our imagination upon which we can see and hear our outcomes being achieved. And, yes, it's like day-dreaming or staring out of the window, and it is essential for trying on for size what we might do in reality. It involves imagining what we want to take place actually happening, which increases our chances of getting what we want. That's because we will have practised in our mind what we want to happen, and we all know that practice makes perfect.

Another major benefit is that if the mental rehearsal feels uncomfortable, then you can find other options that will feel better and, therefore, be more likely to work. It's better to find that something is wrong for you in your own rehearsal than in front of other people. Mental rehearsal is especially useful when PLANNING a lesson, or an important conversation or interview. Think about, or visualize, how it's likely to work, and what unforeseen traps you can foresee! You need to ensure that

- The *way* you engage the person or group will work well for them and you.
- The *contents* will keep them engaged, and get the desired result.

You also need to find out what potential problems and needs might arise, and plan how to prevent them, and/or deal with them. This takes about 10 min in total. Typically we ourselves do it a couple of times, once well in advance and once close to the event, just to make sure. *See also* the Changing Places Strategy in ATTENTION SPAN on pp. 14–15.

✓ *Tips*

☐ You can make these pictures either with you inside yourself and looking out of your own eyes. Or picture yourself as if you were an observer watching from a distance. (Think back to a holiday and imagine yourself on the beach. Are you looking at yourself from a distance or are you inside yourself looking at other people on the beach?)

☐ It is best to use both to get the whole picture. Putting yourself in as many people's shoes as possible, and using all the insights you get, maximizes your chances of success in practice.

Mentors are people who not only guide a person's personal growth and/or work-related growth, but are trusted to do so. Frankly, we believe that everyone should have one (or more), especially at stages in our lives when 'things' around us are changing, or are about to change.

- *Learning Mentors* work with students who have barriers to learning such as behavioural problems, difficulties at home, difficulty adjusting from one school to another, or are generally underperforming. They act as guides, advisors and sounding boards to help students to gain more from education and life.
- *Link Learning Mentors* arrange link meetings for all interested parties to co-ordinate support as well as disseminate good practice to other mentors.

Metacognition is the process of thinking about one's own thinking.

⭐ **Metaphors** are figures of speech implying, but not explicitly stating, a comparison between two objects or actions. Often a more descriptive word substitutes for a more literal one, as in 'they ran like the wind' or 'as pretty as a picture'. When we use metaphors – like stories, anecdotes, allegories, parables, myths, fables or legends – it is a form of DISCOVERY learning where the listener draws the conclusion, rather being told what to conclude. How do they work? Well, telling a story elegantly distracts the conscious mind and allows the unconscious mind to search for meaning and under-standing. Using metaphors or asking students to make up metaphors is a great way to get them thinking more creatively and with greater understanding.

Here are some common categories, simplified for ease of distinction:

- *Fables* are short fictional stories with an underlying moral and often involving animals as characters.
- *Fairy tales* have characters that behave like stereotypes (e.g. princes and princesses), and involve conflict between good and evil in which good eventually wins. They are set in the past, and often contain an important realization for the main character.
- *Myths and legends* feel like real history. (Jung wrote about their connection with our collective unconscious.) They are based upon specific characters (who may or may not have existed) rather than stereotypes (e.g. Zeus – who probably didn't exist – or King Arthur and the round table, who did exist but whose activities are probably rather exaggerated).

✓ **Tip**

☐ If you want students to be objective about their behaviour or performance ask metaphorical questions that enable them to talk less personally, such as 'if this piece of work was a character from history, who might it be?' or 'if what you did was an animal, what sort of animal could it be?'. In some cases they may not even explain their answer, as you can see that they have realized what you wanted them to.

MFL Modern Foreign Languages.

MIDAS Multiple Intelligence Development Assessment Scales developed by Charles Branton Shearer (US) in 1987, give measures based on Howard Gardner's MULTIPLE INTELLIGENCES. There are versions for young children right through to adults.

Mind Maps® are visual ways of presenting information. They can be especially useful for people with dyslexia and other learning difficulties since, when the student is constructing them, the decisions they make about which words and colours and connections to use, help to implant the information more firmly in their memory. Mind Maps were developed in the UK in the 1960s by Tony Buzan, and the rules about how to use them include

- Only use one word to represent each item.
- Use capital letters only.
- Use colours and illustrations.

A simpler idea, without any rules, is sometimes called spider diagrams, as that's what they look like. We, personally, like them, as we are able to use more than one word, and also we like using upper and lower case letters since there is more shape to words than only using UPPER CASE.

✓ **Tip**

☐ The best form to use is the form that helps the student best: they can learn more, and get pleasure in the process, by experimenting for themselves, with a teacher's encouragement if necessary.

Note

You can see a Mind Map® at http://www.mind-map.com/EN/mindmaps/how_to.html and a spider diagram at http://www.bbc.co.uk/schools/ks3bitesize/english/writing/planning_spider.shtml.

Minor (subjects) (US) are degree subjects requiring fewer units than MAJOR subjects and are not strictly needed in order to graduate.

Mixed Year Groups (also called vertical grouping) include children from more than one year when, for example, there is a topic of interest that spans year groups, or when there are insufficient students to warrant a separate class.

MLD Moderate Learning Difficulty.

M-Learning (1) is a general term for learning using mobile phones: it is personal (vs. public) and can capture the attention of otherwise hard to engage learners via text messaging, mobile internet and video messaging (2) is a 3-year European research programme co-ordinated by the Learning and Skills Development Agency (LSDA) to develop products and services which will deliver information and learning that are accessible to everyone with mobile phones, especially young adults (16–24) who are not currently in education or training. It focuses, on e.g. football and music to develop literacy and numeracy.

⭐ **Modelling** works in unconscious and conscious ways:

- *Unconscious* modelling is known also as ROLE MODELLING, where we unknowingly copy the behaviour and thought patterns of someone we admire. Children do this all the time to learn how to behave in general. They copy behaviours and skills, beliefs and values, and so form a similar sense of self or identity to one or both of their parents. This is why so many children grow up to live similar lives and having similar relationships to their parents. Modelling is part of our survival mechanism. We copy those who have evidently stayed alive in order to stay alive ourselves.
- *Consciously* we can learn how to be as good as we want to be in some skill or activity. We can achieve the same success as others by believing the things they believe and doing the things they do. We certainly master skills faster if we model those who know what they are doing. Apprenticeships are built on this principle: if you want to be a great chef then work with a great chef.

✓ *Tips*

☐ Some people 'adopt' those that they model, as GURUS.
☐ Identify a teacher (or teachers) you admire and ask them if you can model them. They may be embarrassed or puzzled at first, but it will be interesting for them also, to find out what makes them as good as they are (see the story about Laurence Olivier on page 88).

  - Observe the behaviours and skills they display and ask them how they achieved those skills and behaviours.
  - Ask them what is important to them about learning, and about what they do. Once you have a full list of their beliefs and values, try them on for size. Do they fit with you, can you adopt them yourself and replace any of your old beliefs with some of these if they feel 'better' to you?
  - Ask what their sense of self is. A simple way to do this is just to ask, 'when you're in front of a class who would you describe yourself as?'. Get them also to choose a fictional character or maybe a teacher they once modelled? Ask them what exactly they admired in this person.
  - Study the behaviours, skills and thought patterns behind all that they do, from planning to preparation, delivery and review.

Example

- One modelling project we liked was conducted by Richard Wiseman, when he became fascinated by why some people were consistently lucky or unlucky, or believed themselves to be so. He found four principles among 'lucky' people, that we can all learn, and learn from (we summarise):

1   Expecting good fortune is often a SELF-FULFILLING PROPHECY.
2   Maximizing your chances of something good happening can be done by
    noticing and acting on opportunities.
3   Listen to 'gut feelings', what your 'heart' tells you and act on hunches (how
    many times after something's passed us by have we heard ourselves say 'I had
    a funny feeling that …'?).
4   Deal speedily and constructively with bad luck – turn it around by thinking
    how things could have been even worse, and think how you'll deal with
    similar situations in future.

See also SOCIAL LEARNING THEORY.

⋆ **Models,** Theories, Forma, Paradigms, Cognitive Maps, Hypotheses, Premises,
Hunches, Conjectures, or even METAPHORS, are all ways of describing how we can
make sense of a set of information. (Yes, there are subtle differences between them,
but apart from our story below, let's just say that they are splitting hairs, and, again see
the story, we prefer to use 'models'.)

Story (or model? or theory?!)

■   Let's imagine we have an aquarium. We want to use it to design shapes so, for
    example, if we wanted a shape that could glide effortlessly through water, we can
    see a long slender fish that could be a model for what we want. Or if we wanted
    a shape that could rise and fall gently, we might 'model' a more spherical puffer
    fish. That's what modelling is about, building a model that's similar.
■   Theories, however, go like this. (And we're sorry for any offence.) You get a whole
    load of fish, chuck them into the tank, and the last one to die is the current the-
    ory! (Just think of the 'theories' that the earth was flat, or that the sun and the
    planets revolved around the earth?)
■   And, depending on which side of the aquarium you are, you might well have a dif-
    ferent or even contradictory 'theory' from others working elsewhere with the
    same material.
■   So, is matter made up of particles? or waves? or strings? They may be different
    'theories', but we'd rather think of them as alternative *models*.

Modern Apprenticeships were introduced in 1995 and renamed APPRENTICESHIPS
from September 2004.

Monitorial System is where students teach and/or monitor other students. Sometimes
there are specific duties, e.g. cloakroom monitoring. Sometimes the monitoring is
more like mentoring.

Montessori schools are independent schools, where the belief is that children teach
themselves, and learn what they need from their environment. This form of education
was founded by Dr Maria Montessori (1870–1952, Italian). Dignity and independence
are key. Students choose tasks for themselves in the environment that is set out for
them. Each school, however, responds sensitively to reflect the needs of their students,
their society and their cultures.

⋆ **Motivation** How do you motivate students to *want* to study and learn? Why do some
students study with energy, enthusiasm and a hunger for knowledge while others need
to be driven by verbal force or threat to even pick up a book? There are many theories
and models around this, and one commonly used is by Frederick Herzberg, where he
defined these two types of motivation as:

1   *Motivators* – the truly motivating factors (e.g. you can eat some chocolate cake
    when you've learned how to bake it).

2   *Hygiene factors* – which de-motivate if they are absent (e.g. now you mention it, I don't want to work here if the room's too cold).

So, people are motivated either to make a gain or to avoid a loss. They will strive to achieve something they want, or to avoid losing something they wish to hang on to.

- On the 'gain' side may be such things as:

   - A good education to enrich my life.
   - Qualifications to get a better job.
   - Knowledge that will help me with my ambitions.
   - A good report to please my parents.
   - A good performance to please the teacher.
   - High results to give me status among my peers.
   - A sense of achievement and a boost to my self-esteem.
   - To show I can do it.

- On the 'avoid a loss' side may be such things as:

   - I want to avoid another telling off.
   - I don't want to be kept in detention.
   - I don't want to be expelled and have to explain that to my parents.

It is obvious that, if a student has a goal or ambition that a relevant education will help them 'gain', then they will be motivated. Indeed, this type of motivation could be classed as self-motivation or intrinsic motivation (coming from inside the individual).

But if a student needs to be motivated by avoiding a loss, then this normally needs an external or extrinsic motivation. Where a student has no intrinsic motivation, where they have no ambition at all, or no ambition that an education would contribute towards, the job of the teacher becomes very hard. Having to be the driving force and the threat behind students is emotionally tiring. If they are at school only because the law says they have to be, you can feel like a jailer trying to keep the inmates in. If they have no ambition and you pose no threat, the job is even harder. And remember, every class and group will have mixed motivations. Each student will have different needs, ambitions and support. It is easy to give most attention to the highly motivated students, and giving time to those with low motivation can seem unfair to those who are willing and eager. However, we cannot write off students. It is our job to do all we can.

✓ Tips

- Where you have a troublesome student a priority is to find something they want to do or achieve, that an education will at least play some part in. If they know clearly what they want to do (e.g. be a footballer, a pop star or a traveller) you will need to find some role for the non-vocational subjects to help in achieving this ambition. For example, when you're a pop star, you'll need maths to check that your manager isn't on the fiddle, yes?
- Never assume what will motivate anyone else – it is too easy to believe, erroneously, that other people are motivated by the same things that we ourselves are motivated by.
- Gaining or maintaining self-esteem and status are two key driving forces for most people. Boosting a student's self-esteem can motivate them to want greater boosts to their self-esteem, and thereby capture their interest and attention.
- Lack of motivation is sometimes triggered by family culture and peer pressure. It's 'cool' not to like school. When this is the case, endeavour to show how those people who influence the student may have fewer choices available to them by not doing well at school – but ensure that it's presented as a positive increase in choices for your student, rather than disparaging comments on their family or friends.
- If you can create a sense of choice and possibility in the world, this will help students become motivated. Those who are without hope of a chance or a choice in life, need more opportunities to choose from, since they've rejected whatever they've so far thought of.

- If a student has no ambition now, explain how education can create more choices for them once they are clear about what they want to do with their lives.
- For those with low motivation, we should endeavour to make learning a 'want to' rather than a 'have to' by finding something in the student's life that an education would contribute to, i.e. ensure that there's always a WIIFM – What's In It For Me?
- We should do all we can to understand their lives, the context in which school is just a part, and to understand the pressures that cause them to be de-motivated.
- Make use of teaching assistants and other staff where possible – you never know who will provide the spark that captures someone's attention.
- Use group work or study buddies to mix the highly motivated with those with less motivation, and by creatively partnering less motivated students, and briefing all parties, success can be around the corner.
- And if it isn't, remember 'If at first you don't succeed, try something *different*. (Don't try, try, and try again – if it didn't work the first time, why would it work now?!)

✔ *Tips for you*

- If ever you feel a lack of motivation, remind yourself what you wanted to achieve when you chose to teach.
- Don't beat yourself up if you can't motivate all students all the time. You will have done your best and your role in life is to teach those who need to learn. It's up to the individual, at the end of the day, to make their life work.
- If you see a student wasting their chance in life, remind yourself of those you *have* helped.
- There are, broadly speaking, three types of student:

  - *Prisoners* resent being there. The best you can do is to turn them into holiday-makers, by finding an angle (individually) that intrigues them and at least makes them willing to be there, rather than under protest.
  - *Holidaymakers* are just there for the ride. The strategy you need is to find the spark that turns them (individually) into learners.
  - *Learners*. Phew! Their agenda is pretty much the same as yours and the school's.

- And, finally, back to Herzberg. He found that in the workplace – so this applies to you and your students equally, yes? – the main motivators were.
- In first place, a sense of achievement.
- In second place, recognition.

  and only then

- In third place, the work itself.

Isn't that why you went into teaching in the first place? It's good to touch base with this from time to time. (And if you are lacking a sense of achievement or recognition, you need to talk through with someone how you will get it back. As Nietzsche said, 'To forget one's purpose is the commonest form of omission'.)

Motor Skills *see* PSYCHOMOTOR SKILLS.

MSI *see* MULTI-SENSORY IMPAIRMENT.

Multicultural Education is not only about providing an education for all students in an equal, fair and relevant way, it is also about shaping the society of the future. While recognizing that there should be no bias or discrimination within the education system it is useful to acknowledge some truths:

- The racial and ethnic mix in the UK has changed rapidly over the last 50 years and not everybody has been able to adjust to the speed of change, and many have not wanted to.
- Much of the cultural infrastructure has yet to adjust fully to this change.

- There is discrimination in society as a whole and schools cannot be an exception to this, but they can act as a model for the rest of society to copy.
- Bias and prejudice take time, sometimes generations, to be educated out of society.
- For a long time multicultural differences were handled by trying to make people the same, rather than respecting and valuing difference.

So what can teachers do to bring about multicultural education?

- Involve parents of all ethnic groups in the activities of the school.
- Recognize that English or Welsh may be a second language and support students and parents who need to adjust.
- Recognize that all students have an ethnic identity that should be respected.
- Support students holding onto, or building, or finding their ethnic identity.
- Demonstrate in your actions and words that you believe in EQUAL OPPORTUNITIES for all.
- Help all students to understand all cultures, backgrounds, faiths and traditions.
- Have all students recognize and value difference, without prejudice.
- Make sure all educational material is inclusive.
- Be prepared to explore constructively any transgressions or racial prejudice.

Multidisciplinary *see* INTERDISCIPLINARY.

Multiple Choice is where a single question is asked, and several specific answers are given for the student to choose from (e.g. do you think this hat is too big, too small or about right?). It is cheap to administer, but cannot examine in depth.

✓ *Tip*

☐ Clearly in the above example the questioner is NOT asking if the hat suits them, or if you like it. In multiple choice you have to answer only from the questioner's options and not your own.

Multiple Intelligences Howard Gardner theorized in 1983 that there was not just one intelligence (see IQ) but perhaps seven:

- *Linguistic* (suitable professions might include journalist, or poet).
- *Musical* (composer, musician).
- *Logical–mathematical* (scientist, doctor).
- *Spatial* (architect, sculptor).
- *Bodily–kinaesthetic* (athlete, massage therapist).
- *Intrapersonal* (thinker, philosopher).
- *Interpersonal* (leader, salesperson).

Subsequently other intelligences have been proposed and much debated, including:

- *Naturalist* (botanist, conservationist).
- *Spiritual* and/or *existential* (priest, guru).
- *Emotional* (counsellor, psychotherapist) *see also* EMOTIONAL INTELLIGENCE.

Assessment tools include MIDAS MULTIPLE INTELLIGENCE DEVELOPMENT ASSESSMENT SCALES.

✓ *Tips*

☐ We believe that everyone has all of these intelligences. Yes, different people may have them in different proportions. And yes, we all have our own preferences; why else would we ignore something we're 'good' at, and persevere with something that's a struggle?

□ To make learning as easy as possible for everyone in a group, teachers who use multiple intelligences present subject matter in ways that blend (to follow the first seven opposite) words and language, music and rhythm, numbers and equations, physical spaces and surroundings, practical hands-on experiences, independent thought and reflection, and social interactions.

✗ *Trap*

□ Pigeon-holing someone (or oneself) as e.g. 'Not Musical', or 'Not Good With People', is shutting the stable door with the horse potentially trapped inside forever. We are all flexible.

Multi-Sensory Impairment (MSI) describes students with more than one sense impaired (e.g. sight, hearing) where changes to the environment or teaching practices are needed to help them to access the curriculum.

★ **Music** can cheer us up or calm us down (unless we don't feel like being cheered up or calmed down, in which case we resist). There is, however, a growing awareness of how specific music can affect learning. We're sceptical about some of the claims, but enough people use music for mood-altering for us to believe that it's worth experimenting with. We've taken these categories from SUGGESTOPAEDIA:

■ *Active Concert* – high-speed, high-frequency background music (e.g. some Mozart) is thought to aid the initial retention of new learnings. Some people think this is because it stimulates the release of adrenalin (the chemical, not the band) and thus creates a state of increased alertness.

■ *Passive Concert* – music at 60 beats per minute is recommended to reinforce new learnings, especially some specific Baroque music (from European composers such as Bach, Corelli, Handel, and Vivaldi working approximately 1600–1750). These pieces are ornate on the surface but have a bass-line of precisely one beat per second, typical of many people's relaxed heart-rate of 60 per minute. It was deliberately composed at the time to produce a relaxed, meditative state. (There are also many new compositions recorded specifically for this purpose.) Some people find that the speed has to be exactly 60 bpm, whereas others are less specific. Some people think that this music attracts the attention of the part of the brain that 'does' boredom so that the rest of the brain can learn. Others believe that it stimulates the production of serotonin, which helps us to feel calm.

✓ *Tips*

□ Try different music, and choose pieces that work for *you*. In that way you will be in the desired state that your class can see and model.

□ Fast music can be great for getting the heart-rate up for physical exercise, post-lunch, or anytime you want your students to get up and going.

□ Fast music that gradually slows can be a good way of matching a high-energy group, and then helping to 'settle' them within a few minutes.

✗ *Traps*

□ Not all Baroque music has this one-beat-per-second rhythm, nor do all recordings play the music at the same speed. Check on the Internet for recommended recordings.

□ Music doesn't work for everyone – we know people who have strong AUDITORY preferences who cannot resist listening to background music and get completely distracted by it.

Myers–Briggs Type Indicator (MBTI) *see* LEARNING STYLES.

N

Name-calling *see* APPEARANCE BULLYING.

NASUWT National Association of Schoolmasters Union of Women Teachers.

National College for School Leadership (NCSL) was launched in 2000 and is based in Nottingham. It provides development and support for England's school leaders, current and potential, in four main areas

- Leadership development, including the National Professional Qualification for Headship.
- Research and development.
- Online learning.
- The Talking Heads online community.

National Curriculum was introduced in 1988 as part of the Education Reform Act in order to specify what should be learned at different stages in a student's development. Initially it did this by specifying what exactly should be taught (rather than learned), and in many cases it also specified how exactly teachers should teach it. The intentions were excellent – that all students should achieve uniformly high standards, but the methods it imposed were prescriptive and, therefore, alienating. It defines subjects that need to be covered at each key stage, the content to be covered at each key stage, and how progress in learning should be monitored. It is likely to be dropped for students aged 14 and above.

National Grid For Learning (NGfL) is a network of educational resources on the Internet for everyone involved with learning and education www.ngfl.gov.uk (as of June 2004).

National Learning Targets for literacy and numeracy were introduced in 1999. There were 11 targets covering ages 11, 16, 19, 21 and on into adulthood.

National Literacy and Numeracy Strategies were developed from 1997–1999 and included National Learning Targets, and interventions such as the Literacy Hour and Numeracy Hour, both of which are now part of the National Primary Strategy or, for secondary schools, part of the overall Key Stage 3 National Strategy.

National Open College Network (NOCN) is the national body for OPEN COLLEGE FOR NETWORKS and is also an AWARDING BODY for adult learning.

National Professional Qualification for Headship (NPQH) *see* NATIONAL COLLEGE FOR SCHOOL LEADERSHIP.

National Qualifications Framework *see* NQF.

National School Improvement Network (NSIN) was established by the Institute of Education for individuals, schools, LEAs and higher education institutions to share ideas, discuss common issues and support one another.

National Skills Strategy was launched as a key part of SUCCESS FOR ALL in 2002–2003 to address the major skills needs in the UK, in partnership with industry and training providers for students and workers aged 14–19 and above.

Nature or Nurture is a much debated (and often confusing) area concerning the relative influence of inherited characteristics (nature) and environment (nurture), on a person's intelligence, personality, behaviour, mental health etc.

- *Nature* refers to those characteristics that have evolved through natural selection and are carried in our genes from one generation to the next. The colour of our eyes, for example.
- *Nurture* describes those behaviours that have developed from our upbringing and environment. From MODELLING others, or being taught and rewarded, it's what we learn through observation and experience. As we are genetically (i.e. by nature) driven to survive, we model *how* to survive from those closest to us who have shown the capability to survive.

Of course, most behaviour is influenced by both nature *and* nurture. A susceptibility to heart disease can be partly attributable to our genes and partly to the diet we have learned to eat.

Since much behaviour is also influenced by the ENVIRONMENT we are in, a change of environment can often have a major effect on behaviour. *See also* LOGICAL LEVELS.

✓ *Tips*

- ☐ 'It's in my genes to be this way' is no excuse for any behaviour, although a lot of nurturing might be necessary to teach other choices.
- ☐ Which has the most influence in a situation is often a chicken-and-egg situation and, by the way, the answer to which came first is ... the egg. (Dinosaurs laid eggs.)

NCSL *see* NATIONAL COLLEGE FOR SCHOOL LEADERSHIP.

NDPB Non-Departmental Public Body which is the current name for what used to be known as a QUANGO. (= Quasi-Autonomous Non-Governmental Organisation.)

★ **Negative Self-talk** is that voice in your head that sounds as if it's trying to help you but all it does is hold you back. It's there whether you like it or not, and seems eager to argue with you and make you feel worse about a situation. It talks you out of decisions you know are right. It uses words like ought to, should, can't and won't.

Examples

- You should never say no to your boss.
- You know you're no good at this.
- Someone like you won't achieve what you're looking to achieve.
- You'll never do anything with students like these.

One technique to override negative self-talk is to adopt a positive mental attitude. No, this doesn't mean to be artificially cheerful. This is simply taking a positive stance to displace the, often wrong, negative voice. For example, stand in front of a mirror and tell yourself what you plan to achieve during the day ahead, speaking out loud. For some people this works well. Others find their negative voice comes at them from a different direction, using a different tone and further undermines their confidence by saying, 'I told you so,' when things do not turn out well. In those cases, here are some ideas for yourself and for students who have been limiting themselves.

✓ *Tips*

- ☐ Identify who the negative self-talk sounds like. Is it your voice or someone from the past? If it's not your voice then thank it for its advice and tell it that you're old enough to make your own decisions now.

- ☐ If it uses words like ought, won't or can't, then puncture its bubble by asking what would happen if you did. For instance, 'You can't tell the class that'. 'What would happen if I did?'. And see what answer pops into your head.
- ☐ When your negative self-talk is criticizing, put its observation into the past tense and then phrase your response in the present tense. For instance if it says you won't succeed because you're always late then say, 'I know I always used to be late and now I'm going to make sure I'm on time'.
- ☐ If it makes sweeping statements and generalizations such as, 'every student will play you up,' then counter with, 'What! Every single one? You mean not one of them will behave? Ever?'

See also SELF-FULFILLING PROPHECY.

Networking is making contacts with people, and making use of those contacts in order to further your aims and objectives. It happens naturally everywhere (it could also be called 'meeting people'), e.g. in families, pubs, clubs, sports clubs, and conferences. It also happens unnaturally when someone goes, e.g. to specific networking clubs. The teaching profession is limited in its potential for networking because teachers meet colleagues from other schools only on training and special events. However, if you are proactive in networking, rather than waiting for opportunities to be presented to you, then it can have advantages.

✓ *Tips*

- ☐ Networking is best when it is reciprocal. If people feel you are trying to make use of them, they will hold back on helping you. Don't abuse someone's generosity of spirit.
- ☐ Be careful how others perceive you networking. If they see your actions as political you may make enemies.
- ☐ Networking is most effective when it comes from having a real interest and pleasure in others.

New New Universities are currently being proposed, controversially, to allow higher education colleges to gain university status. The requirement for conducting research (and awarding research degrees) would no longer be essential for university status.

New Start was a 1997 initiative (part of INVESTORS IN YOUNG PEOPLE) to re-engage 14–17-year-olds who had dropped out of learning or were at risk of doing so. Its work is now part of the CONNEXIONS Service.

New Universities are those formed, often from what were polytechnics, following the Further and Higher Education Act 1992.

NFER National Foundation for Educational Research is an independent educational research institution founded in 1946 and funded by charging for its research and information services. (nferNelson was originally the publishing arm of NFER and is currently part of Granada.)

NIACE National Institute for Adult Continuing Education promotes lifelong learning opportunities for adults.

Nine Events of Instruction *see* GAGNÉ, ROBERT.

NLP Neuro-Linguistic Programming emerged in Santa Cruz, California in the early 1970s, developed by John Grinder and Richard Bandler. It started when they and their students modelled high performers, predominantly therapists. They wanted to identify how exactly these high performers did what they did, so they could teach the techniques to other people. Defining NLP is difficult because there are many definitions, and much debate amongst NLPers about what actually is part of NLP and what is not. Here are two definitions we like:

■ The study of the structure of subjective experience, and its practical applications (i.e. how we structure our experiences and how we can use this knowledge to change our experiences, e.g. happiness, sadness, fear, compassion).

■ It's the instruction book for human beings – it's how we do what we do, and how we can do what other people can do (as we are all pretty much wired the same way).

Norm Referencing *see* ASSESSMENT.

Northern Examinations and Assessment Board *see* AQA.

NPQH National Professional Qualification for Headship. *See* NATIONAL COLLEGE FOR SCHOOL LEADERSHIP.

NQF the National Qualifications Framework provides a series of levels into which all QCA, ACCAC or CCEA accredited qualifications will fit. It is intended to provide a clear and motivating progression for lifelong learning, and to put vocational and academic qualifications on an equal footing. (However, and potentially confusingly, there is also a FRAMEWORK FOR HIGHER EDUCATION QUALIFICATIONS, FHEQ.) All general, vocational and occupational qualifications are accommodated.

■ *Entry Level.*

■ *Level 1 (Foundation).*

  □ NVQ level 1.
  □ VGCSE (grades D–G).
  □ Foundation GNVQ (to 2004).
  □ Foundation Certificate/Certificate (level 1).
  □ GCSE grades D–G.

■ *Level 2 (Intermediate).*

  □ NVQ level 2.
  □ VGCSE (grades A*–C).
  □ Intermediate GNVQ (to 2004).
  □ Intermediate Certificate Certificate (level 2).
  □ 'First' Diplomas.
  □ GCSE grades A*–C.

■ *Level 3 (Advanced).*

  □ NVQ level 3.
  □ Vocational GCE A and A/S levels.
  □ Advanced Certificate.
  □ Level 3 'National' Awards, Certificates, and Diplomas.
  □ GCE A and A/S levels.

■ *Level 4 (Higher Level).*

  □ NVQ level 4.
  □ Higher National Diplomas (HND) and Certificates (HNC).
  □ Degrees.

■ *Level 5 (Higher Level).*

  □ NVQ level 5.

NQT Newly Qualified Teachers. They should normally have a teaching workload that is 10 per cent lighter than other teachers in their school, to allow for, e.g.

■ Regular meetings with their induction tutor.
■ Progress reviews half-termly.
■ Progress reviews with both the induction tutor and head teacher on a termly basis.

They should also have clear progress indicators to help them meet their induction standards by the end of their first year, and clear grievance procedures both at school and LEA levels, in case any of these, or other matters, need to be resolved.

NSIN *see* NATIONAL SCHOOL IMPROVEMENT NETWORK.

Numeracy Hour is part of the Primary National Strategy for all students in years 1–6. The objective is to increase their competence with numbers.

A typical numeracy hour could be:

■ A starter (5–10 min) where the whole class works on mental arithmetic, to rehearse, sharpen and develop their mental and oral skills.
■ The main teacher input and activity (30–40 min) where the teacher explains the objective, and the students then work in groups or pairs or as individuals.
■ A PLENARY (10–15 min) where the teacher works with the whole class to assess understanding and progress made by students, and to identify any misunderstandings. The class summarises key facts and ideas to remember, makes links to other work, discusses the next steps, and sets follow-on work or homework.

Numeracy Strategy is now part of the PRIMARY NATIONAL STRATEGY.

Nursery School is for students typically under 5-years-old, also called kindergarten.

NUS National Union of Students.

NUT National Union of Teachers.

NVC Non-Violent Communication is a form of language increasingly used in conflict situations, developed by Marshall Rosenberg.

Observation is simply noticing what is going on, by collecting information without interfering. In a world where we are inundated with information, we can unknowingly become selective about what we observe, so we need to be deliberate with our observation, depending on the task at hand. Teachers are now taught and encouraged to observe in greater depth, and are expected to plan how and what they will observe, consciously. Observing the individual student to understand where they are at now, is necessary in order to plan to take them onto their next stage.

✓ *Tips*

- To practise your observation skills, make use of social situations. Choose a friend and decide on an area of their thinking or their behaviour that you would like to know more about. Then, without causing offence or spoiling the social occasion, observe not only *what* they do and say, but *how* they do it, to better understand the area you have planned to observe.
- Ask questions to verify the conclusions of your observations – you may think someone looks bored, but that may be how they listen better, for example.
- If you have a student with a particular difficulty, observe them with the intention of understanding where exactly the difficulty kicks in. By planning to observe this, you will have a better chance of addressing the issue.
- If you set up an observation sheet you can both plan what you want to observe, and monitor how effective you have been. List what you intend to notice, and then add what you have in fact noticed.

OCR

1 Oxford Cambridge and RSA Examinations were formed in 1998 from UCLES (the University of Cambridge Local Examinations Syndicate) and RSA Examinations. It is still part of UCLES and offers General, Vocational, and Occupational qualifications.
2 Optical Character Recognition software that 'reads' words when scanned so that, unlike a photocopy, they can be edited.

Ofsted the Office For Standards In Education is a non-ministerial government department set up from the schools inspectorate in 1992, to help improve the quality and standards of education. It achieves this through independent inspection and by providing advice to the Secretary of State for Education. Its original role was to manage the system of inspecting state-funded schools in England, but its role has expanded and they now also review LEAs, sixth form and further education colleges, initial teacher training courses, early years childcare and education, some independent schools and youth services.

An Ofsted inspection gathers information to assess how well a school is doing. It involves data analysis, observing lessons, interviewing teachers, analysing students' work, meeting parents, students and governors and publishing a written report. Inspections used to take place every six years, with new schools being inspected during their second year. (It is now being proposed that inspections are undertaken with less than ten weeks' notice, to inspect how the school normally operates, rather than how it operates when given notice of an inspection.)

If a school is felt to be underperforming, it might be declared as having 'serious weaknesses'. Lack of improvement might put a school into SPECIAL MEASURES. If these don't work, then the school might be closed down under the FRESH START programme.

✓ *Tip*

☐ When an Ofsted inspection is due, some students pick up on the anxiety felt and demonstrated by teachers and other staff. Reassure the students that it is not they who are being measured. Have a positive mindset that the inspection is to help you (all) to do your job even better, for your students.

Olfactory one of the five senses – smell.

OLSAT™ Otis-Lennon School Ability Test™ measures language and conceptual thinking and reasoning comprehension.

ONC/OND Ordinary National Certificate/Diploma are vocational qualification introduced by the Technician Education Council in 1973 and each is at Level 3 of the NQF National Qualification Framework.

Open Classrooms describe learning in communities and workplaces, not just in classrooms.

Open College Networks (OCNs) enable local organizations such as colleges, voluntary organizations, unions and employers to develop and deliver their own learning and training, with nationally recognized qualifications. The national body for the UK's 29 Open College Networks is the National Open College Network (NOCN) which is also an awarding body for adult learning.

Open College of the Arts (OCA) offers distance learning in visual and creative arts, and was set up in the late 1980s by Michael Young (later Lord Young of Dartington) (1915–2002).

Top Tips from Anna Craft

Engage, Inspire, Ignite!

■ *Engage*
I believe that the most fundamental step in learning is for the learner to be interested, stimulated, connected . . . and so a primary responsibility for an educator must therefore be to foster engagement in the learner.

■ *Inspire*
A step beyond engaging the learner is to inspire them, through an array of approaches which might include providing an appropriate environment, offering access to a variety of well-chosen learning modes and resources (including other people), introducing concepts and ideas which stretch the learner's own perspectives and also encouraging learners to take – and own – steps in their learning journeys.

■ *Ignite*
This is the space that perhaps all educators aim for, where the learner is consumed with excitement for learning and where the learner's own interests, passions, understanding and potential are ignited like a fire which then burns with its own intensity, firing other nearby ideas and people and lighting up the possibilities for future learning.

Open School

1 An evening or day where work is on display and the school is open to parents, carers, friends and all who are interested.
2 Open Schools are now known more commonly as COMMUNITY SCHOOLS.
3 The Open School Network offers would-be teachers the opportunity to spend a day in a school for hands-on 'feel'.
4 The Open School was launched in 1989 by Michael (later Lord, of Dartington) Young (1915–2002) offering distance learning for teachers.
5 The Open School Trust is a charity aiming to tackle access and underachievement, particularly in literacy and numeracy, including TELETUTORING for supporting students with special needs.

Open University (OU) is the UK's largest university with two-thirds of its students studying part-time, as they are in full-time employment. It admitted its first students in 1971 and pioneered many DISTANCE LEARNING and E-LEARNING techniques. It was influenced partly by the Dawn University on Anglia TV developed by Michael Young (later Lord Young of Dartington) (1915–2002), who was also instrumental in setting up the OU.

Opening Minds *see* RSA.

Operant Behaviour and Conditioning emerged as B.F. Skinner discovered that how often a rat pressed a bar depended not on a reflex to a stimulus (e.g. a light coming on, or a bell ringing) as Pavlov had suggested, but on what came as a *consequence* e.g. food. Since its behaviour operated on (i.e. affected) its environment, he called it Operant Behaviour. This behaviour (pressing the bar) was reinforced by repeating the consequence (food) – a process he called Operant Conditioning.

Until this time people's behaviour was 'controlled' mainly through negative reinforcement – i.e. punishing negative behaviours. The value of positive reinforcement is still being discovered as it avoids the push-back consequences of punishment (e.g. disengagement, violence, vandalism or truancy).

Example

One of the most effective ways of teaching a dog to 'sit' on command is not to push down its rear, screaming 'sit' increasingly hysterically, but to take it for a long walk, and when at last it sits gratefully of its own accord, to pat its rear, and say 'sit' or 'good sit' in a calm way.

✓ *Tip*

☐ Thinking of your more 'difficult' colleagues or students, what could you reinforce when you catch them doing something *right*?

✗ *Trap*

☐ It's easy to sound patronizing if the praise is forced or false rather than (apparently) spontaneous!

Opportunity and Excellence is a DfES report published in 2003 which sets out a vision to transform the learning experience for young people, so that by the age of 16 they are committed to continued learning, whether in school, college or the workplace, to fulfil their potential. Among its proposals are:

■ Consistent excellence in teaching and learning for 11–19 year-olds.
■ Curriculum changes for 14–16 year-olds.
■ Raising aspirations for 14–19 year-olds.

Options are subjects that students can choose to study, alongside compulsory subjects. They enable students to choose subjects they believe they have a better chance of doing well at, or for which they have a natural affinity, or that may be most relevant to the career they have in mind. (In the US these are called electives, since students elect to study them voluntarily.)

Oral Assessment is testing for learning and understanding through face-to-face conversation and questioning, rather than in writing. *See* ASSESSMENT.

OTTP Overseas Trained Teachers Programme is for graduates with a teaching qualification from another country. Currently there is no training salary so you need to be employed by a school. Training is from a minimum of 'assessment only' to a maximum of 1 year.

OU *see* OPEN UNIVERSITY.

Out of School Clubs, Networks, and Services are often called Kids' Clubs and provide appropriate childcare such as

- *Breakfast clubs* – open before school in the mornings so students, and sometimes staff and parents, can enjoy breakfast there.
- *After-school clubs* – open in the afternoons to about 6 pm where students can do homework, or play, or use the internet while their parents or carers are still at work.
- *Holiday clubs* – open during the day during school holidays, with activities and meals while their parents or carers are working.

Oxbridge a term meaning *Ox*ford and cam*BRIDGE* universities (which were founded in the twelfth and thirteenth centuries).

Oxford & Cambridge Examining Board now part of OCR.

P Scales are used for students whose learning attainments are below level 1, especially where there are learning difficulties. There are eight steps or levels:

■ P1–P3, which show general attainment, e.g.

☐ *Encounter* – where students are simply present during an activity, and willing to tolerate it without any obvious learning outcome.

☐ *Awareness* – where students seem to be aware of something happening, maybe focusing briefly on an event or person.

☐ *Attention and response* – where students show signs of paying attention and responding, on occasions.

☐ *Engagement* – where students pay more consistent attention to specific events.

☐ *Participation* – where students may share, take turns or show signs of anticipation.

☐ *Involvement* – where students actively reach out, or join in.

☐ *Gaining skills* – where students gain or use skills and knowledge.

■ P4 to P8, which show *subject-specific attainment*.

★ **Pacing** If you enter a room of people you don't know, you will probably stay relatively quiet, and look around until you understand what is happening around you. Few people would storm in and try to dominate without first understanding the environment they had entered. What you are assessing is the mood, the type of people, and how they are likely to respond to you. You are assessing how to 'pace', or fit in with, what is happening. It is not until you have paced the group, not all at once, naturally, and feel more comfortable that you can then begin to assert yourself (gently, of course) or start to take the group in a different direction. Anybody joining a political meeting will understand this process. You wait and listen until you understand what is happening, and only then do you voice an opinion once you have been assimilated into the group. If you were to bluster in and voice your opinion without first establishing the mood of the group, they would likely rebuff you, irrespective of the point you were making.

The same principle is true of a class (or a staffroom, friends or family). You need to pace where they are when you or they enter the room and, once assimilated, lead them where you want them to go.

The mood and frame of mind of a class could vary from day to day. Something could happen in the school, in the local area or on the world stage that will influence how they feel. For instance, after 9/11, your students would have been emotionally affected. To have carried on with the class without acknowledging their response would have left them alone with their thoughts, and you alone with your teaching. Pace the obvious. Say something like '9/11 has happened, how do we feel about it?' Without first pacing where people are, they will not follow you. Just as someone who blusters into your space won't get a sympathetic hearing either.

Paedocentric/Pedocentric *see* CHILD-CENTRED LEARNING.

PANDA Performance Assessment and National Contextual Data is an Ofsted tool that gives an overview of each school's performance, compared to other schools in England, using data from Ofsted, the Department for Education and Skills and the Qualifications and Curriculum Authority (QCA). They are management tools to help schools develop plans to raise standards, but are not published for the public.

Parents (i.e. your students' parents) can be your best friends and worst nightmares. If they are not on your side, it is usually because of mixed messages, or miscommunication.

 Tip

☐ There is no alternative to taking time to listen to them and their concerns, and working together to produce some creative solutions to their concerns. (Why creative? Because the existing ones haven't worked!)

Parent–Teacher Associations (PTAs) were primarily used in the UK for fundraising to provide extra resources for a school. But relatively few parents are motivated to play an active role in this. In the US, however, PTAs are much more vocal, and expect to be consulted and listened to on matters of policy and practice that affect their children. They know that having an effective and vibrant PTA is a huge asset for a school. UK PTAs are, at last, becoming more organized and influential, following the US model.

Parent–Teacher Evenings are required under The Schools Standards and Framework Act of 1998. Their purpose is to keep parents informed of student progress and to provide the opportunity for parents and teachers to compare notes and exchange any information that would be of use in the education of the student. The evidence suggests that although parents were keen to have these evenings made compulsory, not many of them attend. For a teacher, meeting parents often provides useful insights into the behaviour of the student. It enables the teacher to compare the student's behaviour at school with that away from school.

Tip

☐ It can be pretty scary, having to meet lots of people, one after another, trying to remember who is who from the year before, so make a few notes after each meeting, not only of any agreed action points, but of who you met. *See* ACADEMIC MONITORING for a more leisurely in-depth alternative.

Participation at its best is where those involved with a project (community, society or school) are not only informed and consulted but also take the initiative, decide and manage. In 2003 the DfES published a consultation document 'Working together: Giving children and young people a say' to help Local Education Authorities, Governing Bodies and schools to involve young people when making decisions that affect them. The aim is to open up opportunities for young people to become active participants in planning their own education, and evaluating their own learning. We are going to hear a lot more about participation.

■ A key model is *Roger Hart's Ladder of Participation*, and we summarize the eight steps:

1 *Participation offered (to adults)* – young people initiate and run projects, bring in relevant adults for decision-making, and involve adults with relevant skills as mentors and coaches.
2 *Self-organized* – young people initiate and run projects with limited or no adult involvement.
3 *Participation invited (by adults)* – adults initiate and run projects and share decision-making with young people who are considered key stakeholders.
4 *Consultation* – adults initiate and run projects and make the decisions, but consult young people and seriously consider their opinions.
5 *Involvement* – adults initiate and run projects, but young people have a meaningful role and participate.

6   *Tokenism* – Projects are adult-initiated and run. Young people may be consulted, but are not provided opportunities for feedback or to shape agendas. Adults may feign that young people are stakeholders.
7   *Decoration* – Projects are adult-initiated and run. Young people may have a limited understanding about events or activities but have no say in organizing.
8   *Manipulation* – Projects are adult-initiated and run. Adults use young people who have no understanding of issues and are not considered key stakeholders.

■ *Harry Shier* believed that for children to be able to express their views openly and confidently, adults working with them must take positive action to enable this and to overturn those barriers that may prevent children's views from being expressed.

■ *Penny Westhorp* suggested a six-step model

1   *Ad hoc*: Low level input, e.g. surveys, suggestion boxes.
2   *Structured consultation*: Two way flow of information, usually in some depth, e.g. workshops, discussion groups.
3   *Influence*: Formal input which includes decision making on, e.g., working parties or as elected representatives.
4   *Delegation*: Young people have responsibility for a particular task.
5   *Negotiation*: Young people have bargaining power in the decision.
6   *Control*: Young people make all the crucial decisions within an organization.

She also suggested a series of questions to ensure the genuine participation of young people in organizations:

☐ *Aims*: What do we hope to achieve by youth participation, for young people and the organization?
☐ *Level*: What kind or level or participation does the organization want? What do young people want?
☐ *Target group*: Given the aims and desired levels of participation, what target groups are we looking for?
☐ *Support*: What will participants need, in order to participate effectively? e.g. information, money, peer support, training.
☐ *Barriers*: What are the barriers to young people's participation? What strategies can we develop to overcome these barriers?
☐ *Evaluation*: How will we know if we are achieving our aims?

Partnership is a belief that existing organizations should be encouraged to work together to ensure that their expertise and contacts can benefit each other, rather than re-inventing the wheel by setting up new organizations or duplicating existing expertise. Partnerships range from the simple (e.g. several local schools working together) to the multi-faceted.

Example – and we *don't* expect you to read all of this.

The Adult and Community Learning Quality Support Programme is funded by the Department for Education and Skills (DfES) as a partnership between the Learning and Skills Development Agency (LSDA) and the National Institute for Adult Continuing Education (NIACE) to provide support for quality initiatives within Local Education Authority (LEA) adult and community learning services, working closely with the Learning and Skills Council (LSC). Phew.

Partnerships for Schools is the non-departmental public body set up in 2004 to offer support and expertise to LEAs spearheading the BSF Building Schools for the Future programme.

Passive and Active Learning

- *Passive learning* entails being passively taught at (sorry for the grammar, but this expresses what we mean), remembering information and being able to repeat back what has been dictated or presented to you. The student is seen as a receptacle into which the teacher pours facts and information, hopefully, but not necessarily, creating knowledge.
- *Active learning* involves learning by DISCOVERY – making a contribution, being prompted into thinking and reasoning, understanding what is beneath information and acquiring knowledge.

Passive Concert – *see* SUGGESTOPEDIA.

Pastoral Care literally relates to a shepherd taking care of sheep. Teachers have a duty of care to all students. There is more to a student than academic achievement. We need to have in mind the possibilities of BULLYING, difficult RELATIONSHIPS, TRUANCY, ill health and other factors that could affect the student. However, we must be aware of boundaries. We have no right to intrude or impose unless it directly affects the student's education. We need also to be aware of how our actions could be misunderstood or misinterpreted.

✓ *Tip*

☐ If ever you think action needs to be taken of a pastoral nature then confer with the head, the SENCO or a colleague. A discussion will help you to decide on appropriate action and act as evidence that your actions were properly motivated, rather than you acting alone, and being exposed if things go badly.

PBL Problem-Based Learning is where we work out what we need to learn and then, with the help of a trained facilitator (e.g. a teacher) we learn it.

PC Political Correctness is being aware of social acceptability (which of course varies from social group to social group, and varies over time) by avoiding saying or doing things that could

- *Exclude people*: e.g. we can 'staff' the telephone line, is more inclusive than 'man' the telephone line.
- *Marginalize people*: e.g. we can refer to women as 'women' (= adults) rather than as 'girls' (= children) or 'girlies'; or we can avoid making assumptions that marginalize people, for example, assuming that someone with disabilities is, therefore, 'handicapped'.
- *Insult people*: e.g. by picking up on a social disadvantage or physical feature, i.e. we can avoid calling someone a 'pauper', 'cripple', 'fatty', etc. (Note too, that these are all at the very wounding level of Identity – *see* LOGICAL LEVELS.)

✓ *Tips*

☐ Some people are very crusading about the need for political correctness at all times and in all situations, whether the remark is directly to them, in their company, or accidentally overheard, especially if they themselves feel disadvantaged or discriminated against. It is therefore prudent, and polite, to avoid excluding, marginalizing and insulting anyone.
☐ It's potentially a minefield and since we are all human and have grown up in a past that was different to the present (inevitably), if and when we cause offence, it's simple to

1 Apologize.
2 Ask how the other person would prefer us to behave or speak in future.
3 Assure them that you'll do this, then.
4 Move swiftly onto another unrelated subject, since the matter has been dealt with.

See also BULLYING, EQUAL OPPORTUNITIES.

PD Physical Disability.

PD Days Personal Development days *see* INSET.

PDQ

1   Professional Development Qualifications.
2   Common slang as in 'I need this PDQ' (= Pretty Damn Quickly).

PE Physical Education, i.e. sport and other below-the-neck rather than in-the-head activities.

Pedagogy is the traditional teacher-led education of children. *See also* ANDRAGOGY.

Peer Pressure can be as much a force for good as it can for bad, even though we tend to refer to peer pressure when a student has been 'led astray'.

✔ *Tips*

☐   Put a de-motivated student with a group who are a little more motivated, to see if peer pressure can work in a positive way (although make sure the opposite doesn't happen by putting them with a group that is light-years away in terms of motivation).
☐   Explain to students how peer pressure works; i.e. part of a group's dynamic that members try to be as alike as possible in actions, interests, behaviours, values and beliefs in order to build trust and confidence in each other. Let them know that these pressures are common and natural. (*See* LOGICAL LEVELS.)
☐   Explain how some members of a group use peer pressure to force others to do things that they wouldn't normally do.
☐   Make them know that people will sacrifice their values in order to stay as part of the group and they will do things they may later regret.
☐   Above all, explain that they do not have to follow all of the actions of the group to remain part of it – they do have a choice.
☐   Help them to make decisions that suit them and not the group.
☐   Ensure that they understand how to be assertive without being aggressive, to get what they need.

★ **People Skills** enable us to understand and get on with other people. Many very successful lives and careers have been built largely on people skills when someone has no qualifications at all. It's not just *what* we do, but *how* we do it, that counts. Of course, qualifications provide greater choice for a student looking for a career, but there is equally no doubt that people skills make a massive contribution in how successful a student can be, not just in their careers but in life in general. The most important aspect of people skills is being able to put ourselves in someone else's shoes, and see ourselves as others see us. It is one of the most profound lessons we can teach. (*See Tip* 'Changing Places' in ATTENTION SPAN on pp. 14–15.)

It is easy to think that people skills are a gift of nature, something you are born with and blessed with. They can, however, be taught.

✔ *Tips*

☐   Never stifle inappropriate behaviour outright; explain *how* it might not be appropriate and in which circumstances it could be an asset.
☐   Build a student's SELF-ESTEEM by recognizing their strengths and pay special attention when they relate to others with thought and understanding.
☐   Provide opportunities where students can express themselves.
☐   Ask them to look at situations from other perspectives, as if they were somebody else, and if their behaviour is inappropriate ask how others would look at that behaviour.

- ☐ Get them to list their positive qualities that others, peers and adults, respond to.
- ☐ Have them tell each other what they think of each other's behaviours and how they would appreciate them even more (*see* FEEDFORWARD).
- ☐ Have them say what qualities they would look for in a friend and then measure themselves against that list.
- ☐ Until schooling covers 'how to be successful or fulfilled' these soft skills will remain secondary – except by your students learning from you and using you as a ROLE MODEL, even unconsciously.

Performance Based Instruction enables the learner to behave in pre-specified ways after the learning has taken place, e.g. enabling someone to write, edit and print letters using word processing software. It is almost identical to CRITERION REFERENCED Instruction.

Performance Management is a set of processes to improve the quality of teaching for everybody, especially the students. Every school has a School Development Plan, and within this are objectives and priorities. These provide the framework for performance management. By having these set objectives and a regular review of achievement, teachers are then able to improve their performance and professional development. The outcomes of these reviews can be used to inform grade and, therefore, pay decisions. Ofsted will review performance management to ensure that there is a close link between the objectives for school improvement and those agreed with individual teaching staff. Ofsted will also ensure that the objectives are challenging and well focused.

Performance Management Outcomes (PMOs) are, simply, targets.

Peripatetic Teachers are literally 'walking about', i.e. not based in a single school, but visiting regularly, e.g. music lessons, or supporting a specific child.

PFI Private Finance Initiative, is where a private company, or consortium, invests the money in, for example, a new school (or hospital) which it then leases or rents to the local education (or health) body. It saves the public sector raising large sums of capital. There is, however, some unease about the public sector paying for the private sector's leasing or rental profits.

PGCE Professional Graduate Certificate of Education (originally *Postgraduate* Certificate of Education) courses are full-time one year, part-academic, part-practical, and lead to Qualified Teacher Status. They are suitable for people who like putting theory into action (versus the GTP, for people who prefer learning on the job). Different courses allow students to specialize in, for example, primary or secondary education, with specific subjects. It is the most common entry route for teaching and can be based in colleges, universities and schools. While it is typically one-year full-time, it can be taken part-time, or extended to two years full-time if extra specialist subject-learning is needed. It usually involves classroom experience in at least two schools.

Philosophy for Children is in many ways the opposite of learning by rote. Rather than digesting facts in order to recall them, philosophy for children teaches them to question, think and understand. It teaches them to analyse the rationale behind facts and actions, cause and effect, how to listen and appreciate someone else's point of view, how to discuss and present counter arguments, how to disagree and make a case in a calm and logical way. It is a difficult subject to measure and examine, although the long-term benefits are likely to be great.

Phonemes *see* PHONICS.

Phonics are a key part in teaching spelling and in reading words (which later can be combined into sentences). It uses sounds (phonemes) and written representations of sounds (graphemes) which correspond reliably with letters or groups of letters. There are, it is generally agreed, 44 phonemes (24 consonants and 20 vowels) and 120 main graphemes (60 consonant, 60 vowels) in English.

Piaget, Jean (1896–1980) was an influential Swiss biologist and philosopher who pioneered theories of children's COGNITIVE DEVELOPMENT. Many of these have been, since the 1970s, coming under the microscope and his guru-like status is now being re-examined. Anyway, his general theoretical framework is Genetic Epistemology (how knowledge develops in humans). He believed there were four key development stages (which we simplify here):

1   *Sensorimotor* (birth–2 years approximately) where thinking is largely about movement (i.e. motor) and so children need lots of physical stimulation, play, and objects to move.
2   *Preoperation* (3–7 years approximately) where thinking is largely intuitive and internal.
3   *Concrete operational* (8–11 years approximately) where thinking is largely logical and depends on concrete reference experiences: children can be encouraged to move away from purely describing events, into thinking in terms of more complex hierarchies, classifications, types or patterns.
4   *Formal operational* (12–15 years approx.) where thinking involves concepts and ideas.

✓ *Tips*

☐   Tailoring material and activities to a student's natural capabilities is essential. We would never expect a baby (sensorimotor stage 1) to be able to hold a conversation about abstract concepts (formal operations stage 4). It could bore or disengage a child at stage 3 to think only of one-off events ('so what?') without a broader pattern of understanding to relate them to.
☐   Always enable a student to participate actively and feel acceptably challenged. But avoid asking them to perform tasks that are either way above their current cognitive capabilities, or way below.
☐   Remember, also, that in any group there will be students with a range of cognitive capabilities.

Plan Do Review *see* THINK PLAN DO REVIEW.

⭐ **Planning** is an essential for success in education, as in life. As they say (whoever 'they' are) if you fail to plan, then you plan to fail. In education there are three main levels of planning – long, medium and short-term.

■   *Long-term* plans could include how the school intends to develop, how you plan your career to develop and what a student wants in their future.
■   *Medium-term* plans may include how you take a student from one area of learning to the next, how you get qualifications to enable you to reach your long-term goal, or how you can motivate a student to change their path.
■   *Short-term* planning is mostly focused on specific immediate needs, such as lesson planning, arranging your weekend, and addressing a student's immediate needs.

✓ *Tips*

☐   Ensure that you spend time *each day* on short, medium and long-term plans, otherwise you'll always be fire-fighting and not having a sense of 'getting somewhere'.
☐   Even two minutes long-term planning a day can help to achieve long-term successes.
☐   Plans that are written down have much more chance of being achieved.

- ☐ Plans that are periodically looked at and changed have even more chance of being achieved that those that are made and not re-visited.
- ☐ Planning not only the content of a lesson, but the *state* you want the students to be in can pay enormous dividends.

    1 Start by understanding what state (of body) *they'll* be in at the start of the lesson (e.g. tired, as it's Monday morning; or frisky, as they'll have been very active just before).
    2 Decide how you want them to be at the *end* of the lesson (e.g. excited that they've successfully discovered something and understood it; or a bit spaced out with a 'wow' of understanding at a deep level).
    3 Then plan the steps from start to finish. It's unlikely that you could get from Frisky to Spaced Out in one step:

        - e.g. Frisky → Actively engaging → Involved → Thoughtful → Spaced out (i.e. A gradual settling-down).
        - or Tired → Thoughtful → Involved → Spaced out (i.e. Calm, low-energy).
        - or Frisky → Actively engaging → Excited (i.e. High energy throughout).
        - or Tired → Thoughtful → Involved → Actively engaging → Excited (i.e. A gradual upping of energy).

    Then

    1 Think what state *you* need to be in, to get them from one state to the next.
    2 What to *do* to get them from state to state.

This enables you to go with the flow of the group, not try to force material where it just doesn't feel right.

✗ Traps

- ☐ Effective planning can feel limiting to some people. It seems like it takes away their flexibility and stops them going with the flow. But planning increases your ability to be flexible where it counts – in *how* you do things. ('Success is having *fixed goals*, but *flexible means* of achieving them' to paraphrase William James.)
- ☐ Planning can seem to take a lot of time. However, effective planning proves to be a very time-efficient investment for the medium and long-term.

See also MENTAL REHEARSAL, THINK PLAN DO REVIEW, RESILIENCE.

PLASC the Pupil Level Annual School Census is statutory for all maintained schools, academies and city technology colleges. The data are intended to improve the management of learning, for the DfES, LEAS and schools. From 2004, maintained and direct grant nursery schools may also make a return.

Plato (approx. 427 BCE–347 BCE) was an Athenian philosopher who had a massive impact on the development of learning and education especially in mathematics, science and philosophy. He also believed that the interests of the state were best served if children were raised and educated by society as a whole, rather than just by parents.

Play is fundamental to the learning process, especially, but not exclusively, for younger students. Through play, children learn and practise verbal communication skills, thoughts, ideas, concentration, social, spatial and co-operative skills. Also, for so-called grown-ups, being playful at work is much more fun that being solemn: we all thrive when engaged on a human level, don't we?

Here are some of the many different types of play:

- *Socio-dramatic*: co-operation between at least two children through words, actions and body language.

- *Role play*: a child takes on actions that are within their experience or imagination and 'becomes' another person for the period of play (and helping them to de-role afterwards is vital, e.g. by saying 'I'm Robin, and I'm not playing at being Guy Fawkes any more, and what I'm looking forward to is…').
- *Imaginative or fantasy*: playing out a story, possibly with objects and costumes.
- *Exploratory*: where the children may be given props and other resources, but no instructions, so they can use their imagination and creativity.
- *Physical*: to develop necessary motor skills.
- *Free flow*: where there is no end product and the child has total control.
- *Structured or directed*: usually focuses on a process, where following that process is needed for the play to achieve pre-determined outcomes.
- *Therapeutic*: can also be one-to-one with pre-determined outcomes, and it is especially useful for children with behavioural and emotional difficulties.
- *Spectator or observational*: the child doesn't *appear* to be doing anything – they simply watch others play, to try out or model for themselves later.
- *Parallel*: children use the same resources but are playing separately, as in a climbing frame.
- *Solitary*: where they play alone.
- *Collaborative*: improvising a drama, for example.

✓ *Tips*

☐ Ensure that a wide variety of play is used, to stimulate your students – of all ages – and yourself.
☐ Explore new forms, and not just the type that you yourself prefer or preferred.

Plenary is a lesson or meeting of an entire class, or school, as opposed to smaller group meetings, e.g. 'we'll all split into our groups now, and get back later for an end-of-class plenary together'.

PMLD Profound and Multiple Learning Difficulty.

PMO Performance Management Outcomes are, simply put, targets.

Polytechnics were colleges that could apply for university status following the Further and Higher Education Act 1992. Most did. (And 'Anglia Polytechnic University' still proudly proclaims its 'poly' principles of open access and employability.)

★ **Portfolio Career** is earning your living not from a single job, but from a number of different jobs at the same time. For example, some people work simultaneously as authors, consultants and broadcasters. In teaching, a supply teacher could earn money in different ways when not called upon to teach, but a portfolio career is unlikely to become common in teaching. However, when talking to students we must remember that many forecasters see portfolio careers as the model for the future. Students are unlikely to follow the route of one job for one organization for life. In fact, we are sceptical that the concept of a career will survive: we will have a succession of jobs or projects that, hopefully, interest us.

★ **Positive Instruction** Before explaining the importance of giving instructions in the positive we would first like you to take a moment and *don't* think of a pink elephant. How well are you doing?! Well, in case you hadn't guessed, in order *not* to think of a pink elephant you must first *think* of a pink elephant, in order not to think about it! Similarly, if a child is walking with a cup of water and you say, 'don't spill the water,' their mind pictures spilling the water, and as their body follows the picture, they spill the water. Similarly 'don't run in the corridor' or 'don't go too near the edge' or 'don't keep shouting' are all likely to have the opposite effect to what was intended, yes?

(This is because when the brain is instructed 'don't…it sort of freezes, not knowing what to do. And so whatever it hears next, it gratefully obeys! Incidentally, have you noticed how dentists do this a lot: don't *worry*, this won't *hurt much*, it won't take *long*, etc.)

Teachers use 'don'ts' quite a bit – don't make a mess, don't make a noise, don't fail the exam, don't mess about, don't mess up your education. Where possible, and it is always possible, give instructions in the positive so that the immediate picture that you create is the behaviour you *want*, not the one you don't want.

Examples

■ Walk steadily to keep your drink still (vs. don't run and spill…).
■ Walk more than one metre from the edge (vs. don't go too near the edge…).
▥ Keep calm and relaxed. (vs. don't worry…).

✓ Tips

☐ Experiment with your own internal voice. When you are trying to achieve something make sure your internal voice is giving you instructions in the positive.
☐ Notice how quickly students obey (reasonable) requests if you ask them using positive instruction.

Possibility Thinking is a type of DIVERGENT THINKING, also called What If? thinking, used, for example, in BRAINSTORMING as a way of generating new options.

Here are some 'possibility' questions we might ask ourselves:

■ What assumptions have we made, and what could happen if these assumptions are wrong?
■ What other assumptions might be valid?
■ How else could we achieve this goal?
■ What do we expect to happen, and what might happen if that isn't the case?
■ What could surprise us, and how might we respond?
■ How would we get back on course if we are knocked off course?
■ What could happen that we haven't yet thought about?
■ What could go wrong?
■ What choices do we have that we haven't thought of?
■ What if we were the world expert in this – what would he or she do?
■ What if we were (say) Albert Einstein or Richard Branson – what would they do?

(This technique has been much developed in education by Anna Craft, one of our Advisory Panel.)

Prefect is a student given specific responsibilities and authority by the teaching staff. Their primary role is to help with the organization of other students. They are there also to support teachers, e.g. in helping to show parents around, and this role helps to develop leadership skills.

Prep (Preparatory) Schools *see* PUBLIC SCHOOLS.

Primary National Strategy (more commonly known as the Primary Strategy) was launched in 2003 as a vision for the future of primary education, building on the principles of the KEY STAGE 3 NATIONAL STRATEGY launched two years earlier. Key features include:

■ Empowering primary schools to develop their own curriculum and, therefore, character, while networking together to share good practice.

- Setting challenging but realistic targets for each student at Levels 4 and 5 at Key Stage 2, with LEA targets being set afterwards (rather than schools striving to achieve targets set by the LEA).
- Developing partnerships with parents and the community.
- Schools increasingly in control, and Government acting more as an facilitator, especially to strengthen leadership and professional development, for example.

(It has subsumed the literacy and numeracy strategies.)

Primary School used to be for students from 7–11-years-old. Although now supposedly replaced as a name by Key Stage 2, many primary schools still exist, some also covering Key Stage 1 (i.e. 5–7 years as well as 7–11 years).

Private Finance Initiative – *see* PFI.

Private Tuition is providing additional tuition to a student for a fee. As with private education, there is always a debate about payment for tuition; is it fair, does it put other students at a disadvantage? However, some students benefit greatly from either general help or subject-specific additional teaching. If one of your students is receiving private tuition it is best for you to be aware of what they are being taught and how they are being taught it so that you can ensure it is compatible with their mainstream education. Work with the private tutor if possible. It is not normally permitted to charge your own students for additional tuition without the full knowledge and agreement of the school authorities.

✓ *Tip*

☐ If one or more of your students is needing supplemental help, maybe ask yourself, why? We know of one teacher who was told that six out of eight students in a particular group were having difficulties understanding their lessons, and that their parents had to pay for private tuition. Instead of being curious to find out how he could help them more, or just help them, he responded 'well, that's how I've always taught, and if they're unable to follow, it's they who are at fault'. *See* LEARNING STYLES and TEACHING STYLES (especially, please, if you are that teacher!)

Problem-Based Learning *see* PBL.

Professional Unity is

1   A body campaigning for a single union for all classroom teachers.

and

2   The concept of all teaching and non-teaching staff working together.

Professor is a holder of a specialist chair at a university, or head of a university department. (In the US it covers all lecturers at universities or colleges, hence a common US definition we find shallow but amusing – 'someone who talks while others sleep'.)

Programme of Study (or syllabus) is a summary of subjects to be studied in a particular course, to achieve specified outcomes.

Programmed Instruction was devised by B.F. SKINNER who realized that testing a student's understanding of a lesson, at the end of that lesson or later, was less effective than offering material to be learned in much smaller steps, where students get feedback on their performance, step by step. In some situations the answers might even be given at the end of the question, to enable the student to understand the goal to be reached, and to find their own way to that goal. The actual sequencing of the steps is critical, and has been found helpful at all ages, and especially with students with AUTISM.

Prospectus is the marketing document that shows what students, parents and staff applicants can expect from a school or other educational establishment. It provides information on, for example, subjects covered, admissions and behaviour management policies, and its ethos and how it puts it into practice. It should provide information of examination results and value added, and may also include a governors' report. It should be published during the year preceding the annual admission so that parents and students can make judgements about the standards within the school. This will help them make choices, where choice is available.

PRU *see* PUPIL REFERRAL UNITS.

PSAT (US) Preliminary Scholastic Assessment Test is often called the practice SAT and is taken in the 10th and 11th grades. It is also the qualification for entry into military academies.

PSHE Personal, Social and Health Education.

Psychometric Tests measure, e.g., intelligence, personality and vocational aptitude. Many organizations use psychometric testing as part of their recruitment and promotion policy. No test claims 100 per cent accuracy, and they are best used as a guide to areas of an individual's psychological characteristics that the selection panel might investigate further.

✓ *Tips*

☐ You cannot 'pass' or 'fail' a psychometric test. It's more like a photograph of who you really are.
☐ Relax when you take them, as they are (largely) impossible to double-guess.
☐ But there are books available to give you practice, so at least you are part-prepared.

Psychomotor Skills aka Motor Skills are measured by how 'well' (e.g. how fast, precisely or accurately) a person can physically do something. (Not 'think' something – that's Cognitive skills. Not 'feel' or 'emote' something – that's Affective Skills.)

PTA *see* PARENT–TEACHER ASSOCIATIONS.

Public Schools are

▪ Long-established private or independent schools in the UK. (The first was thought to be Winchester in 1382.) Entrance is generally at age 13 and, where places are in demand, selection is made according to the student's performance in the 'common entrance' exam. Prior to age 13, the student, if in the private sector, will have been at a 'prep' (or 'preparatory') school.
▪ State (or City or Town) maintained schools in the US.

★ **Punishment** in society is complex, mainly because it tries to achieve a number of aims:

▪ Protect the public by taking the criminal off the street.
▪ Reparation for society and for victims of crime.
▪ Rehabilitation of the offender.
▪ Discouraging the offender from committing another crime.
▪ Deterring others from criminal acts by making an example of the offender.

If there has been an act committed in school that warrants any of the above, then the undesirable behaviour necessitates action in line with your BEHAVIOUR POLICY. (In education, the use of punishment should be a last resort, after educational approaches have failed. We should focus on reform and not retribution.)

✓ *Tips*

- ☐ Avoid punishing as much as you can by rewarding and encouraging: positive behaviour–prevention is better than cure.
- ☐ Never act on the spot out of anger or revenge. Losing your cool may be a reward in itself for the student. Be in the right emotional state (neutral) before you punish.
- ☐ Never punish by associating punishment with schoolwork, e.g. never say 'you've done wrong, so write an essay'. This makes essays into punishments.
- ☐ Punish in private and reward in public. (Public punishment can cause humiliation, a desire for revenge, and instant heroes.)
- ☐ Punish by withdrawing something that the student values and wants to keep, e.g. responsibilities, privileges, or freedom (detention).
- ☐ Before you punish be clear about your outcome and the way in which you will measure that outcome being achieved.
- ☐ Always consult with colleagues to find best practice, and check that your actions are appropriate.
- ☐ If in doubt, ask the student (or group of students) what punishment would be appropriate and review their response to it afterwards (they are often *more* punitive than would be proportional to the 'offence').
- ☐ Check with the student, after the punishment, that their behaviour will be different in the future, e.g. 'what have you learned?' and 'how exactly will you be able to act differently the next time this happens?'.
- ☐ All through the process, notice and manage your emotional state.

Pupils are students, in schools.

Pupil Referral Units are for students who, for a variety of reasons (e.g. behavioural problems, having been excluded) cannot attend mainstream school. They work closely with schools, parents and other agencies to help the student to re-enter mainstream education better resourced to learn successfully.

Pupil : Teacher Ratio is defined by needs and circumstances. For example a 1 : 30 or 1 : 40 ratio is common in some classes. In nurseries the ratio is often 1 : 10 to 1 : 15. But to ensure Health and Safety on a school outing it may be 1 : 20 or 1 : 10 or even 1 : 1 depending on the nature of expected risks.

PWD People with Disabilities – *see* DIFFERENTIATION AND EQUAL OPPORTUNITIES.

QAA The Quality Assurance Agency for Higher Education has – among other responsibilities – the Framework for Higher Education Qualifications (FHEQ), in England, Wales and Northern Ireland.

QCA Qualifications and Curriculum Authority is responsible for standards in education, training and qualifications – in schools, colleges and at work. It was established in 1997 from the National Council for Vocational Qualifications (NCVQ) and the School Curriculum and Assessment Authority (SCAA).

QTS Qualified Teacher Status has been awarded to all trainee teachers since 2002 who have met all of the standards and requirements set by the Teacher Training Agency:

- *Professional values and practice* – attitude, commitment, having a high expectation of students, and promoting positive values, attitudes and behaviour in students.
- *Knowledge and understanding* of the subjects you are trained to teach.
- *Teaching skills* – planning, monitoring, assessment, and teaching and class management.
- *Literacy, numeracy and ICT* (information and communication technology) skills.

Qualifications come in two categories

1   Precise ones e.g. a driving licence qualifies you to drive a car; or a CORGI accreditation qualifies you to work with potentially dangerous gas equipment.
2   Others (e.g. many exams) that only qualify you to take more exams.

See also MOTIVATION.

QUANGO Quasi-Autonomous Non-Governmental Organisation became derided as a term because there were so many of them set up by successive governments. And so NDPB Non-Departmental Public Body is currently the acceptable term. (And yes, there are thought to be many more NDPBs than there ever were QUANGOs.)

★ **Questioning Skills** are so important for teachers, aren't they? The way you ask a question determines the answer you receive. You can either open up a discussion, or close it down. Here are some examples:

- *Open questions*: these cannot be answered by a 'yes' or a 'no'. They begin with what, where, how, when, which, who and why. If you want to open up a discussion then use open questions to create plenty of space in which to answer. 'What seems to have happened?' will allow the person answering to focus on what they feel is most relevant. 'What do you enjoy most about school?' creates the space for them to express their preferences. 'Why do we learn about all the religions?' is an open invitation that will trigger varied responses.

✓ *Tips*

☐   If you get one word answers to open questions – e.g. dunno or nothing – try slipping an 'exactly' into your question, e.g. 'What exactly seems to have happened?'
☐   If someone says they 'don't know', but you suspect that they do have more to say, try 'I know you don't know, but if you *did* know, what might your answer/thoughts/opinion be...?' Allow plenty of time for them to think. It also helps them to visualize the answer if you look up and/or point towards the ceiling as you say this. (This works 99 per cent of the time with open questions.)

- ☐ *Leading questions*: begin with the same words as open questions but are directive. An open question could be, 'what does the bus look like?' whereas a leading question could be, 'what can you say about the colour of the bus?'. The open question gives you the freedom of the bus whereas the leading question focuses the answer onto the colour.

- ☐ *Closed questions*: limit the possible answers even more than leading questions and can be answered by a 'Yes' or a 'No'. (Although they *could* be answered with short phrases like 'I am' or 'That's correct', they could also use 'Yes' or 'No' if they wished to.) An example of a closed question is 'Is the bus red?'.

- ☐ *Why?* In open and leading questions, 'why' questions differ from the others. The others tend to elicit factual information. 'Why' questions seek the rationale behind the facts. 'Where did you go on holiday?' will create a different type of response to 'why did you go there?' because 'why' demands an understanding of motivation and decision-making processes. 'Why' questions are an effective way of getting students to consider the actions of others. 'When was the Norman Conquest?' is a question that needs a memory to answer whereas, 'why did William invade in 1066?' requires the student to have a greater understanding of motivations, pressures and political situations. (The same depth of questioning can be achieved by asking 'why' questions without the 'why' e.g. 'what was behind the invasion in 1066?' or 'what were the reasons behind …?').

- ☐ Have you ever been somewhere where the conversation is flowing until someone gently says 'Why?' and it's suddenly dead quiet, with everyone frozen mid-sentence? That's because 'why' throws a conversation into reverse – it's like slamming the brakes on, and throwing the car into reverse gear. 'Why' means 'explain yourself' or, to some people, 'Why on earth do you say/think *that*!'. We have a friend who gently cocks her head to one side, puts a twinkle in her eye, and gently and effectively, instead of using the 'w' word, just asks 'Because …?'.

Questions that test the ability of students to re-call information are often called lower-level questions, whereas questions that elicit their ability to understand and use their knowledge are called higher-level questions. (*See* BLOOM'S TAXONOMY.)

✓ *Tips*

- ☐ Before asking questions be certain of your objective and ask a question that suits that objective. Then ask yourself 'what even *better* question could I ask?'.

- ☐ If you don't get the reply you want, look at the way you asked the question as well as the capability of the person giving the answer.

- ☐ It is useful to know your normal way of asking questions. Either record yourself, have someone listen to you or pay extra attention to your questioning style when you're asking questions, and notice which type of questions come most easily to you. Then you can decide how to gain more flexibility in your style.

- ☐ After asking a question it is important to give the student time to answer. This may mean an uncomfortable period of silence but it is vital for the student to form their own answer. Being impatient or interrupting the silence will negate the value of asking the question in the first place. *See* WAIT TIME.

- ☐ However, if the pressure of the silence is intimidating, you could always offer to leave the question with them to think about for a few minutes/hours/days as appropriate. People think at different speeds.

- ☐ By saying, 'that's interesting, can you tell me why you think that?' in response to an answer, opens up more of a discussion and reveals the student's thinking process behind the immediate response.

- ☐ Many teachers find that statements can be more effective at stimulating discussion than questions e.g. instead of asking 'So how good a king was Henry V?', you could ask students to discuss the statement 'Henry V was a good king'.

◻ Another way to get someone to think deeper, is to place them in a dilemma that they have to think their way out of. It's easy to do, with a 'tag question'. Just tag something like 'isn't it?' or 'can't you' onto the end of a statement. Try these on for size:

- ▪ You got a bit carried away then, didn't you?
- ▪ You could do better than that, couldn't you?
- ▪ I think you should tell me what's been going on, don't you?
- ▪ You might spot another one at the beginning of this article, mightn't you?!

 Trap

◻ Be careful of asking *multiple questions*. These are a string of questions, e.g. 'have you been on holiday, was it nice, you look brown, where did you go?' Usually only the last question is answered.

Rs, the FIVE were originally devised (as three) by Bill Lucas (one of our advisory panel) as essential for lifelong learning, and learning to learn. Alistair Smith, Guy Claxton and the Campaign for Learning have also made contributions to develop these Rs:

- Be Ready and prepared to learn, physically and mentally.
- Be Resourceful to get what you need, to learn best.
- Learn to Remember, i.e. how you can make your memory work best for you.
- Be Resilient and keep trying new ways when stuck.
- Always Reflect on what you have done well, and how you could do even better.
- Be Reciprocal and expect some give and take with whoever or whatever you are working with.
- Be Responsive, or flexible, to the unexpected twists and turns called life.

See also RESILIENCE, and REFLECTIVE PRACTICE.

Rs, the THREE are commonly Reading, Writing and 'Rithmetic (no wonder spelling is a mystery to many people!). Originally they were Reading, Reckoning (problem-solving involving numbers or quantities) and Wroughting (making things practically, as in wrought iron).

★ **Radiators and Drains** is a concept we hear increasingly nowadays. There are, it suggests, two kinds of people:

- *Radiators* who are givers, radiating warmth to others.
- *Drains* who are takers, draining the energy of those around them.

It's useful to remember that we can all 'do' both of these if we choose to, but that most of us have one or other as a 'default'.

✓ *Tips*

- ☐ Enjoy being with radiators, but remember to look beneath the warmth for *content*, and beware of FAVOURITISM.
- ☐ Lower your expectations of warmth from drains, and respect them for the content of what they do and/or how they do it, rather than how they appear.

★ **Rapport** is what happens naturally and automatically when you are getting on with someone. It is a harmonious relationship even when that relationship lasts for a short time. It enables you to sense more easily what is happening in other people's minds by putting yourself in their shoes, and it is therefore easier to communicate and to be accepted.

If you watch people, and you can't hear what they are saying to each other, you can normally tell if they're getting on well by the way they are sitting. Rapport leads people to match or mirror each other in as many ways as they can, e.g. posture, mannerisms, eye contact, opinions, values and voice qualities. That's how you know who somebody on the phone is talking to – you can recognize the telephone voice that they use to match this particular caller.

✓ *Tips*

- ☐ This naturally occurring rapport can also be created consciously, by (subtly) matching or mirroring the other person in some way.
- ☐ When dealing with a class we can match their interests – not necessarily by trying to keep up with their tastes in music, but by showing a genuine understanding and interest in their aspirations and outcomes.
- ☐ You can practise building rapport in social situations. Simply match the other person in as many ways as you can, and notice how it changes the quality of your relationship.
- ☐ When matching, stay subtle – if they wave their hands around, you can just point a finger.

RE Religious Education is determined by local education authorities as it is the only compulsory subject, even though parents have the right to withdraw their children from the classes. (But students cannot withdraw themselves.) The 1988 Education Reform Act (England and Wales) requires that the main content of religious education in non-denominational schools is Christianity, while taking account of the other principal religions represented in the United Kingdom.

(There must also be a daily act of collective worship in schools in England and Wales (not Scotland) which often takes place as part of an ASSEMBLY.)

Independent schools are not covered by Education Acts, and policies will be agreed by their governors.

REAF Royal Society of Arts Examinations and Assessment Foundation.

Reception Class or Year is the final year of foundation stage, i.e. the first year in school.

Redbrick Universities is an often derogatory term referring to all universities except Oxford and Cambridge (Oxbridge).

Referral Orders are given by the Youth Court to young people who have committed a first-time offence and who have pleaded guilty to it (i.e. accepted responsibility for their actions). They last between 3 and 12 months, and should not interfere with the young person's education. There are two parts to carrying out the order. First, to support the young person so that they do not re-offend. Second, for the young person to undertake reparation to the victim of their crime, or to the community if there is no specific victim. All interventions are decided at a YOP (YOUTH OFFENDING PANEL), at which the young person plays a full part. You may well be contacted before this panel so that the young person's educational needs can be taken into account.

Reflective Practice has been practised for centuries, but in 1983 Donald Schön introduced the idea of the 'reflective practitioner'. Reflective practice, or reflection, is essentially thinking about what has happened, and then examining the beliefs, actions, beliefs about actions, and plans for future action on a continuous basis. Reflective institutions could certainly be called LEARNING ORGANIZATIONS.

★ **Reframing** is changing the perception of something by the way you think of it. For example, if you had a photograph and put it in a scratched and dull coloured frame it would look different than if you put in it a bright and shiny frame, although the photograph would still be the same. Reframing is helping yourself or someone else look at a situation in a different way, by the way you present it. For instance, if something goes wrong you can either look at it as a problem or an opportunity to do something different. Or if you find yourself with a difficult class you can either see the coming year as being very demanding, or as a way of stretching and improving your teaching skills. Reframing is finding the silver lining behind the dark cloud. The key to reframing is in finding a positive side to a situation.

Example

We were conducting a workshop and we asked everyone to go into their syndicate groups. And we mentioned, in a throwaway remark, that we hated the term 'syndicate' as it sounded so, well, cold and clinical. One of the group jumped up and shouted 'but I *love* that word – it reminds me of Chicago in the 1930's with all the syndicates trying to outdo each other!' And, with that picture in our mind, we now *like* the word 'syndicate'.

Refusers (or school refusers, or school phobics) are students who do not attend school for emotional reasons. Unlike truants who, in the main, decide they have somewhere better to go, refusers and phobics experience anxiety and stress at the thought of attending. The reasons for non-attendance can be similar to other phobias, e.g. the dislike of open or confined spaces, poor relationships with peers and teachers, bullying, academic pressures, a fear of specific lessons where they might reveal ignorance and lose self-esteem, problems at home or other traumas.

✓ *Tip*

☐ Early identification, extensive pastoral care and having a member of staff specifically trained to deal with such cases reduces the educational damage caused to refusers and phobics.

Relationships are the essential framework within which communication and learning take place. Whether or not it's teacher with students, teacher with colleague or teacher with head, unless you first take time to establish the relationship it is very difficult to achieve anything else. If you bluster into a classroom without any sensitivity to the atmosphere or mood that existed before your entrance, it will be difficult to take the students with you on the journey towards learning. You might be able to present them with a lot of information but how much they retain will be limited. If you read about PACING and RAPPORT you'll see the part that matching and mirroring play in building relationships. Taking time to build a relationship will pay you back handsomely in the amount of learning that takes place.

✓ *Tips*

☐ Pace the obvious; note what they would have noticed about the day and acknowledge it, e.g. 'it's very hot today and we'd all like to be at the beach, yes? however, since we all need to be here, let's think about...

☐ Show an interest in their interests. 'It's fantastic that the school team did so well and we're all pleased about that, yes? and now it's time to...

☐ The relationship framework creates the trust, empathy, safety and willingness to take risks that are essential for full learning.

Religious Education *see* RE.

Religious or FAITH SCHOOLS were originally the only schools in the UK, as offshoots from local monasteries or churches. Nowadays these are in a minority, but there is provision in the education system for them to select students and run their studies and activities according to the laws of a specific religion. Most faith schools want evidence that the family of a prospective student is active and committed in their religion before gaining a place. All faith schools tend to be sensitive to all sections of the community and are willing to work in partnership with the general community and other religions. (Being a faith school does not exempt them from the NATIONAL CURRICULUM.)

Remodelling (or to give it its full title, Remodelling the School Workforce) is the initiative to raise standards by helping teachers to concentrate on teaching. For example, teachers will have 10 per cent of their timetabled teaching time (that's equivalent to half a day a week) for planning and preparation, instead of having to find this time 'at home'. Support staff, such as TEACHING ASSISTANTS, with appropriate training where necessary, are increasingly taking over many administrative functions and other non-teaching duties such as invigilating exams. (NB while this is part of a drive to reduce the workload on teachers, some are concerned about 'unskilled' staff in the classroom, while others welcome the support.)

Remote Teaching is where the teacher is in one location, and the student is at the other end of a video link. In this way teaching expertise can be utilized, regardless of location.

★ **Resilience** (*see* RS, THE FIVE) is essential for every student and teacher. There will be times when teaching will get on top of you. You could be feeling less than enthusiastic. Maybe something in your personal life hasn't been going well. Then something happens at school and you have that sense that you need some space, but there you are with a classroom full of students all demanding to be stimulated. By you. Here are some ideas for increasing your resilience:

✓ *Tips*

□ Ask yourself what resources you need to deal with the situation, and talk with someone about how you might get them.

□ Remember the other times when your back has been against the wall and you've pulled through.

□ Remember times when you've been resilient, and what exactly you did to become resilient.

□ Take a deep breath and make yourself smile, inside as well as outside (sounds daft, but it works even if you're smiling at how daft it sounds).

□ Think of all the worse situations people face around the world and notice you're not facing anything so bad.

□ Create a picture in your head of how it will be once the situation has been resolved and there's no more need for resilience (and be curious how you managed to resolve it!).

□ *Keep* thinking of how it will be once the situation has been resolved.

□ Remember that Winston Churchill said 'when you're going through hell, keep going'!

Re-Sits From February 2004 candidates are allowed unlimited re-sits of GCE, VCE and GNVQ units, and their best attempt will count towards the final award. This was announced by the Joint Council for General Qualifications (JCGQ) in 2003, following a recommendation in the Tomlinson Report. Previously only the better of a candidate's last two attempts could be used.

Response Partners *see* STUDY BUDDIES.

★ **Restorative Justice** is a term often used to cover all sorts of community-based restorative approaches, where all the parties with a stake in a specific conflict or offence come together to resolve collectively how to deal with the situation, and to move on. Offenders have the opportunity to acknowledge the impact of what they have done, and to make reparation. Victims have the opportunity to have their harm or loss acknowledged and amends made. It is a carefully mediated process, whereby all parties can safely speak and be heard, with the victims fully involved in the problem-solving. It is increasingly being used in cases of violent crimes, and also in schools. Why? Because studies across the world show a 35%+ reduction in re-offending, compared to traditional court justice. Some schools use it only, e.g. for extreme cases that might otherwise result in exclusions or legal action. Others adopt a whole-school approach, and use it for staff conflicts also.

It's relatively new in the UK, although growing fast, and early indications are that some schools have reduced exclusions by two-thirds. (This is significant for a community, because 60 per cent of students out of school are thought to be involved in crime.)

✓ Tip

☐ Belinda Hopkins' approach is very accessible for schools.

Revision *see* STUDY SKILLS.

Ritalin is a medication sometimes used to have a calming effect in the treatment of students with ADHD (ATTENTION DEFICIT HYPERACTIVITY DISORDER) and ADD (ATTENTION DEFICIT HYPERACTIVITY DISORDER). As with any medication, Ritalin may have side effects e.g. appetite loss, irritability, depression and 'zombie'-like behaviour. The use of Ritalin, or other medications, would only occur after consultation with your Special Educational Needs Co-ordinator (SENCO) and a qualified specialist.

RJ *see* RESTORATIVE JUSTICE.

★ **Role Models** are how we learn to behave in different situations, by imitating other people, instead of hearing about it or reading about it. You, as a teacher, will inevitably be a role model for the academic side of school, and you will also be a model for the behaviours, values and standards that will support your students in life outside of school as well. You, and their peers, and other adults – especially movie and music and sports stars – will have a huge influence on them, whether you like it or not, or know it or not.

✓ Tips

☐ 'Don't do as I do, do as I *say*', does not work (*see* BODY LANGUAGE). Respect and authority come from the values we demonstrate and, therefore, the students' assessment of us as people. It doesn't come from our knowledge, age, status or ability to reward or punish. Authority comes from our standards and the consistency of those standards.

☐ If you want your students to be organized, punctual, well presented, enthusiastic and hard working, you must be that way yourself.

☐ Act like the sort of person you would like them to be.

☐ Being true to yourself is all it takes.

☐ Never speak ill of other students, teachers, or parents. They may be positive role models for some or all of the students, and you will have set yourself up as someone whose opinion is not to be trusted.

☐ If you make a mistake, find a way to acknowledge it and then move on to another subject. Remember a mistake only becomes an error if you don't do something about it. It's also called 'learning'.

☐ The best role model you can be, arguably, is as a learner:

  ■ While having a clear objective and destination for the lesson, show you are willing to learn new ways of getting there.

  ■ Ask questions in a way that shows you are curious, and are excited about learning something new.

  ■ Go with the class on its discovery as a co-learner, a co-traveller.

- Students will be motivated by helping you to learn something.
- You will also be modelling that it's all right not to know something.

See also GURUS.

Rote learning is memorization through repetition, mechanically and, most importantly, without understanding being necessary. It is the ability to repeat back information without having any knowledge about what may be beneath or behind it. Unbelievably, this ability to repeat back used to be one of the highest measurements of education that existed. Knowing historical dates, lists of Kings and Queens, place names and multiplication tables used to be of key importance. This type of teaching and learning is now looked upon as being old fashioned but it still exists, as it's a useful part of the toolbox for learning lower-level skills. (*See* BLOOM'S TAXONOMY.)

Rousseau, Henri (1712–1778) was a Swiss (not French as often cited) hugely influential philosopher, writer and theorist, whose thinking inspired many events, such as the French Revolution and Romanticism (the expression of emotional experiences rather than classical structures). His novel Émile (1762) launched a new theory of education that emphasized, in true Romantic fashion, expression instead of repression. It saw children as naturally good, and in need not of a rigid and standardized education, but of one that satisfies their needs, at each stage of their development. (*See* CHILD-CENTRED LEARNING.) He also believed that physical activity is an essential outlet for children's curiosity. And that the more stimulating a child's environment is, the more effectively a child can learn. And that children should learn how to reach their own conclusions – they should not be force-fed other people's ideas by a teacher. (*See* DISCOVERY LEARNING.) He was also passionately concerned about the wider implications for society, when educating individuals.

RSA is not the Royal Society of/for Art/Arts (which don't exist) nor the Royal Society (which does exist). It is the 'Royal Society for the encouragement of Arts Manufactures and Commerce' – a charity founded in 1754. It 'encourages the development of a principled, prosperous society and the release of human potential'. Until 1986 it also was responsible for the RSA Examinations Board. A key project is 'Opening Minds' – a three-year pilot in schools to re-focus education on competencies and technology.

RSA Examinations Board is now part of OCR. (The RSA introduced vocational examinations in 1855 for those who had left school. In 1859 it began its music examinations. Arguably it was best known for its qualifications in music and secretarial skills by the time it became independent of the RSA in 1986.)

RTP Registered Teacher Programme is normally a two-year course, customized to individual needs, for people who have 2 years' higher education qualifications (e.g. DipHE, HND). They are employed by a school as an unqualified teacher, and will need to study for, or complete, a degree. There are also specific GCSE/A LEVEL qualification requirements. A salary/training grant may be payable.

Russell Group, The of universities is an informal self-selected group of 20 of the larger, older, research-based universities in the UK. It aims to protect and promote excellence in UK higher education. (Meetings take place in the Russell Hotel in London, hence the name.)

   If you're curious, the twenty are Bath, Birmingham, Bristol, Cambridge, Cardiff, Edinburgh, Glasgow, Leeds, Liverpool, Manchester, Newcastle, Nottingham, Oxford, Sheffield, Southampton, Warwick, Imperial College London, King's College London, University College London, and London School of Economics & Political Science.

S Levels was the commonly used term for special (S) papers at A level, and are now known as Advanced Extension Awards.

SAIT Society for Auditory Intervention Techniques was formerly known as the Society for Auditory Integration Training. It was formed in the US in 1992, and their purpose is to help people with hearing difficulties, using training techniques and equipment. Since their results are somewhat controversial, any student with suspected hearing-related learning difficulties should be referred to a doctor via your SENCO Special Educational Needs Co-ordinator.

Sarcasm is saying the opposite of what you really mean, as a form of mockery. (The Greek origin of the word is sarkasmos, meaning to tear flesh, or bite your lips in rage.) For instance, if a student presents a piece of scrappy work and you say, 'my word, that is neat,' that is sarcasm. Sarcasm needs a victim. A common response to being the victim of sarcasm is silent acceptance followed by a calculated wait in order to get back at the perpetrator. This apparent silent acceptance can mask a great deal of pain. You can do a lot of damage with sarcasm and the resentment can last a lifetime.

✓ *Tips*

- ☐ Sarcasm is not a mainstream tool for learning.
- ☐ Sarcasm can be a form of BULLYING, trying to appear big by making others feel small. Sarcastic people often have self-doubt and are trying to bring others down in order to feel better about themselves.
- ☐ If you are a victim of sarcasm remember that the perpetrator was trying to be funny, but wasn't.
- ☐ You can deal with sarcasm by 'topping' it, taking what is said and extending it. For instance, if someone says how tidily you've dressed on a day when you've just thrown something scruffy on, mirror the sarcasm and just say, 'you should see me on a bad day' and then immediately change the subject.
- ☐ Invite the person with the sarcastic approach, maybe in a quiet moment, to speak to you honestly and openly as you feel they've got valuable things to say, and you want to feel you are on the same wavelength as they are.

✗ *Trap*

- ☐ Sarcasm is not always destructive! So long as you have a good relationship with your students, mutual sarcasm (without destructive intentions) can be a fun channel of communication so long as there's a twinkle in everyone's eye. It can also be a challenging way of learning by opposites (e.g. 'so you all want to stay for another hour do you?' or 'so you really think this is the best you could have done?')

SAT Scholastic Assessment Test (US) is a college admission test. (*See also* ACT: some US colleges will accept either test, whereas others will accept only one.)

SATS Standard Assessment Tests? Standard Assessment Tasks? were originally 'standardised assessment tasks' intended for teachers to use with their students. But they never happened, and even though national curriculum testing was introduced instead, the term 'SATS' has stuck. Anyway, they are a form of summative assessment that measure students' levels of knowledge, skills and understanding at the end of Key

Stages 1, 2, and 3 in England, and Key Stages 2 and 3 in Wales and Northern Ireland. (At Key Stage 4 students are measured by national qualifications.) Scotland has national tests at similar ages, but they are conducted internally at the time when their teachers believe their students are ready for them.

In Key Stage 1 students are tested in maths and English, and papers are marked by their own teacher, with a grid of specific skills to assess to ensure that marking processes and levels are consistent from school to school. In Key Stages 2 and 3 students are also tested on Science. (After Key Stage 1, SATS are marked outside of the school.) SATS measure the performance of both students and teachers, and unfortunately some use SATS as a political football to measure the policies of the educational hierarchy.

✗ Traps

- ☐ The NATIONAL CURRICULUM and SATS are both relatively new and both are under constant review.
- ☐ As with all tests, there can be a temptation to teach only in order to pass the tests. There is education beyond the SATS, and students only worry about them if their teachers make a big deal about them.
- ☐ There is much debate about the usefulness of testing children at Key Stage 1 as testing can create stress and make young students averse to exams and testing. Teacher assessment may prove to be a better form of measurement at this early stage, as currently exists in Wales, Scotland and Northern Ireland, but not in England.

Scaffolding is a structure around a building that helps the builders complete their task. And, that's exactly what happens when learning is scaffolded. You do not build the building yourself – that's the students' job. You (may) help them to get organized, support them when things get tough, ask them what resources they need, point out that they might question their last decision, refocus them on their objectives, offer resources they didn't know about, suggest they might need a break but NOT do the task for them. (David Wray is acknowledged as the key developer of this technique.)

Here's how, for example, scaffolded writing might be appropriate:

- The whole class experiences a text, which they all then discuss.
- The teacher then demonstrates the writing process with the whole group, for the students to model.
- Each student then does scaffolded writing with, e.g. teacher support and questioning, and maybe using a WRITING FRAME.
- Students then gain the skills and confidence to write independently.

Schemes of Work are available at, for example, www.standards.dfes.gov.uk (as at July 2004) to help teachers with lesson ideas. Each unit sets out learning objectives, suggested teaching activities, resources available to achieve these objectives and student learning outcomes.

School is where (in the UK) children become students from age 5 to at least 16. In the US this term is also used for all-the-education-I-had-before-paid-employment (i.e. schools, college and university) as in 'when I was in school I had more time to hang out with friends'. Also, in the US, it means university department as in 'my law school was the University of Michigan Law School'.

School Action is when a school must tell parents that they are planning to give their child extra or different help because of their special educational needs. (In pre-school this is called EARLY YEARS ACTION.)

School Certificate and Higher School Certificate were the General School Examinations established by the University of London in 1918.

School Council is a body of elected representatives who ensure that issues are raised and addressed before they become problems. Some councils have representatives from each school year. Some are facilitated by students themselves, others are facilitated by a member of staff. Some have staff representatives and some have parent representatives. They should have clear terms of reference so that their role and responsibilities are clear, and encourage genuine PARTICIPATION.

School Day Minimum weekly lesson times are suggested by the DfES, excluding time for collective worship, breaks and registration:

21 hours for students aged 5–7.
23 hours for students aged 8–11.
24 hours for students aged 12–16.

See also FIFTEEN PER CENT.

School Development Plan (SDP) is, hopefully, created from the chalkface up – what each teacher and group of students, then each department, plans to achieve in the next school year (for an annual plan) or in the next 3 or 5 years (for a longer-term plan, for example). This is then negotiated with the head, governors and any other interested party so that it can be 'bought into', rather than imposed from on high. It is essentially a costed business plan:

1   What we plan to achieve.
2   How we will measure these achievements.
3   How we will allocate resources in order to achieve our plans.
4   And how we will monitor progress.

Many schools still impose these from the top downwards (e.g. the leadership team, or the head alone) rather than develop them from the chalkface upwards.

 Tip

☐   The preferred term is now School Improvement Plan, which reflects Ofsted's expectation that schools should have a plan to improve specific things which can then be measured – by Ofsted. Some teachers object to the implication that their school is in need of Improvement, and prefer Development.

School Improvement Network *see* NATIONAL SCHOOL IMPROVEMENT NETWORK.

School Improvement Plan (SIP) is the new improved term for SCHOOL DEVELOPMENT PLAN.

School Leaving Age was raised to 16 years in 1972 after being at 15 years since 1947. There is much debate about the age at which a student should leave. Much of the debate centres on vocational and career opportunities once a student has left. Some people favour lowering it to 14 years, with a vocational apprenticeship to follow. Others have suggested raising it to 19 years but one must question the purpose of keeping people at school if they don't want to be there.

School Refusers *see* REFUSERS.

Schools Inspectorate is now part of OFSTED.

Schwartz Report Professor Steven Schwartz was asked by Charles Clarke, the Secretary of State for Education and Skills, to conduct an independent review of the options which English higher education institutions should consider when assessing the merit of applicants. It is due to report at the end of 2004, but an interim recommendation was that institutions should retain the right to make their own judgements in assessing applicants, rather than having to accept instruction from outside.

SCITT School Centred Initial Teacher Training is a practical one year post-graduate course designed, lead, run by and based in schools, often in partnership with, e.g. higher education and local education authorities. The emphasis, from the very start of the course, is on real-life classroom environments with an established teacher acting as a mentor. Many teaching assistants find the SCITT course a suitable progression towards teaching because it provides more school-based experience with students. Core subject knowledge is delivered in lecture form, and trainees have to complete both written assignments and school-based tasks. They are also assessed by their tutors and by external examiners from an institute of higher education in order to receive their Professional Graduate Certificate of Education (PGCE). The trainee is paid a small sum while training and student grants may be available.

SDP *see* SCHOOL DEVELOPMENT PLAN. (also the Social Democratic Party, which merged with the Liberal Party to form the Liberal Democrats)

SEBS Social Emotional and Behavioural Skills. (and also a DfES pilot programme of the same name, in over 250 primary schools)

Secondary Modern Schools were a major part of the state secondary school system, along with TECHNICAL and GRAMMAR schools, prior to the advent of comprehensive education in the 1960s. Students were selected for grammar and technical schools by the ELEVEN PLUS exam, and those not selected went to secondary moderns. They hardly had a good image, therefore.

Secondary Schools are for students aged 11 and over, and include COMPREHENSIVE, GRAMMAR and SECONDARY MODERN schools. They are all intended to become SPECIALIST schools by the mid-2000s.

Secondary Transfer Syndrome is the drop-off in performance and motivation many students, possibly as many as 40 per cent, experience when moving from primary to secondary school. A similar drop off can occur from infants to primary.

The reasons include

- Anxiety about the move from an environment where they are the oldest into one where they will be the youngest all over again.
- Where a number of primary schools act as feeders to a large secondary school, students have to adjust to losing old friends, and establish new relationships.
- Moving from an environment where they have control and status into one that is strange can make anyone feel insignificant and lost.
- The long summer break disengages students from learning in any case.
- The loss of the teachers, the building and familiar surroundings that have become associated with learning means almost starting from scratch again.
- A change in teaching styles and subjects from primary to secondary can be daunting.
- Constantly moving from one classroom to another, rather than having only one classroom, can be unsettling.
- Many people, in any case, just don't like change.

Initiatives that could help the transition are:

- A visiting day where primary students experience secondary school before the long summer break, so better informed mental rehearsal can take place.
- Having a one-on-one meeting with the secondary Head and HEAD OF YEAR prior to leaving primary school, to discuss expectations and anxieties.
- Better communication and understanding between primary and secondary teachers.
- Visits to the secondary school's after-school-clubs and extra-curricular activities.
- Better liaison and dovetailing of the final work at primary and the new work at secondary, with some joint activities.

- The use of primary–secondary co-ordinators to support the transition.
- Transfer of appropriate data and information from one school to the other.
- Primary students attend a sample of secondary school lessons.
- Parents are made aware of this potential drop-off so that they can pay special attention to support their children.

Selection is a contentious issue within education.

- Faith schools are permitted to select students based on attendance at a place of worship and commitment to a religion.
- Grammar schools select on academic ability and potential.
- Independent schools select on the basis of ability to pay and (sometimes) an entrance exam.
- Specialist schools are permitted to select up to 10 per cent of their intake on the basis of aptitude for specific specialist subjects (but not on ability; although the difference between aptitude and ability is difficult to grasp).
- And schools in OFSTED special measures are allowed to select-out students.

The reasons some schools wish to select students are that:

- Schools are measured by academic achievement and the 'better' the students, the higher the school's results. But the knock-on effect of selection on neighbouring schools is generally thought to be detrimental.
- They want to increase the achievement ethos within their schools, to create a critical mass of committed achievers to create a culture of success.
- Well-motivated and capable students are more satisfying to teach (for some teachers).

Selection would seem to be contrary to the concept of equal opportunity and fairness to all. As long as we permit selection and measure school performance based more on results than VALUE ADDED, it is difficult to see how an abuse of the selection criteria can be avoided.

Self-assessment is a way of students being objective about their own work and performance. By agreeing objectives and then having the student measure and mark themselves, against those objectives, you will enable them to

- Take responsibility and reflect on their own performance.
- Create their own development plan.
- Acknowledge problems privately, without risk to self-esteem.

It is also useful to have them review the work of another student, preferably one they do not know too well. This will give them a comparison with peers and, where necessary, a model to aim for.

Self-directed Learning is where students decide for themselves what and how to learn. They choose their own learning outcomes and appropriate learning strategies, while overcoming obstacles and monitoring their progress along the way.

⭐ **Self-esteem, Confidence, Efficacy, Image, Respect and Worth** are terms that have become interchangeable even though they have slight differences in meaning.

- *Self-confidence:* is a reliance and certainty in your own powers and abilities.
- *Self-efficacy:* is belief in your capability to produce the necessary performance.
- *Self-esteem:* is holding a good opinion of yourself, approving of the way you are and who you are, but not to the detriment of others.
- *Self-image:* is your perception of how you look, and how you appear to others. (People with eating disorders often see themselves as being bigger or smaller than they actually are.)

- *Self-respect:* is how much you like yourself.
- *Self-worth:* is similar to self-esteem but with a sense of measurement to your qualities.

The common umbrella term for thinking and feeling well about yourself is self-esteem, and it is of the utmost importance for learning. The more we can do to build a student's positive sense of self, i.e. their self-esteem, the more likely they are to apply themselves to their studies and avoid some of the pitfalls in life such as drugs, smoking, truancy and aggression. Students with high self-esteem tend to be confident when working on their own, are helpful to others, are proud of accomplishments, are enthusiastic and want to succeed and support others.

✓ *Tips*

- ☐ Do all you can to build self-esteem as the primary motivator for yourself and your students – if we can't respect ourselves, how can other people respect us?
- ☐ In an image-conscious world, students compare themselves to the most attractive and most successful in their age group, so encourage them to value their own strengths in absolute terms, not comparative. (A common way to have *low* self-esteem is to find someone who's had years of experience at something you're just starting, and compare yourself to them. A good way to *raise* the self-esteem is to ask how they think they compare to that person when they were just starting out.)
- ☐ When attempting to raise a student's self-esteem, base your comments and observations on reality. If you lavish praise where it is not due then you will be seen as insincere.
- ☐ Arrogance, conceit or a sense of superiority are normal indicators of low self-esteem. The bully almost always has low self-esteem.
- ☐ Do not confuse egos – the need to be admired – with self-esteem. Many 'famous' people have enormous egos and low self-esteem.

A Story We Like

Carl Rogers, the very successful psychotherapist, was asked how he did what he did. He replied 'before a session with a client I let myself know "I am enough". I am not perfect – because perfect wouldn't be enough. But I am human, and there is nothing that this client can say or do or feel that I cannot feel in myself. I can be with them. I am enough'.

See also LOGICAL LEVELS, NEGATIVE SELF-TALK.

Self-fulfilling Prophecy is making something happen because you expect it to. It works for both positive and negative expectations. Many fortune tellers use self-ful-filling prophecy and by telling a client that something is going to happen, the client is then more likely to make that prophecy come true, and wonder at the foresight of the fortune teller.

If a teacher has low expectations for a particular student this affects the student in two ways:

- First, the student picks up on the teacher's low expectations, and complies (or rebels behaviourally).
- Also, because the teacher has low expectations they put less effort into working with the student. When this happens it is often followed by, 'there you are, I knew they wouldn't make it'.

See also EXPECTATIONS, MENTAL REHEARSAL, and NEGATIVE SELF-TALK.

Semester (US) is the same as term (UK). US universities often have six semesters: the 'regular' semesters are fall (= autumn) and spring semesters, each approximately 15 weeks. A winter semester is approximately three weeks; and there can be three summer semesters, with a three-week pre-session and two five-week semesters.

SEN Special Educational Needs. A student is defined as having Special Educational Needs if they have a learning difficulty – whether because of high ability or low ability – and can, therefore, benefit from special teaching. This includes students with, e.g. physical limitations, emotional vulnerability, severe dyslexia or autistic spectrum and other developmental disorders. *See also* LEARNING DIFFICULTIES.

SENCOs are Special Educational Needs Co-ordinators, who have the responsibility for managing the effective delivery of the education psychology service, learning support, behaviour support, SEN assessment and parental liaison and support. A SENCO may be a specific member of staff, or in a small school the head or deputy may take on this role. In a large school there may be a team of SENCOs.

Senge, Peter *see* LEARNING ORGANIZATIONS.

Senior (US) final-year (normally fourth-year) undergraduate. ('Senior year' is the fourth undergraduate year in the US.)

Senior High School (US) *see* HIGH SCHOOL (US).

★ **Sensory Acuity** describes the skills of taking in information through the five senses. Teachers might, for example, be very sensitive to what people say, but not so sensitive to noticing their body language and non-verbal signals. Or they could be sensitive to how people look, and less able to understand how they feel. Developing our sensory acuity increases our ability to understand, relate to and empathize with other people. Encouraging students to develop their sensory acuity broadens their awareness of what is around them.

✓ *Tips*

☐ If you have recognized your preference for specific senses, make a point of practising the others. For instance, if you are very visual then sit with your eyes closed and notice what you can *hear*. Or if you are very auditory, then turn the sound down on the television and notice what you *see* that you may not have noticed had you been mainly listening to the sound;

☐ Look at your favourite authors and identify which senses they use the most and how you could enrich their narrative by introducing other senses or by using a different balance of sensory language;

☐ Taste foods you have never tried before. Visit a perfume counter in a store and notice how you would describe one smell compared to others;

☐ Encourage your students to use all five senses wherever possible, especially in talking and writing, and in noticing what they would not normally have noticed;

☐ Build all of this into HOT SEATING.

Sensory Preferences *see* LEARNING STYLES.

Sets and Setting (i.e. putting students into sets) *see* ABILITY GROUPS.

Sex and Relationship Education (SRE) is taught in either science lessons or PSHE or both, from Key Stage 1 to Key Stage 4. It covers – as appropriate to the age of the students – the physical, emotional and moral elements of sex and relationships. It is hoped that problems such as teenage pregnancies (we have the highest in Western Europe), divorce, relationship breakdowns, sexually transmitted diseases and the emotional turmoil many young people experience during their physical development can be reduced. Part of the function of SRE is to correct misinformation. (Parents have the right to withdraw their children from SRE. Students cannot withdraw themselves.)

SGNVQ Scottish GNVQ.

SHA Secondary Heads Association for secondary school and college leaders.

Shared Reading And Writing *see* LITERACY HOUR.

Shier, Harry *see* PARTICIPATION.

Sin Bin is slang for LEARNING SUPPORT UNIT.

SIP School Improvement Plan *see* SCHOOL DEVELOPMENT PLAN.

SIT

1   Slosson Intelligence Test, measures verbal cognitive ability.
2   Structure of Intellect Theory, is a 150-factor theory of intellect and intelligence constructed by J.P. Guilford (1897–1988) from various psychometric tests.

Situated Learning describes how human knowledge develops in the course of every-day activities. It is the opposite of 'inert knowledge' which can provide answers to exam questions but which is not easily usable by students when trying to solve a problem that requires that knowledge. *See also* 'ACTIVE LEARNING' under PASSIVE AND ACTIVE LEARNING.

SKA three types of learning, namely

- Skills (= Manual or Physical).
- Knowledge (Cognitive).
- Attitude (Feeling and Emotions).

Skills, capabilities, abilities and competencies are *how* we can put

1   Knowledge.
2   Into action.
3   For a specific purpose.

Skinner B.F. (1904–1990, US) was the 'father' of BEHAVIOURISM, *see also* OPERANT BEHAVIOUR AND CONDITIONING; and PROGRAMMED INSTRUCTION.

SLCN Speech, Language and Communication Needs.

SLD Severe Learning Difficulty.

SNVQ Scottish NVQ.

Social Learning Theory is a multi-faceted approach developed by Albert BANDURA that describes the importance of observing and modelling the actions of others:

1   *Observation* – noticing what happens around you and within you.
2   *Memory* – absorbing, coding and therefore retaining the learnings from the noticing.
3   *Activity* – putting the learnings into action, trying them on for size.
4   *Motivation* – including external encouragement and internal self-motivation.

It is the theoretical basis for many types of behaviour modelling and modification programmes, especially with aggressive and socially inappropriate behaviours. It encompasses three components:

1   Cognitive (thoughts).
2   Behavioural (actions).
3   And environmental factors.

(Many models are *either* cognitive, *or* behavioural *or* environmental. This one acknowledges all three.)

Socratic Learning (and Questioning, Debating and Discussion) draws out of students what they already know or are capable of formulating, rather than just telling them things didactically. This approach is named after the Greek philosopher Socrates (469?–399? BCE) and encourages students to develop their own opinions and values by considering thought-provoking open questions. (*See* QUESTIONING SKILLS.) It enables students to solve problems, make decisions, think critically, apply their own knowledge to a situation and develop, understand and articulate ideas.

Soft Skills *see* PEOPLE SKILLS.

SOI-LA The Structure of Intellect Learning Abilities Test.

Sophomore (US) is a second-year undergraduate.

Spatial Ability is the ability to judge distances between objects, and between the observer and those objects (e.g. parking a car in a small space). (It can also be the ability to recognize patterns and systems, and to know if the system is unbalanced and what is necessary to make it balance.)

Students with poor spatial ability may have difficulties with activities such as jigsaws or construction, or catching or throwing objects. They may also struggle with map-reading, and may be the ones who get lost on school outings.

Those with good spatial ability often demonstrate it in team sports such as football or cricket where an 'instinctive' knowledge of where their team mates are, and a precise 'knack' with the ball, makes them 'play makers'. It is as if they are one step ahead of everyone else, in knowing how the game is developing. Good spatial ability also shows itself in art where details come together to make a balanced whole.

Speaking and Listening are part of the NATIONAL CURRICULUM, and cover verbal communication, e.g. giving and receiving information, how to put your views across, and how to be attentive to the views of others. (There have been reports that these skills are less developed in the current generation than in previous generations, possibly due to more solitary TV and computer usage.) Although these skills are detailed under English, they are fundamental to all subjects as they help students' reasoning, problem-solving and discussion. (Embedded within this programme is an acceptance of variety in language, which itself is a model for tolerance and acceptance in all walks of life.) Interestingly, it's called Talking and Listening at Key Stage 1, and Speaking and Listening at Key Stages 2, 3 and 4.

Special Educational Needs *see* SEN.

Special Educational Needs Co-ordinators *see* SENCOS.

Special Measures is the term given to a school that OFSTED reports as failing to give its students an acceptable standard of education, or likely to fail. The governing body, with the headteacher and staff, will draw up an action plan to address the reported concerns within a maximum of two years. Frequent inspections, often each term, will monitor progress. If the measures fail to work, the school may be closed and a new school opened under the FRESH START scheme.

Special Needs *see* SEN (SPECIAL EDUCATIONAL NEEDS).

Special Schools offer education to students with specific difficulties who would not be adequately catered for in mainstream schools. These difficulties include, e.g. autism, hearing or vision impairment, and emotional or behavioural difficulties, as well as moderate to profound learning difficulties. There are pros and cons to having these students in non-mainstream schools, discussed in EXCLUSION.

Specialist Schools are secondary schools in England set up, since 1994, in partnership with private sector sponsors and with additional Government funding. They teach the National Curriculum, but augment this with subjects in their chosen area. It is planned that *all* secondary schools will become specialist schools (currently about

50 per cent are) by the mid-2000s. Current specializations, in order of 'popularity', include Technology, Arts, Sports, Languages, Science, Business & Enterprise, Maths & Computing, Engineering, Humanities & Music. They typically work within a grouping of other schools, not only for the benefit of the other students but also to involve adults from the community.

Spelling in English is more difficult than in languages that are more phonetic. Here is a strategy for spelling developed by Robert Dilts based on MODELLING expert spellers as part of an NLP project. What he noticed was that inaccurate and hesitant spellers tended to spell by sound, whereas accurate spellers visualized (i.e. actually *saw*) the word (i.e. the row of letters) in their head. When these 'experts' wanted to spell a word they re-viewed it in their mind's eye, and simply read it off. Try this for yourself, maybe?

1   Write a word on a piece of paper knowing it to be correct. Look at it and notice how it feels to see the word correctly spelt.
2   Place the letters of your word on a tabletop or screen *in your imagination* in your head, preferably to the left and just above normal eye level. Double check that your imaginary word and the word on the paper are exactly the same. Check that it feels right when you look at it.
3   Looking up at these letters in your imagination, change their colours or shapes. Try grouping them in smaller clusters. Add sounds or smells or whatever pleases you.
4   And then when they feel 'right', write down the word on a new piece of paper, or spell it aloud, backwards! (Since you are just 'reading' the order of the letters, it makes no difference if you start at one end or the other, does it? And it's much more fun for younger students to play subversively with the order.).
5   Congratulate yourself on all the letters you got right.
6   If any letter still needs some attention go back into your imagination and maybe bolden it, or add music or lights, until it feels 'right' again.
7   Repeat from 4 above.

Spider Diagrams *see* MIND MAPS®.

Spiral Curriculum is where you design learning experiences for your students, repeating things several times, but in greater depth each time. It is a type of CONSTRUCTIVIST LEARNING, building layer upon layer, to develop familiarity with the material. For example, you might start with an overview, and later examine component parts once the students have understood the 'big picture'. And then you might examine how some of the parts affect the big picture in more detail.

SpLD Specific Learning Difficulty which refers to a diagnosed difficulty such as DYSLEXIA or DYSPRAXIA.

Sport is an area where it is difficult to determine clear policies. There is certainly a strategy for students to have two hours physical education a week, and there is growing recognition that the sedentary lifestyles lived by some students is creating obesity and long-term health problems. (As with adults, too.) We need to increase student awareness of health issues and encourage them to take more exercise, and yet it does not seem to be happening. The health of our children is getting worse, in line with the decline in national sporting achievement, perhaps. Many schools refuse to have competitive sports for fear of creating losers (and yet they are happy to have students compete academically). Sport has traditionally been a practical way to learn skills such as leadership, competition, teamwork, co-operation, fair play and how to deal with setbacks and remain motivated. None of this is easy without adequate local sports provision and appropriate school grounds.

Springboard Programmes are INTERVENTION PROGRAMMES for students having trouble with numeracy. They operate in small groups, often facilitated by a teaching assistant.

SQA Scottish Qualifications Authority.

SRE *see* SEX AND RELATIONSHIP EDUCATION.

SSC Sector Skills Councils are responsible for developing the skills that specific sectors need (e.g. building, food manufacturing) by involving employers, government, trade unions and professional bodies.

SSDA Sector Skills Development Agency is responsible for the network of Sector Skills Councils (*see* SSC) and promotes effective cross-sector partnerships where appropriate.

SSS Scotopic Sensitivity Syndrome is a visual perceptual disorder. *See* IRLEN SYNDROME.

⭐ **Staff Meetings** can make a positive contribution to the running of, and communication within, a school, or achieve little except to waste time, energy and commitment. The key to successful staff meetings is having all those present focus on student, school and learning agendas and to leave their personal agendas outside. Irrespective of the atmosphere or tone of staff meetings, it is essential to be learning-focused and forward-looking.

✓ *Tips*

☐ If a colleague tries to take the meeting away from the matter in hand, say e.g. I know that's interesting but how does that affect the students or our reason for being here?'.

☐ If you want to make a suggestion, then connect it to an agreed outcome. For example, 'bearing in mind our need to get the new syllabus agreed, how would it be if...'.

☐ Remember to use phrases such as 'possibly we could...' or 'maybe it would...' (*see* FEEDFORWARD).

☐ Always behave in a way that suits where you want to go in your career, if that is different to where you are now. If you want to be a deputy head or head then behave like one.

☐ If you don't have strong feelings on a particular question then say, 'I don't have strong feelings, I'll be happy with the group decision'. This will show you to be a team player.

☐ If you are unhappy with the agenda, say what you would prefer, and why, before the meeting rather than during it.

☐ If there isn't an agenda, explain how meeting outcomes are as useful to you as learning outcomes, in preparing and keeping focussed.

Stafford Review of Exam Standards in 1995 prompted, among other recommendations, the setting up of the UNITARY AWARDING BODIES that now offer both academic and vocational qualifications.

⭐ **Staffrooms** come in different shapes and sizes, and with different smells, sorry, atmospheres. Some you long to go to, others you avoid unless you have to. Here are two extremes:

■ *Basic Belief – there is a scarcity of good things* – not enough to go around – so I'll hang on grimly to whatever I've got, and no-one's going to get any of mine! An atmosphere or culture of scarcity will have these 'qualities':

☐ There is not enough of anything to go round.
☐ You have to hold onto everything or else you'll lose it.
☐ It's best to keep yourself to yourself and not trust anyone.

- Ownership of chairs and space needs to be protected vigorously.
- Keeping information and knowledge to yourself is essential (except for gossiping just a little too loudly).
- Saying you don't get involved in politics, while creating 'situations' for others.
- Competing where competition need not exist.
- Covertly gaining favour and support, and making allegiances.

■ *Basic Belief – there is an abundance of good things* – more than enough for everyone:

- The more you give away the more you get.
- Sharing is beneficial for all.
- What goes around comes around.
- What's good for the students and the school will be good for me.
- The more I help others the more help I'll receive.
- I'm here to learn too, which means asking and receiving gracefully.

Example of abundance approach

A science teacher we know had never understood one aspect of physics that she needed to teach the following day. She opened up to a colleague, who got really excited explaining it to her. She stopped him, and asked him if he'd come and teach her class – and her! She reported that for the first time ever, she understood the physics idea. And, as a co-learner in the class, she modelled curiosity and a hunger to understand, better than just 'saying it' could ever have done. (A 'scarcity' approach would have been to keep quiet about not understanding, keep other teachers out of 'her' classroom, and pretend to know what she was teaching when it was obvious to her that she didn't, and would have been obvious also to her students.)

✓ *Tips*

- Whatever the atmosphere or culture of the staffroom, be true to yourself.
- If you are by nature abundant, then model that for others even if you get no immediate response.
- Giving away rarely costs you anything.
- Do not be drawn into being what you don't want to be.
- Understand how others see the world, *and* stick to your own principles.

Standard English is

■ Spoken English without a discernible accent.
■ Written and spoken English that is conventional and slang-free, so that it is as comprehensible as possible to as many people as possible, worldwide.

(English is probably no longer the world's standard language, however. 'American' has taken over with the dominance of American movies, television and music.)

Stanford–Binet tests are INTELLIGENCE TESTS. There are versions for pre-school through to adults, producing three scores:

■ *Verbal* – vocabulary and verbal.
■ *Performance* – picture completion and arrangement.
■ *Overall* – a combination of verbal and performance.

State Schools *see* MAINTAINED SCHOOLS.

Statement If a Special Educational Needs Co-ordinator (SENCO) believes a student has special educational needs, they can apply for provision for the student from the local education authority. This process cannot progress without the co-operation of parents or carers so it is important for them to be involved in the process.

The education authority will provide for the assessment of need, and should make funds and resources available to ensure the student receives the appropriate help. Part of the assessment is the collation of professional reports from external sources. When the education authority makes provision it is called making a 'statement' of special educational needs. This is a legal entitlement as set out in the 1981 Education Act. The student is described as being 'statemented'. The statement is a list of the needs and entitlements that the school is obliged to provide. A statemented student is also expected to have an Individual Education Programme (IEP) and an Individual Behavioural Programme if necessary (IBP). These should be drawn up and provided by the school. The statement is reviewed once a year by the SENCO, the teacher, a parent and an outside advisor. Whereas funds used to be allocated specifically for each statemented student, schools are now provided with a pot of money according to their overall needs regarding statemented students. Since having a student 'statemented' involves expense and obligations for the school, there are some that resist having a student assessed for statementing in the first place.

Steiner Schools are independent schools which focus on learning through play and creativity, and avoid formal teaching until the child is six or seven. Even up to age 18 they teach in a family-like setting with an emphasis on creativity. There is an holistic approach to spiritual, physical, social and moral development as well as academic achievement. They are sometimes called Rudolph Steiner schools, or Steiner–Waldorf schools, as they follow the Waldorf Curriculum, developed by Rudolph Steiner, the Austro-Hungarian (now Croatian) philosopher and occultist (1861–1925). Incidentally 'Waldorf' comes from the Waldorf-Astoria cigarette factory in Stuttgart which asked Rudolf Steiner to form a school for their children.

Sternberg, Robert (b. 1949) is a US psychologist whose theories cover creativity, intelligence, thinking styles, education and, yes, love. A major contribution to intelligence theory was his redefinition of intelligence to include practical knowledge. *See* TRIARCHIC THEORY OF HUMAN INTELLIGENCE.

Story Sacks can make reading more engaging for young students. You can buy them already prepared, or make your own. There is a sack of some description (a large bag would do), a story book that suits the age of the students, and props of various sorts that relate to the story. The props could be puppets, pictures, costumes or any item that occurs in the story. Then, as you read the story together, you reveal the items as they occur in the story.

✓ *Tips*

☐ Sacks you buy are put together by other people. Sacks you make can involve your students, by making or collecting all the items yourselves.

☐ You could expand the story sack with videos and CDs, especially if you are making your sack around a story of local interest.

☐ The whole group can tell the story they have created to other audiences, to increase participation.

Storyboard is a sequence of pictures that show, in chronological order, a plan for an event as it will unfold. It is like the format used for cartoon strips, and is extensively used to map out movies prior to producing them. For instance, if you were making a storyboard of a wedding, the picture in the top left hand corner could be the best man and groom arriving; the picture to the right of the first picture could be the two men standing in the church; the third could be the bride arriving; and so on. This representation helps students who have a visual preference and for whom logical sequences are important. It also helps students who find planning difficult, with its step-by-step approach.

Streaming is putting students of similar capability into ABILITY GROUPS or sets, not just from time to time for specific lessons, but on a more-or-less permanent basis. The idea is to have each stream progress at a pace that suits the students in the stream. The danger with streaming is making those in some streams feel inferior or without hope, if the concepts of 'higher' and 'lower' streams is ever voiced. After all, if they feel the teacher is giving up on them they might well give up on themselves.

See ABILITY GROUPS.

★ **Stress Management** is always too late, because the damage has been done. Of course, teaching is rewarding, but even a well-behaved class (and staffroom!) will be stressful at times. It is imperative that you take responsibility for your own well-being. Do not put yourself at the end of the queue when it comes to pastoral care. Do not put up with people BULLYING you. The key to stress management is nipping it in the bud, or, better still, prevention.

✓ *Tips*

□ Expect the unexpected, and deal with it calmly (otherwise you have to deal with feelings of panic as well).
□ Always discuss potentially stressful situations with others, to find new ways of managing them.
□ Recognize which students have deliberately tried to create stress in you and either talk to them about it, or find a strategy for dealing with it so that it doesn't affect you.
□ Be clear about your positive goals in teaching and keep them clearly in mind, rather than focus on potentially stressful events.
□ Plan and prepare in depth so that there is no self-created stress and pressure.
□ Take breaks.
□ Have a well-balanced life with interests (and friends) outside of teaching and make sure at least one day of the weekend is spent doing what you enjoy doing.
□ Have a good diet, and drink lots of water: know what you and your body need most and ensure that you get it.
□ Take exercise and be aware of doing whatever you need to do, to be in good health.
□ Don't over-stay at school – you'll give the impression of not coping, to yourself as well.

However, if you are already 'with' stress (and by this we mean unacceptable stress, rather than a good 'buzz') you might try:

■ Asking yourself the question 'what do I need that would help?' and listen to the answers.
■ Meditation, yoga, karate, tai chi and similar, are proven to reduce stress for some people.
■ If you have a particular student causing stress in you then talk it over with a friend or colleague, rather than keeping it to yourself.
■ Go for a walk or some other form of exercise.
■ Keep away from alcohol and drugs as stress relievers – they don't work beyond the first few seconds, and tend to compound the problem.

STT Speed of Thinking Test.

Student Associates is a scheme launched by the Teacher Training Agency in 2003. Undergraduates who are interested in teaching as a career spend two week-long placements in schools, to help them decide if teaching is or is not for them.

Student Counsellors are available for students in universities and colleges (and some schools) who need advice, or a sounding board, for personal and educational problems that they cannot resolve themselves. Each establishment has its own policy and processes when it comes to calling upon the services of trained counsellors.

⭐ **Students** are people whose job is to learn. We use this word interchangeably with 'learners' and 'pupils' all of whom

- As individuals have their own thoughts, feelings, beliefs, values, preferences, needs and identities.
- Collectively, are part of various learning and teaching organizations and systems (e.g. schools, colleges, universities, workplaces) and whose needs as individuals may be seen as:
  - ☐ Central (as in most learning systems).
  - ☐ Peripheral (as in, thankfully, fewer and fewer teaching systems).

Study Buddies are students paired together by the teacher to act as mutual support for learning. They are also known as co-learners and response partners. It is common to partner those with lower ability and motivation with those with slightly higher ability and motivation. Although this may seem unfair on the student who has the higher ability for the task, they will gain a deeper level of learning through supporting and teaching their buddy. The lower ability student will model the attitudes and behaviours of their buddy and, hopefully, be motivated and resourced to improve.

Study Skills are essential (for students and everyone else!) in order to

- Make the most of available time.
- Make the most of available brain power.
- Especially when there's so much to be read, learned and understood.
- And life to be lived as well.

And so your students will benefit from learning *how* to study and learn, alongside 'normal' lessons. There are hundreds of techniques and approaches, many of which are incorporated in ACCELERATED LEARNING.

- *Revision* is re-viewing work already done, in preparation for exams. For many students, revision can be a solitary, boring and arduous process. Here are some ways to help make study and revision more enjoyable and effective.

✓ *Tips*

- ☐ Use MIND MAPS® for note-taking and re-vision.
- ☐ Learn speed-reading and photo-reading.
- ☐ Think aloud and read aloud, as it involves your ears as well as your eyes.
- ☐ Have a realistic written time plan (and if it looks attractive, that can't hurt) rather than staying up late, cramming like mad.
- ☐ Have a STUDY BUDDY, or better still a group of them, as talking and discussing and asking questions can be more productive (and more fun) than sitting alone. It can also be fun to ask each other questions by turning study and revision into a quiz show, Or take it in turns to play the role of 'teacher', and teach the others, and ask and respond to questions.
- ☐ If something's less than fascinating, promise yourself a small treat when you've finished (*see* MOTIVATION).
- ☐ Re-view your notes (briefly) after one day, one week, and one month, to help the information to be more easily recalled in the longer term.
- ☐ And always, but always, discuss any study difficulties with someone who can help with ideas, suggestions, or support.

> **Top Tips from Gill Brackenbury**
>
> ■ Have lots of short breaks.
> ■ Above all, use all your senses – get hold of coloured gel pens with different smells.
> ■ Draw a humorous character next to a difficult formula.
> ■ Stick mini notes on your door/drumkit/posters.
> ■ Organize your work into a file with head dividers.
> ■ Draw Mind Maps® of each topic learnt and stick them around your room.

Substitute Teacher is the US equivalent of a Supply Teacher.

Success for All is a programme announced in 2002 to equip individuals with the skills and education they need to succeed. The four themes are

■ Meeting needs and improving choice through e.g.

    □ The SKILLS STRATEGY.
    □ Centres of vocational excellence.

■ Putting teaching, training and learning at the heart of what we do through, e.g.

    □ DfES Standards Unit–setting up the leadership college and developing strategies for teacher and trainer qualifications, remuneration, recruitment.
    □ Re-engineered 14–19 learning and training.
    □ Developing leaders, teachers, lecturers, trainers and support staff through, e.g. the NATIONAL COLLEGE FOR SCHOOL LEADERSHIP.

■ Developing a framework for quality and success.
■ Intervention with poor performers.

Suggestopaedia/Suggestopedia was devised by Georgi Lozanov in the 1960s. It aims to create optimal learning by using music and a relaxed environment as part of the key 'suggestion' that learning is easy, quick and fun – rather than so difficult and slow that the teacher has to present the material in small chunks which have to be practised again and again. (He talked of creating a 'state of relaxed alertness'.)

Material is presented in sequence, with stage 4 taking about three-quarters of the allotted time:

1 *Presentation* (overview of new material for learning).
2 *Active Concert* (material read emotionally along with certain high speed high frequency music, to 'install' it).
3 *Passive Concert* (material read neutrally and quietly to certain lower speed background music, to 'reinforce' it).
4 *Activation* (exercises and practices for students to explore the new material and its applications).

See also MUSIC.

Supply Teachers are employed to cover for staff shortages, and for permanent teachers who are absent through illness or other circumstances. The skill of the supply teacher is to provide continuity of learning, and to build a RELATIONSHIP with the students.

Supply teachers earn more for each day they teach than they would if they were employed permanently but there is no guarantee of work. Many of them work through an agency. If used extensively, supply teachers make a big hole in a school's budget, and continuity for the students is difficult.

Sure Start is an initiative set up and funded by the government to break cycles of poverty and educational underachievement. It aims to provide seamless multi-agency support for children and parents in disadvantaged areas. It includes a free part-time early education place for all 3 and 4-year-olds whose parents want one. Help is available for those with special needs, as are health advice, play activities, learning services, child care services, and support for families, parents, grandparents and other carers.

★ **Surprises** The unexpected will happen. What we do not know is what or when the surprise will be. No matter how well we plan, a sudden illness, a disruption or an unexpected visitor will come out of the blue. You can be certain that not all of your classes will go according to your lesson plan.

✓ *Tips*

☐ Control your own frame of mind. When the unexpected occurs, allow yourself to be knocked off balance for a maximum of, say, ten seconds. It's normal and natural. If appropriate, say something that paces what's just happened, e.g. that was a surprise for me, wasn't it? This will also give you time to think what you might do next.

☐ Do not expect you or your lessons to be perfect. Be as good as you can be in the circumstances.

☐ Have your lesson plan and fixed goals but realize that everyone has to be flexible with 'how' they achieve their objectives.

☐ Remember that no-one dies because of teaching surprises – they just get knocked off balance and then find a solution, or take a break to think of a solution.

☐ Be willing to say, 'I don't know the answer or how to cope with this.' Ask the class for answers and make your recovery plan a group activity. And don't feel 'stupid' – how can everyone be expected to know what's around the next corner?

☐ Always, even in the busy schedule, build in some slack time to make room for the unexpected. It will always happen.

☐ Find a way of learning from the unexpected, and then it will have a positive pay-off for you, and increase your motivation to deal well with surprises.

Syllabus is a PROGRAMME OF STUDIES.

Synthesis is constructing something new from existing parts, e.g. designing something that achieves specific objectives, or rearranging what already exists in order to satisfy new needs.

✓ *Tip*

☐ To examine someone's ability to synthesize, ask questions beginning with, e.g. synthesize, create, design, invent, devise, what if? (See also BLOOM'S TAXONOMY.)

Systems/Systemic Thinking is seeing beyond what appear to be isolated and independent incidents, to see deeper patterns. It is recognizing connections between separate events so that you are better able to understand and influence them. It is understanding the effect on the whole system, and the elements in a system, of changing one element.

Examples

■ We are all familiar with feeling very tired, knowing that the tiredness will create an illness of some sort that forces us to rest our bodies. (The body is a system and parts of it do not function independently without having an influence on the other parts.)

■ You cannot give one child at a party a cake without finding the other children suddenly become upset in order to get their cake.

- A class of students is a system. You cannot deal with one student without making a change of some sort to the other students. That change may not be great, but there will be a change.
- The education system is by definition a system. A class, a family, an individual are all systems. Any contact with any part of any of those systems will have an impact on the rest.

✓ *Tip*

□ When taking action always consider what that action may lead to, what will be the ramifications, what else within the system may be affected.

TA *see* (1) TEACHING ASSISTANTS and (2) TRANSACTIONAL ANALYSIS.

Tacit Knowledge is the knowledge we acquire without consciously knowing we have acquired it. It comes from our observations and interactions with our work, family and social environments. It's often the result of INFORMAL LEARNING.

TACS Teacher Associate Credit Scheme is a pilot programme for people who are interested in seeing if teaching is for them. If they are studying for a degree that does not lead to Qualified Teacher Status, and if they satisfy the ITT entry requirements, it enables them to work in schools to build an experience-based portfolio.

TAG Talented And Gifted students. Because they can seem self-reliant they can be overlooked and then become disaffected.

✓ *Tips*

□ We believe that each and every person has their own Talents and Gifts, to be continually discovered and nurtured.
□ We never believe that a student is 'no good' at something – we personally accept responsibility for not yet having found a way of engaging that student.
□ We never believe that we 'don't have time' (e.g. for finding ways to engage students), as *investing* time pays huge dividends in both time and energy savings, and reduces frustrations on both sides. A stitch *in time* saves nine. (*See* TIME MANAGEMENT)
□ We always ask 'So what needs to happen for you to find this subject easier/more interesting/less boring etc.?' rather than trying to guess, or to impose our own preferences onto someone else.

★ **Talents** are all around us if we choose to see them; and everybody has talents of some sort. It is important for students' self-esteem to have their talents recognised and, as you will see in SELF-ESTEEM, this is a prerequisite for good academic performance. The difficulty with talent is that we all too often tend to view it within a specific context. A sports teacher will respond to talent of a sporting nature. A maths teacher will respond to excellence in maths.

✓ *Tips*

□ If you are taking a subject in which a particular student has little aptitude, ensure you refer to their talents in other areas. Do all you can to make a student associate your subject with feeling good about themselves.
□ Value all talents equally, irrespective of context, if you want to build SELF-ESTEEM.
□ Recognize your own talents in all areas of your life and keep reminding yourself of them, especially after a hard day!

Talking and Listening is now in the National Curriculum for Key Stage 1 – *see* SPEAKING AND LISTENING.

Talking Heads is a network for headteachers in England. *See* NATIONAL COLLEGE FOR SCHOOL LEADERSHIP.

TEA-Ch Test of Everyday Attention for Children – *see* ATTENTION SPAN.

Teacher Support Line used to be called TEACHERLINE. *See* TEACHER SUPPORT NETWORK.

Teacher Support Network is a national organization that provides practical and emotional support to teachers, lecturers and their families www.teachersupport.info (as at June 2004). It also runs the TEACHER SUPPORT LINE (formerly Teacherline) on 08000 562 561.

Teacher Training *see* ITT.

Teacherline is now called TEACHER SUPPORT LINE. *See* TEACHER SUPPORT NETWORK.

Teachernet is a huge online resource, developed by the DfES, at www.teachernet.gov.uk (as at June 2004).

Teachers facilitate learning. They don't impart it, or give it – it's not theirs to give. (Well, their own learnings are available to give, but they are probably not completely appropriate for other people's consumption.) Teachers motivate, inspire, understand, engage, support, form relationships, train, coach, encourage, persevere and above all are constantly learning. A teacher shapes the future, by playing a major part in the fulfilment of many lives. Yes, it can be demanding, and yes, it should be rewarding because there are few occupations that are more important. (But if you feel like the person in this 'joke', get help quickly):

Q. What is a teacher?
A. A bitter and twisted person who used to think they liked children.

Teachers Magazine was launched in 1999 by the Department for Education and Skills, for teachers in England. There are versions for both the primary and secondary sectors, for teachers, heads of department, senior teachers and head teachers.

★ **Teaching** is (and there are hundreds of other definitions) making learning easy.

Teaching Assistants (TA) are also known as classroom assistants and learning support assistants and work under the direction of, and provide learning support to, teachers. Their role is increasing in importance and scope, and there are several routes for them to study to become teachers, if interested. They may have general roles, or specific responsibility for specific students, often with learning difficulties or special needs. They may have organizational responsibilities (e.g. preparing classroom materials) as well as educational responsibilities.

Teaching Space is where exactly in the classroom a teacher teaches. It is, importantly, not the part of the classroom from which, for example, the teacher reprimands a student. It is good practice to keep these two spaces very separate, so that when a teacher heads towards the teaching space, the class knows what will be expected of them. Similarly, when the teacher heads towards the reprimand space, to deliver a reprimand, the class knows what's coming, and often the offending behaviour will cease before the reprimand needs to be delivered. It is particularly important not to 'contaminate' the teaching space with reprimands, or any other potential unpleasantness, so as to avoid associating unpleasantness with teaching and learning.

★ **Teaching Styles** (Before reading this section, it might be useful to read LEARNING STYLES.)

We process information through our five senses in an individual way in order to learn. We all have personal learning preferences, e.g. needing to see the big picture before being able to pay attention to the detail; or needing to see a lesson within a context. The more we satisfy our students' personal learning preferences, the more they will learn.

Example

One student we know was classed as a 'dreamer' by the teaching staff (this was a derogatory observation). But when we observed him 'dreaming' it was always in classes where the teacher read to the class. It was evident that he was very low AUDITORY and when a teacher was reading he needed to look away to make pictures in his head in order to understand.

Some teaching styles, from the thousands of theories, models and ideas that are available, include – and all have their place:

- *Talk and Chalk:* auditory and visual and probably without any KINAESTHETIC.
- *Discovery:* appeals to the creative and kinaesthetic as well as visual and auditory.
- *Authoritarian, formal and didactic:* lean towards learning by rote, and favours those with a strong auditory memory. (This can suit students who are good at exams but less effective at really understanding the learning.)
- *Child-centred:* needs the teacher to have the flexibility to match the needs of the student.

✓ Tips

- ☐ Your teaching style(s) should be flexible to meet students' learning style needs and not the other way round.
- ☐ You will always have a variety of learning styles within a class so keep varying your teaching styles to enable everyone to learn from you – be generous with your flexibility.
- ☐ Never assume that students have the same learning style as you. Know your own preferences and the ways you filter information, and recognize that they will only suit some of your class.
- ☐ Use their BODY LANGUAGE to judge their engagement and change your style if they are not engaged.
- ☐ A high proportion of teachers are, it seems to us, high AUDITORY whereas a high proportion of disaffected students are high KINAESTHETIC – and they need to be *actively* engaged!

See also CLASSROOM STAGECRAFT.

Team Spirit and group spirit encourage students to do their best for both personal and group goals. Working within a group develops a student's awareness of others, teaches communication skills, forms friendships and creates a dynamic that will help the group to be self-regulating, self-supporting and able to resolve issues without needing a teacher.

✓ Tips

- ☐ Games, sports, charity events, ability groups and projects are all effective ways for team building.
- ☐ If you yourself can be part of the team or group without losing authority, you will benefit from the mutual support – and if this is not possible with your colleagues or students, please ensure that you have support from outside school (or change your school!).

TEC

1   Technician Education Council was established in 1973 by Margaret Thatcher, when Secretary of State for Education & Science, to satisfy employers' skills requirements. It established a unified system for technical education and introduced Ordinary National Diplomas (ONDs) and Higher National Certificates and

Diplomas (HNC/Ds) and eventually took over the validation of further and higher education courses.

2 Training and Enterprise Councils, superseded by Learning and Skills Councils in 2001.

Technical Schools were part of the state secondary school system, along with SECONDARY MODERN and GRAMMAR schools, prior to the advent of comprehensive education. Students with a more academic aptitude were selected for grammar schools, and those with a more practical aptitude were selected by technical schools, by the 11 PLUS exam. (Those not selected went to secondary moderns.) In reality, very few technical schools existed.

Technology Colleges can be SPECIALIST secondary schools, or FE Further Education colleges.

Teletutoring is literally tutoring or teaching at a distance, e.g. by sending and receiving assignments and feedback by email, post, or text messaging.

Terms currently are three per year – autumn, spring and summer. There are also (controversial) proposals for a six-term year, with seven-week terms and a five-week break in the summer. This is to avoid student and teacher overload.

Tests, Examinations, Exams are designed in principle for 'testing' 'examining' or 'evaluating' a student's abilities, but there are other factors that can cloud 'results', e.g.

■ The student's ability to understand the task itself.
■ Their capacity to see, hear and comprehend the instructions and materials.
■ Their mental and motor abilities to execute the task.
■ Environmental distractions, e.g. too hot, cold, noisy, airless.
■ Personal distractions, e.g. hungry, thirsty, personal concerns.

There is, therefore, much discussion as to what exactly they are testing (e.g. a student's ability to remember exact information under time pressures when too hot on a Friday afternoon after a week of other tests?) and how reliable the results are (e.g. would the student's results be the same on a cool Monday morning?).

Theories *see* MODELS.

Think Plan Do Review is an elegant PLANNING strategy for learning, teaching and, actually, life:

■ *Think* about the topic, lesson, holiday – or whatever you are planning. Think about *all* the options that are open to you, or might be if you wanted them enough, and all the possibilities that other people might see, that you haven't seen, yet. Think about all the aims that you might want to achieve, and the benefits to all those involved including you.
■ *Plan* how you could achieve all that you want to achieve

　□ Outcomes.
　□ Methodology.
　□ Timescales.
　□ Resources needed.
　□ Evidence that you've achieved what you've set out to achieve.
　□ Communication to all involved parties, so that they feel involved and not excluded.

■ *Do* what you've planned, checking from time to time that you are (all) still happy with the plan.

- *Review* what worked well for you, what you've learned, what you might do better or differently in the future. (This REFLECTION is an integral part of key learning theories, where the learning is integrated with the event, i.e. the event isn't complete until the review has taken place.)

This is based on David Weikart's 'Plan Do Review' process developed in the US in the 1960s, which is still an important component of the HIGH/SCOPE curriculum.

Thinking Skills are mental processes for handling information. They help us to make choices and to be creative, for example. BLOOM'S TAXONOMY is a useful guide. Other examples of a more everyday nature could include

- *Elaboration* – e.g. building on ideas.
- *Flexibility* – e.g. seeing other perspectives easily.
- *Fluency* – e.g. producing ideas.

See also CONVERGENT THINKING, CREATIVITY, CRITICAL THINKING, COGNITION, and METACOGNITION.

THRASS® is a widely used PHONICS/LITERACY programme.

Time Line is a linear representation of time.

Examples

- A sequence of pictures of monarchs on the wall, in the order in which they reigned.
- If you were discussing a political event, you could lay out the sub-events in the order in which they took place, to show how one action triggered another.
- If you were covering evolution you could lay out a time line on the floor, to scale, so that students could see how recent the arrival of human beings was in the history of our planet.

It is potentially an excellent multi-sensory activity:

- The pictorial representation helps those students whose dominant sense is VISUAL, and those who need to see a context in which to understand events.
- The physicality of separating the events helps KINAESTHETICALLY too.
- And, naturally, the explanations and discussions are full of AUDITORY stimulation.

★ **Time Management** is somewhat essential for a teacher, especially if your WORK–LIFE BALANCE is important to you. And no-one else can manage your time for you (although they might well try!). So, take control.

✗ Traps

- ☐ People who DELEGATE often tell us not only *what* they need us to do but *how* to do it. By all means accept *what* they ask for (although you might want to be familiar with HOW TO SAY 'NO'). But work out your own way of *how* to do it. It probably will take less time and be more satisfying, as you'll be doing it 'your way'.

By the way, we're fascinated by the parallels between time, and money:

- ☐ You can 'spend', 'waste', and 'fritter away' both time and money.
- ☐ You can also 'invest' time, and 'save' time as a result – it really 'pays dividends'.
- ☐ But you can't live forever on 'borrowed' time, and unless you 'manage' it wisely you can 'run out' and end up stressed or worse.

✓ Tips

- ☐ Make the task fit the time, rather than the other way round.
- ☐ Always discuss what you can and can't do, realistically (*see* the first *Tip* under CREATIVITY on p. 38).

☐ Avoid saying

1   'Yes' and then (to yourself).
2   'Why on earth did I say Yes to that?!'.

Try, instead, saying something like 'I'd love to, but let me get back to you once I check my diary/schedule'.

☐ Remember, if you don't manage your own time, no-one else will.

Time Out is a sporting term meaning to take an ad hoc break to regroup and rethink tactics. (It is sometimes indicated by forming a 'T' with your hands.) In education it is useful when a student (or teacher) needs to take a break, maybe to calm down, or to consider how to defuse a situation, for example. The use of time out can break an unpleasant atmosphere or indicate that a class needs to rethink its behaviour. Some students are given a time out card that specifies an agreed quota of time outs that they can use in a day. So, for example, if a student is under stress at home, they might have a card that allows them to take two 5-minute breaks a day, and by simply showing the card to a member of staff, they don't have to explain all over again what's going on.

TLA Three Letter Acronym – believed to be easier to remember and pronounce than the full name e.g. BBC (British Broadcasting Corporation), LSC (Learning and Skills Council), LEA (Local Education Authority) and TLA itself.

T-Learning is learning using interactive TV.

TLF Teaching and Learning in the Foundation subjects is a key part of the National Strategy for KEY STAGE 3 and covers teaching approaches to (typically) art and design, design and technology, geography, history, modern foreign languages, music, physical education and religious education.

Tomlinson Working Group on 14-19 Reform was set up to address the problem that some 50 per cent of young people are labelled, educationally, as failures at age 16. The group, chaired by Mike Tomlinson, the former head of Ofsted, has a brief to report on long-term solutions by the end of 2004.

Training Bursaries (formerly known as Training Salaries) are paid to some trainee teachers with funds provided by the Teacher Training Agency. Courses must be at post-graduate level, lead to QUALIFIED TEACHER STATUS and be provided by an institution in England.

Training Salaries *see* TRAINING BURSARIES.

★ **Transactional Analysis** (TA) is a model that describes the communication exchanges between people and, therefore, types of relationships and how to improve them. It was developed by Eric Berne (1910–1970), the Polish psychiatrist and psychologist who migrated to Canada at the age of 5. TA has continued to develop in many ways but we will keep essentially to the original thinking as this provides a simple and elegant model.

It is much used in therapy, counselling, and organizational development. In education it is frequently used to understand and modify relationships between teacher and student, student and student, and teacher and head teacher. The value of the model is to become aware of our normal and automatic responses to other people and situations, and to know that we have other choices in the way we can respond.

Berne's model is based on the personality having three 'ego states'. Each of these is a system of thought, feelings and behaviours. The labels applied to these ego states are Parent, Adult and Child. We all have all three of them and may access any one or any combination to suit the situation we are in. When it is time to play, we can play. When it is time to be serious, we can be serious. Here are the basic categories, without the subdivisions that form part of the fuller model:

■ *Parent ego state*: This part of us is predominantly *opinions*, based often on the huge collection of mental recordings gathered from the parental figures of our early years that we store and comply with without question. (*See also* NEGATIVE SELF-TALK.) As the name implies, most of the information came from our parents although other authority figures (like teachers) can add to the 'tapes' that run through our head and influence our behaviour.

■ *Adult ego state*: This part of us is predominantly *facts*. It thinks logically for itself. It gathers in information, and makes rational decisions. It listens to both the Parent ego and the Child ego, evaluates all the data, and makes predictions.

■ *Child ego state:* This part of us is instinctive and natural, and is formed in our early years not from words but from feelings and experiences.

Examples of transactions

■ *Adult to adult*: is logical, based on facts. Full stop. Transactions (i.e. discussions, conversations, memos) are relatively short, and likely to be conclusive with clear actions agreed. It may not be a lot of fun but it is a good way to discuss a student's problems or ambitions with another member of staff or a parent. Adult is also a good state to be in when planning, getting organized or reviewing performance. Note that there is no emotion, attitude, fun or playfulness here. Just facts.

■ *Parent to parent*: is where both parties discuss what they 'believe' is 'best' in their 'opinion'. The conversation is not likely to be short or conclusive, unless both sides have the same opinion (in which case it will quickly switch into an adult-adult plan of action). But it may not be well thought through as the facts (adult) and feelings (child) will have been under-represented.

■ *Child to child*: This is likely to be a lot of fun but may not produce results.

■ *Parent to child*: This is a key interaction where status and age try to create a sense of control. It can come across as nurturing, or patronizing (e.g. 'I think you should all work harder' could work in several ways, depending on body language, intonation and the perception of the audience). The common responses to this are either compliance, or rebellion.

✗ **Trap**

☐ A teacher projecting authority may well observe a sea of apparently compliant faces in front of them, but behind this veneer could be ingenious rebellion taking the most cunning of forms.

Transdisciplinary *see* INTERDISCIPLINARY.

Transmission Model of human communication (notably Shannon and Weaver working in the 1940s in Bell telephone laboratories in the US) was taken from the fields of information theory and cybernetics, and is now thought to be largely misleading when applied to humans. Why? Well, Shannon and Weaver suggested three stages of communication:

1 *Technical*: i.e. how accurately the message is transmitted.
2 *Semantic*: i.e. how precisely the meaning is 'conveyed'.
3 *Effect or effectiveness*: i.e. how effectively the received meaning affects behaviour.

They suggested that improving the technical accuracy of human communication would lead to semantic or effectiveness improvements at the other levels. Maybe in telephony, but highly unlikely in humans. (Just think, if someone who doesn't understand English asks you to repeat something, you can articulate it beautifully, or shout it loudly, but as long as they don't understand English, they don't get the message.) *See also* MODELS.

Triarchic Theory of Human Intelligence was developed by Robert STERNBERG as a three-part model which describes and measures mental ability in the real world, rather than in the classroom. The three sub-theories (and we simplify) are the:

- *Componential* – the information-processing abilities that generate behaviours.
- *Experiential* – which relates the behaviours to the person's previous experience of similar situations.
- *Contextual* – which takes into account how the person has used or chosen their environment, to shape their behaviours.

Truancy means, literally, being a vagrant or beggar, and truanting students need a considered individual approach to prevent this – as an extreme – from happening. Statistics show that one in five of England's secondary students are truanting for fifteen half days a year on average. One in seven primary school students are away from school for an average of eight half days a year. As many as fifty thousand students truant each year, many with the knowledge and sometimes with the encouragement of their parents. (In one month recently during a truancy sweep, half of the twelve thousand students caught were with a parent.)

Truancy affects not only students' levels of achievement, and their future employability, but it also has an impact on students who do not truant, because truancy devalues schools and learning.

Why do so many students not want to go to school?

- Lack of MOTIVATION – the student sees no value in going to school.
- The school is not engaging the student.
- The student has no ambition that they believe school will take them towards.
- Lack of parental authority or support.
- Peer pressure or family culture makes learning 'uncool'.
- Parents take cheaper holidays during term times (very strongly discouraged).
- Some students find themselves in the role of carer for a parent or a sibling.

What can a school do to reduce truancy? Certainly they can try to reinforce the 'have to' approach, since attendance is compulsory until the end of year 11, but this can alienate students even further.

Schools need to find ways of engaging each student individually, or the student's mentality will be that of a prisoner rather than a learner.

✓ *Tips*

- ☐ Engage parents as much as you can and 'sell' parents on the benefits to the family and their children of regular school attendance, and keep the lines of communications open.
- ☐ Use incentives for good attendance.
- ☐ Confer with colleagues to identify problems, and jointly find a solution.
- ☐ When a truant does attend school, do not punish or ridicule them. As long as it's appropriate to the rest of the class, praise attendance.
- ☐ Find new ways of making school attendance more engaging.
- ☐ Discuss truancy with the student, but from the standpoint of what needs to change in order that the student does want to attend.
- ☐ Ask students who do attend to work with you to encourage the truants.
- ☐ Reward students for punctuality and attendance in order to establish the habit of attendance.
- ☐ Set up a '100 per cent club' with rewards for those with perfect attendance records.

☐ Take time out to deal with occasional truants to make sure they do not become regular truants.
☐ Make use of mentors to help students.
☐ Contact the carers of regular truants the moment they do not attend to establish a pattern of immediate action and consequences for their actions.

See also REFUSERS.

TTA Teacher Training Agency whose function is to attract able and committed people to teaching, and to improve the quality of teacher training in England.

Tutor is a teacher working with an individual or small group.

UCAS Universities and Colleges Admissions Service.

UCET The Universities Council for the Education of Teachers is the national forum for contributing to the formulation of policy relating to the education of teachers and to the study of education in the university sector. Its members are UK universities and colleges of higher education involved in teacher education.

UCLES University of Cambridge Local Examinations Syndicate has three units

- OCR (Oxford, Cambridge and RSA Examinations) which provides general and vocational UK qualifications for schools, colleges and employers.
- Cambridge ESOL (English for Speakers of Other Languages) provides examinations and qualifications for language teachers.
- CIE (University of Cambridge International Examinations) provides international school examinations and vocational awards.

UCS Undergraduate Credit Scheme is a pilot scheme similar to TACS.

Ufi aims to promote e-learning anywhere, at any time and at any pace, to everyone in the UK, providing the opportunity to learn and put individuals in a better position to get jobs and improve their career prospects. Their learning services are delivered through LEARNDIRECT which provides access to courses both on-line and in 2,000+ learndirect centres. Ufi ('Yoofee') was originally known by its full name, the University for Industry. It was launched by the Government in 1998 to address the skills needs of learners and employers, and was immediately criticized for sounding too elitist ('university') and too limited ('industry' excludes public organizations, e.g. health, education, police, local government).

ULEAC University of London Examinations & Assessment Council was commonly known as London Examinations or London Exams. It was set up in 1991 and is now part of EDEXCEL which in turn is part of London Qualifications.

ULSEB University of London School Examinations Board which replaced the University Entrance & School Examinations Council in 1984.

Uniform is a prescribed mode of dress for students. There is no national policy and decisions are taken at school level, with increasing influence by the students themselves. (Why else study textiles, fashion, art and design?)

Advantages:

- It creates a school identity and an image.
- It projects cohesion, order and organization.
- It stops wealthier students 'power dressing' and overshadowing those less fortunate.
- It may reduce bullying based on the misfortune of others if that misfortune shows itself in the way they dress.
- It helps create a team.
- It makes students easily identifiable in public and on outings.

Disadvantages:

- The cost can be significantly higher than high street clothes, if specialist outlets are mandated.
- Even with a uniform, an individual will find a way of expressing themselves in the way they dress.
- It can cause resentment from those wanting to be individual.
- It can give a limiting message about uniformity and stifle those with flair and individuality.
- For the appearance-conscious, it can be a further reason to dislike school.

Unions for teachers are mainly ATL Association Of Teachers And Lecturers, NASUWT National Association of Schoolmasters Union of Women Teachers NUT National Union of Teachers and PROFESSIONAL UNITY a body campaigning for a single union for the teaching profession.

Unitary Awarding Bodies are the three awarding bodies which offer a wide range of both academic and vocational examinations and qualifications:

- AQA (Assessment and Qualifications Alliance).
- Edexcel.
- OCR (Oxford, Cambridge and RSA Examinations).

Universal Education means education for everybody, not just for an elite.

UUK Universities UK (formerly CVCP).

VAKOG is an acronym for the five senses and ways in which we understand and express ourselves and others – VISUAL, AUDITORY (hearing), KINAESTHETIC/KINESTHETIC (touch, movement, feelings, internal sensations), Olfactory (smell) and Gustatory (taste). An acronym of the first three ('VAK') is commonly used to describe three learning style preferences – Visual, Auditory and Kinaesthetic.

Value Added is the measure of the improvement in students' performance that adds to the accuracy of LEAGUE TABLES, compared to only measuring absolute performance at one point in time. League tables until 2003 took no account of students' development. With the introduction of this measure, some schools previously judged to be poor have been reassessed as good or excellent.

VCE Vocational Certificates of Education are vocational equivalents of GCSEs and A levels. (*See* NQF for details.)

Vertical Grouping *see* MIXED YEAR GROUPS.

VGCSE Vocational General Certificate of Education (the vocational equivalent of GCSES) is at levels 1 and 2 on the NQF NATIONAL QUALIFICATIONS FRAMEWORK.

VI Visual Impairment.

Visual is one of the five senses, sight.

Visualization *see* MENTAL REHEARSAL.

Vocational Certificate of Education *see* VCE.

Vocational Education aims to educate and train students in preparation for specific careers. Students are taught skills to be used when they go to work. Vocational education tends to be practical in nature but not exclusively so. It fills the gap left by the demise of industrial apprenticeships where people left school to join a company as an employee in a trainee capacity. As apprentices, they were paid low wages while they worked with experienced people, learned from them and carried out many of the menial tasks. Apprenticeships often had an academic, or further education, element where the apprentices would attend classes or lectures. Vocational education now also aims to fill the gap created by there being too few tradespeople, craftspeople and technicians to meet the nation's needs. This is a huge about-turn from 1958 when the Carr committee reported that employers were overwhelmingly opposed to schools providing vocational instruction for students! (*See also* COVES CENTRES OF VOCATIONAL EXCELLENCE.)

 Tip

☐ Many students who do not have academic interests may well have abilities that will predispose them towards more vocational courses.

See also APPRENTICESHIPS.

Vocational Guidance is acting as a sounding board and giving advice to students on future careers based on qualifications, interests, aptitudes and opportunities.

Voluntary Activities *see* EXTRA-CURRICULAR ACTIVITIES.

VRQ Vocationally Related Qualifications are developed by individual awarding bodies, accredited by the QCA, and have a vocational focus.

VSO Voluntary Service Overseas is the organization founded by Mora and Alec Dickson for people who want to make a difference outside the UK. (CSV Community Service Volunteers is a parallel organization for people wanting to volunteer in the UK.)

Vygotsky, Lev (1896–1934) was a Belorussian psychologist who believed that what a child can do with the assistance of others is a more accurate indicator of their mental development than what they can do alone. His social development theory states that cognition and consciousness within an individual are the result of social interaction with other individuals. Every function in the child's cultural development appears twice

- First, on the social level between people.
- And later, on the individual level inside the child.

As an example, pointing a finger is initially a meaningless movement. But as people respond to it, it becomes a movement that has meaning to these individuals. *See also* ZPD ZONE OF PROXIMAL DEVELOPMENT, and COGNITIVE DEVELOPMENT.

WAIS-R® is the The Wechsler Adult Intelligence Scale, Revised.

Wait Time is the time a teacher pauses after asking a question, before moving on to a different student, adding more information (i.e. giving a hint), or answering the question themselves. It seems that a wait time of three seconds or more significantly improves the achievement and attitudes of students, especially for open and higher-level questions (*see* QUESTIONING SKILLS).

✗ Trap

☐ If a student cannot recall an answer, giving more time may be putting them under undue pressure, and it may be boring for the other students. (Good luck on getting the right balance! Rely on your instincts to continue to serve you well.)

Waldorf Schools, Education, Curriculum *see* STEINER.

WCST-64 is the Wisconsin Card Sorting Test which assesses conceptual thinking.

Welsh Assembly has introduced, and abolished, several initiatives in order to enhance their education provision, e.g.

- They have abolished tests for 7-year-olds.
- They have abolished school league tables.
- They have re-introduced means-tested university grants.
- They are piloting a BACCALAUREATE exam.

Weschler tests cover intelligence, memory, individual achievement and adult reading. They are probably best known for their intelligence tests e.g. WISC® and WPPSI-R®.

Westhorp, Penny – *see* PARTICIPATION.

What If? Thinking – *see* POSSIBILITY THINKING.

Whiteboards are touch-sensitive large white screens that allow you to interact with, and operate, a computer by touching or 'writing' on the screen. (The set-up also requires a projector to project the computer image onto the touch-sensitive whiteboard.) You can point at active elements on the screen, using a finger or electronic 'pen' (depending on the technology) and the action is transmitted to the computer. You and the class can, therefore, interact with the material you display. You can also enter text via a keyboard, and see the results projected immediately. They are not cheap, but can provide a truly engaging way of working with words, images, calculations, videos, webcasts and whatever your (meaning yours and your students') imagination can suggest.

Whole Body Learning is where not only listening and thinking are involved, but hands-on experiences make it as close to a five-sense experience as possible. For example, reading something aloud as we write it down also involves our mouth, and our ears. This significantly increases our ability to remember. *See also* BRAIN GYM® and HOT SEAT.

✓ Tip

☐ 'Information is only rumour, until it's felt in the muscle.' (Anon, West Samoa)

Whole-class Teaching is taking all the students as a whole without breaking them into ability groups or sets.

Wide Ability refers to a group with different levels of ability. It is increasingly used instead of the term 'mixed ability'.

WISC® is the Wechsler Intelligence Scale for Children.

WJEC Welsh Joint Education Committee is an Awarding Body.

Work Experience is the opportunity for students to work in a business or organization to gain knowledge of what going to work, and being at work, is like. Although schools have business contacts that provide these opportunities, it's sometimes the student's family who create the opportunity. It is important that students really do experience work, as the name suggests, that interests them, rather than do only mundane jobs like endless photocopying. It is important to debrief the student on their return on what they enjoyed, what they did not and what the experience has taught them about the next steps towards their own future.

★ **Work–Life Balance** is increasingly being addressed both at school and national policy levels, with more opportunities for part-time working, flexible hours, and maternity, paternity and compassionate leave. The key is that a stressed worker is not a productive worker. The key is, also, that a person stressed from family or friend problems, cannot focus on their work. It's all very well saying we shouldn't bring our problems into work with us, or take our work problems home with us, but *how*?! It really is not possible, so we have to be flexible. We have to ask for help or support, discuss options, and make suggestions, until a suitable arrangement (for both sides) is reached.

✓ *Tips*

☐ Discuss your needs at the earliest opportunity – a half-day off spent nipping a problem in the bud might be a great investment of everyone's time.

☐ Everyone is human, and has human needs, so discuss what your needs are first, rather than what the solutions should be.

☐ If you feel that the solution is an unacceptable compromise, then say so. By all means give it a try for a specified length of time, and diarize a meeting to review the situation, but make it clear that this is a trial period. (And, naturally, you hope it will work out fine.)

✗ *Trap*

☐ If you feel forced into a compromise, you may well end up leaving in order to get the work-life pattern you require elsewhere, and both you and your employer will have had unnecessary disruption. So, if you are an employer, think of the time and cost of finding a replacement, who might well want a sensible work-life balance in any case. (And would you employ someone who didn't value this?)

World English *see* STANDARD ENGLISH.

★ **Wounded Learner** is a student who has become disengaged from learning through poor teaching, unrecognized learning difficulties, verbal attacks or external problems. Or maybe they've had an illness or missed early school and can't make up lost time. Teaching styles might not have suited their learning style. When they do attend school they may keep quiet and let time pass, or become disruptive. Some may never have engaged, in order to dis-engage, in the first place. We have a responsibility to heal the wounds, or at least distract attention, with new pleasures.

✓ *Tips*

□ There are no easy answers.

□ Wounded learners do not normally respond to 'have to'.

□ Build a RELATIONSHIP and find some ways of showing that you are on their side.

□ Usually the student knows what it would take for them to engage and heal, if you ask them.

WPPSI-R® is the Wechsler Preschool and Primary Scale of Intelligence, Revised.

Writing Frames are templates that provide a format for students to fill in, so they can concentrate on *what* they want to write, rather than having to worry about formatting as well. (They are a type of SCAFFOLDING.) For example:

1 We have just been discussing...
2 And the arguments in favour of this were...
3 And the arguments against this were...
4 And, considering these arguments, what I think is...

WHITEBOARDS are useful for introducing these to a class, and having writing frames available on computers is becoming more common. (There are lots of free templates available on lots of Internet sites.) They need not be used beyond the point where individual students can develop their own writing structures.

YA Young Apprenticeships (piloted from September 2004) are for 14–16-year olds who will spend a minimum of two days a week in the workplace, with the remainder in school or college, hopefully studying for GCSEs including vocational GCSEs.

YJB Youth Justice Board is the non-departmental public body overseeing the Youth Justice System, aiming to prevent offending by children and young people.

YOP Youth Offending Panels are set up by the local YOT (YOUTH OFFENDING TEAM), with community volunteers, to decide with young people who have committed a first-time offence and pleaded guilty to it (i.e. accepted responsibility) how best to satisfy the conditions of their REFERRAL ORDER.

YOT Youth Offending Team is a multi-disciplinary team (typically social work, education, health, probation, police) within local social services responsible for preventing offending by children and young people aged 10–17, and working with those who have offended and their families.

Youth Parliament meets several times a year in Birmingham to discuss youth-related issues and feed into government policy.

ZPD Zone of Proximal Development

1   As originally proposed by Lev VYGOTSKY it is the increase in what a child can do with help and interaction from others (adults or peers), compared to what they might achieve independently without help. The zone can be increased by increasing the learning interaction opportunities that the child has.
2   Sometimes it refers to the learning that a student can most easily do next, to build upon their existing knowledge and skills.